Snow ♥ Drop

Volume One
by Choi Kyung-ah

English Adaptation
by Sarah Dyer

TOKYOPOP®

Los Angeles • Tokyo • London

MANGA

.HACK//LEGEND OF THE TWILIGHT
@LARGE
A.I. LOVE YOU February 2004
AI YORI AOSHI January 2004
ANGELIC LAYER
BABY BIRTH
BATTLE ROYALE
BATTLE VIXENS April 2004
BIRTH May 2004
BRAIN POWERED
BRIGADOON
B'TX January 2004
CARDCAPTOR SAKURA
CARDCAPTOR SAKURA: MASTER OF THE CLOW
CARDCAPTOR SAKURA: BOXED SET COLLECTION 1
CARDCAPTOR SAKURA: BOXED SET COLLECTION 2
  March 2004
CHOBITS
CHRONICLES OF THE CURSED SWORD
CLAMP SCHOOL DETECTIVES
CLOVER
COMIC PARTY June 2004
CONFIDENTIAL CONFESSIONS
CORRECTOR YUI
COWBOY BEBOP: BOXED SET THE COMPLETE
  COLLECTION
CRESCENT MOON May 2004
CREST OF THE STARS June 2004
CYBORG 009
DEMON DIARY
DIGIMON
DIGIMON SERIES 3 April 2004
DIGIMON ZERO TWO February 2004
DNANGEL April 2004
DOLL May 2004
DRAGON HUNTER
DRAGON KNIGHTS
DUKLYON: CLAMP SCHOOL DEFENDERS
DV June 2004
ERICA SAKURAZAWA
FAERIES' LANDING January 2004
FAKE
FLCL
FORBIDDEN DANCE
FRUITS BASKET February 2004
G GUNDAM
GATEKEEPERS
GETBACKERS February 2004
GHOST! March 2004
GIRL GOT GAME January 2004
GRAVITATION
GTO

GUNDAM WING
GUNDAM WING: BATTLEFIELD OF PACIFISTS
GUNDAM WING: ENDLESS WALTZ
GUNDAM WING: THE LAST OUTPOST
HAPPY MANIA
HARLEM BEAT
I.N.V.U.
INITIAL D
ISLAND
JING: KING OF BANDITS
JULINE
JUROR 13 March 2004
KARE KANO
KILL ME, KISS ME February 2004
KINDAICHI CASE FILES, THE
KING OF HELL
KODOCHA: SANA'S STAGE
LAMENT OF THE LAMB May 2004
LES BIJOUX February 2004
LIZZIE MCGUIRE
LOVE HINA
LUPIN III
LUPIN III SERIES 2
MAGIC KNIGHT RAYEARTH I
MAGIC KNIGHT RAYEARTH II February 2004
MAHOROMATIC: AUTOMATIC MAIDEN May 2004
MAN OF MANY FACES
MARMALADE BOY
MARS
METEOR METHUSELA June 2004
METROID June 2004
MINK April 2004
MIRACLE GIRLS
MIYUKI-CHAN IN WONDERLAND
MODEL May 2004
NELLY MUSIC MANGA April 2004
ONE April 2004
PARADISE KISS
PARASYTE
PEACH GIRL
PEACH GIRL CHANGE OF HEART
PEACH GIRL RELAUNCH BOX SET
PET SHOP OF HORRORS
PITA-TEN January 2004
PLANET LADDER February 2004
PLANETES
PRIEST
PRINCESS AI April 2004
PSYCHIC ACADEMY March 2004
RAGNAROK
RAGNAROK: BOXED SET COLLECTION 1
RAVE MASTER
RAVE MASTER: BOXED SET March 2004

ALSO AVAILABLE FROM 🐾 TOKYOPOP®

REALITY CHECK
REBIRTH
REBOUND
REMOTE June 2004
RISING STARS OF MANGA December 2003
SABER MARIONETTE J
SAILOR MOON
SAINT TAIL
SAIYUKI
SAMURAI DEEPER KYO
SAMURAI GIRL REAL BOUT HIGH SCHOOL
SCRYED
SGT. FROG March 2004
SHAOLIN SISTERS
SHIRAHIME-SYO: SNOW GODDESS TALES December 2003
SHUTTERBOX
SNOW DROP January 2004
SOKORA REFUGEES May 2004
SORCEROR HUNTERS
SUIKODEN May 2004
SUKI February 2004
THE CANDIDATE FOR GODDESS April 2004
THE DEMON ORORON April 2004
THE LEGEND OF CHUN HYANG
THE SKULL MAN
THE VISION OF ESCAFLOWNE
TOKYO MEW MEW
TREASURE CHESS March 2004
UNDER THE GLASS MOON
VAMPIRE GAME
WILD ACT
WISH
WORLD OF HARTZ
X-DAY
ZODIAC P.I.

NOVELS
KARMA CLUB APRIL 2004
SAILOR MOON

ART BOOKS
CARDCAPTOR SAKURA
MAGIC KNIGHT RAYEARTH
PEACH GIRL ART BOOK April 2004

ANIME GUIDES
COWBOY BEBOP ANIME GUIDES
GUNDAM TECHNICAL MANUALS
SAILOR MOON SCOUT GUIDES

CINE-MANGA™
CARDCAPTORS
FAIRLY ODD PARENTS MARCH 2004
FINDING NEMO
G.I. JOE SPY TROOPS
JACKIE CHAN ADVENTURES
KIM POSSIBLE
LIZZIE MCGUIRE
POWER RANGERS: NINJA STORM
SPONGEBOB SQUAREPANTS
SPY KIDS
SPY KIDS 3-D March 2004
THE ADVENTURES OF JIMMY NEUTRON: BOY GENIUS
TRANSFORMERS: ARMADA
TRANSFORMERS: ENERGON May 2004

TOKYOPOP KIDS
STRAY SHEEP

For more information visit www.TOKYOPOP.com

10103

Translator - Jennifer Hahm
English Adaptation - Sarah Dyer
Associate Editor - Bryce P. Coleman
Retouch and Lettering - James Dashiell
Cover Layout - Anna Kernbaum
Graphic Designer - Deron Bennett

Editor - Julie Taylor
Managing Editor - Jill Freshney
Production Coordinator - Antonio DePietro
Production Manager - Jennifer Miller, Mutsumi Miyazaki
Art Director - Matt Alford
Editorial Director - Jeremy Ross
VP of Production - Ron Klamert
President & C.O.O. - John Parker
Publisher & C.E.O. - Stuart Levy

Email: editor@TOKYOPOP.com
Come visit us online at www.TOKYOPOP.com

A  Manga

TOKYOPOP Inc.
5900 Wilshire Blvd. Suite 2000
Los Angeles, CA 90036

Snow Drop Vol. 1

ISBN: 1-59182-684-5

First TOKYOPOP printing: January 2004

10 9 8 7 6 5 4 3 2 1

Printed in the USA

Snow ♥ Drop

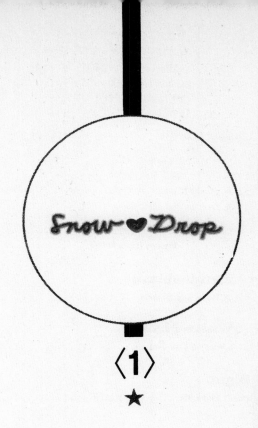

〈1〉

★

C·O·N·T·E·N·T·S

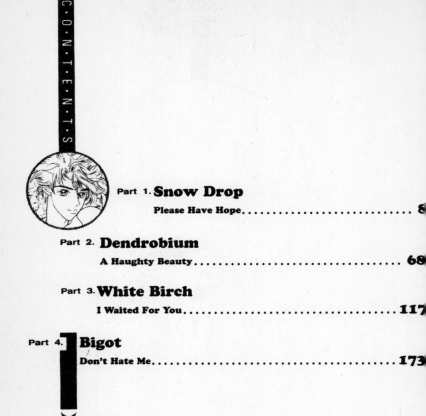

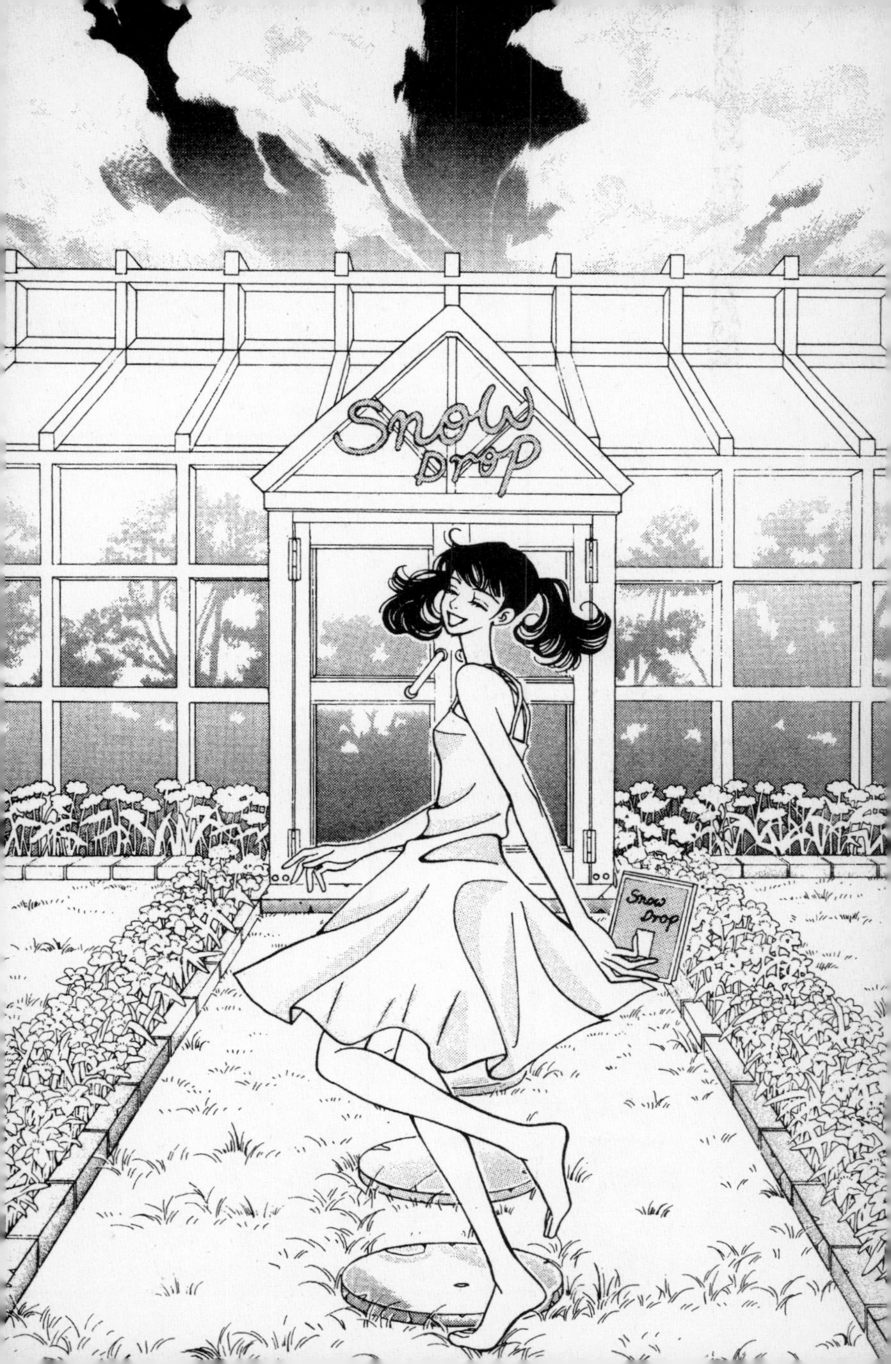
Snow Drop
Snow Drop

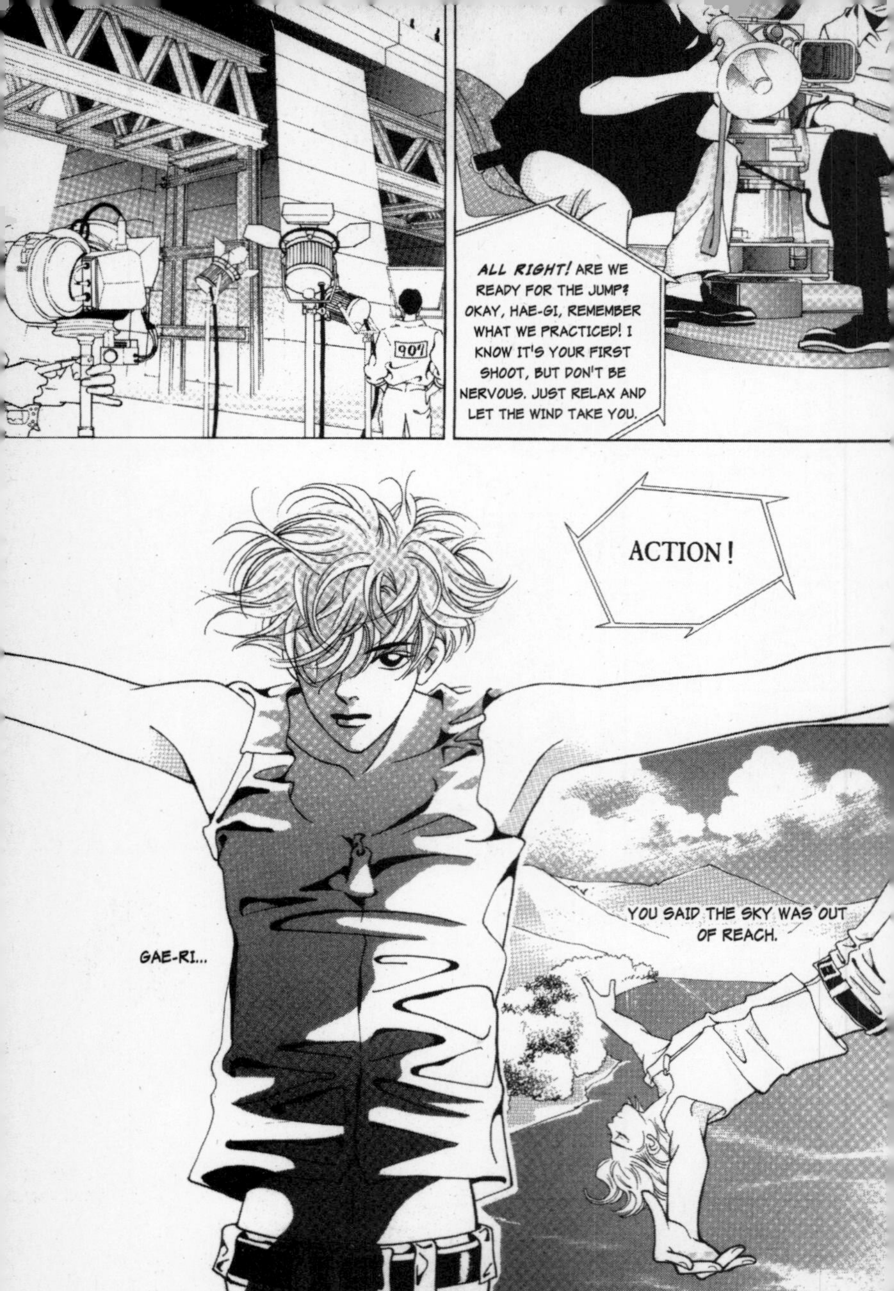
ALL RIGHT! ARE WE READY FOR THE JUMP? OKAY, HAE-GI, REMEMBER WHAT WE PRACTICED! I KNOW IT'S YOUR FIRST SHOOT, BUT DON'T BE NERVOUS. JUST RELAX AND LET THE WIND TAKE YOU.
ACTION!
GAE-RI...
YOU SAID THE SKY WAS OUT OF REACH.

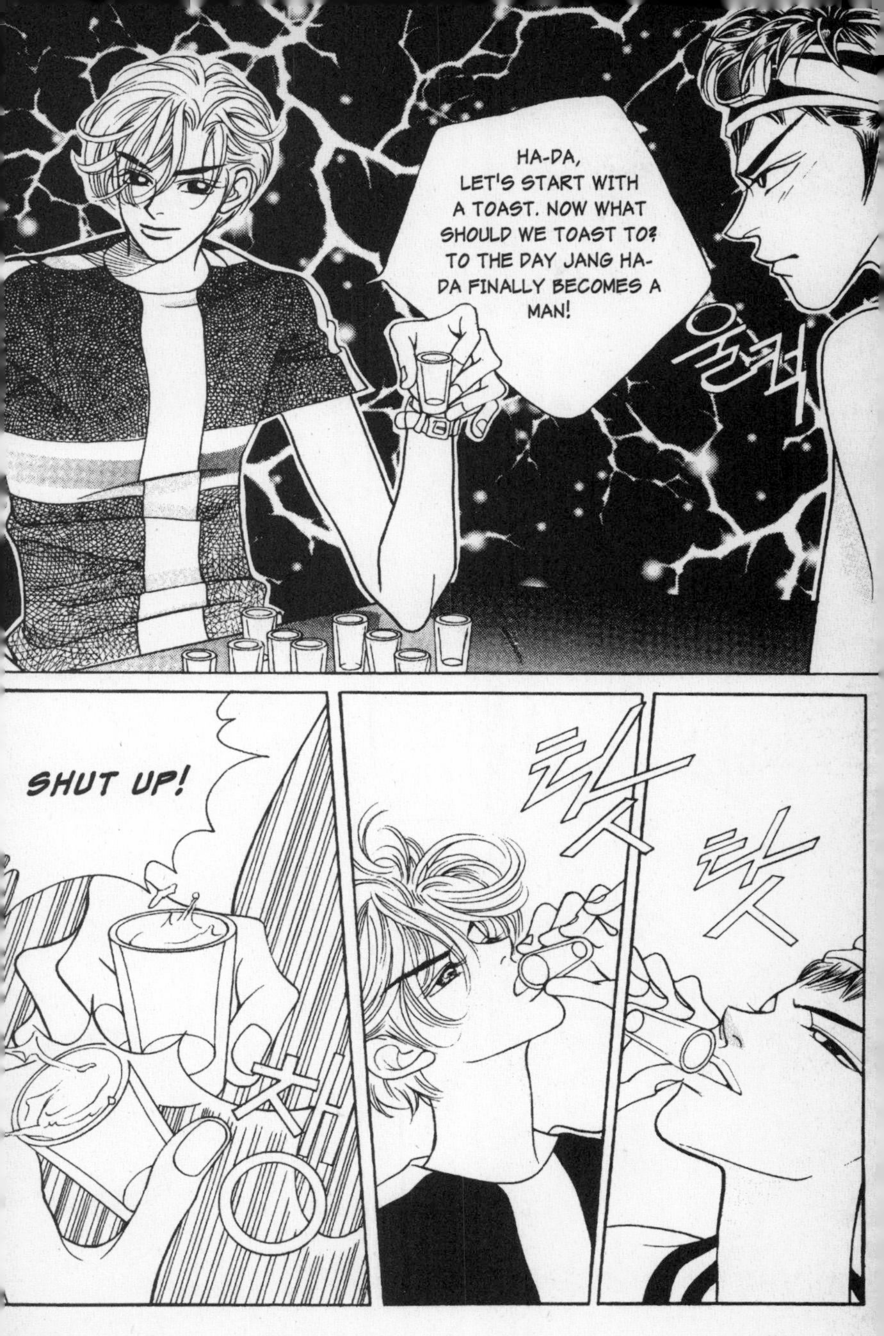
HA-DA, LET'S START WITH A TOAST. NOW WHAT SHOULD WE TOAST TO? TO THE DAY JANG HA-DA FINALLY BECOMES A MAN!
SHUT UP!

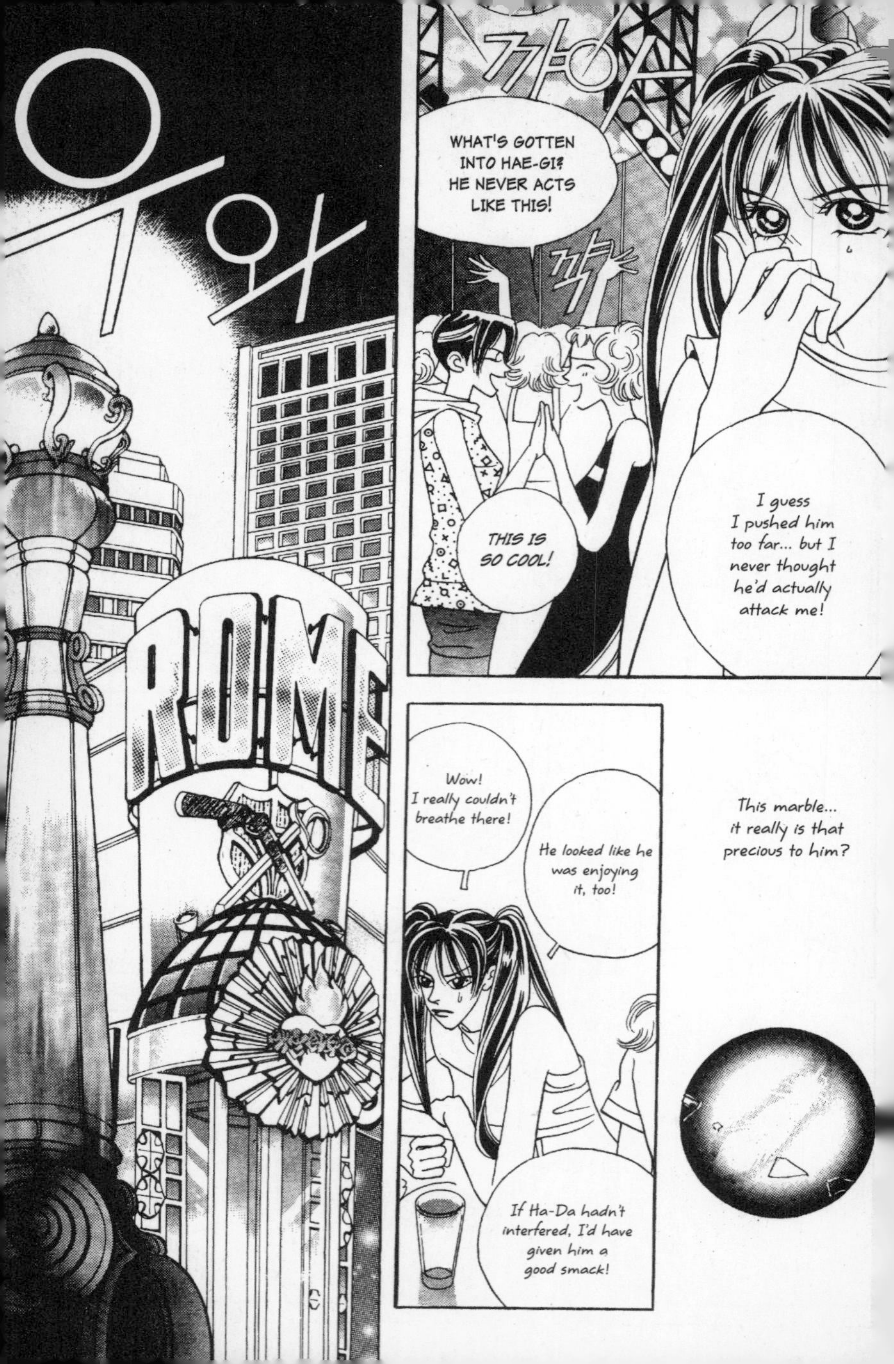
ROME
WHAT'S GOTTEN INTO HAE-GI? HE NEVER ACTS LIKE THIS!
THIS IS SO COOL!
I guess I pushed him too far... but I never thought he'd actually attack me!
Wow! I really couldn't breathe there!
He looked like he was enjoying it, too!
If Ha-Da hadn't interfered, I'd have given him a good smack!
This marble... it really is that precious to him?

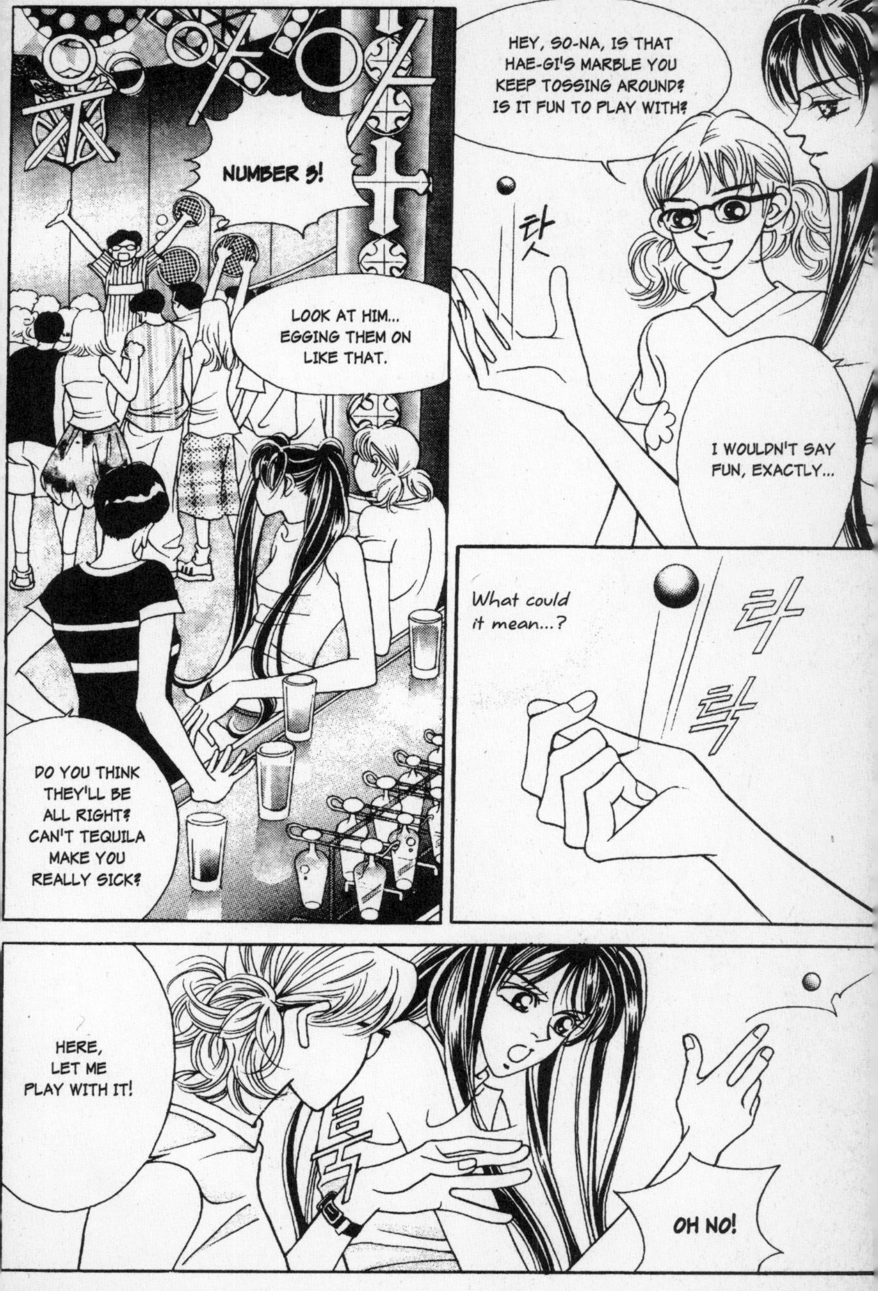
NUMBER 3!
LOOK AT HIM... EGGING THEM ON LIKE THAT.
DO YOU THINK THEY'LL BE ALL RIGHT? CAN'T TEQUILA MAKE YOU REALLY SICK?
HEY, SO-NA, IS THAT HAE-GI'S MARBLE YOU KEEP TOSSING AROUND? IS IT FUN TO PLAY WITH?
탓
I WOULDN'T SAY FUN, EXACTLY...
What could it mean...?
타
탁
HERE, LET ME PLAY WITH IT!
툭
OH NO!

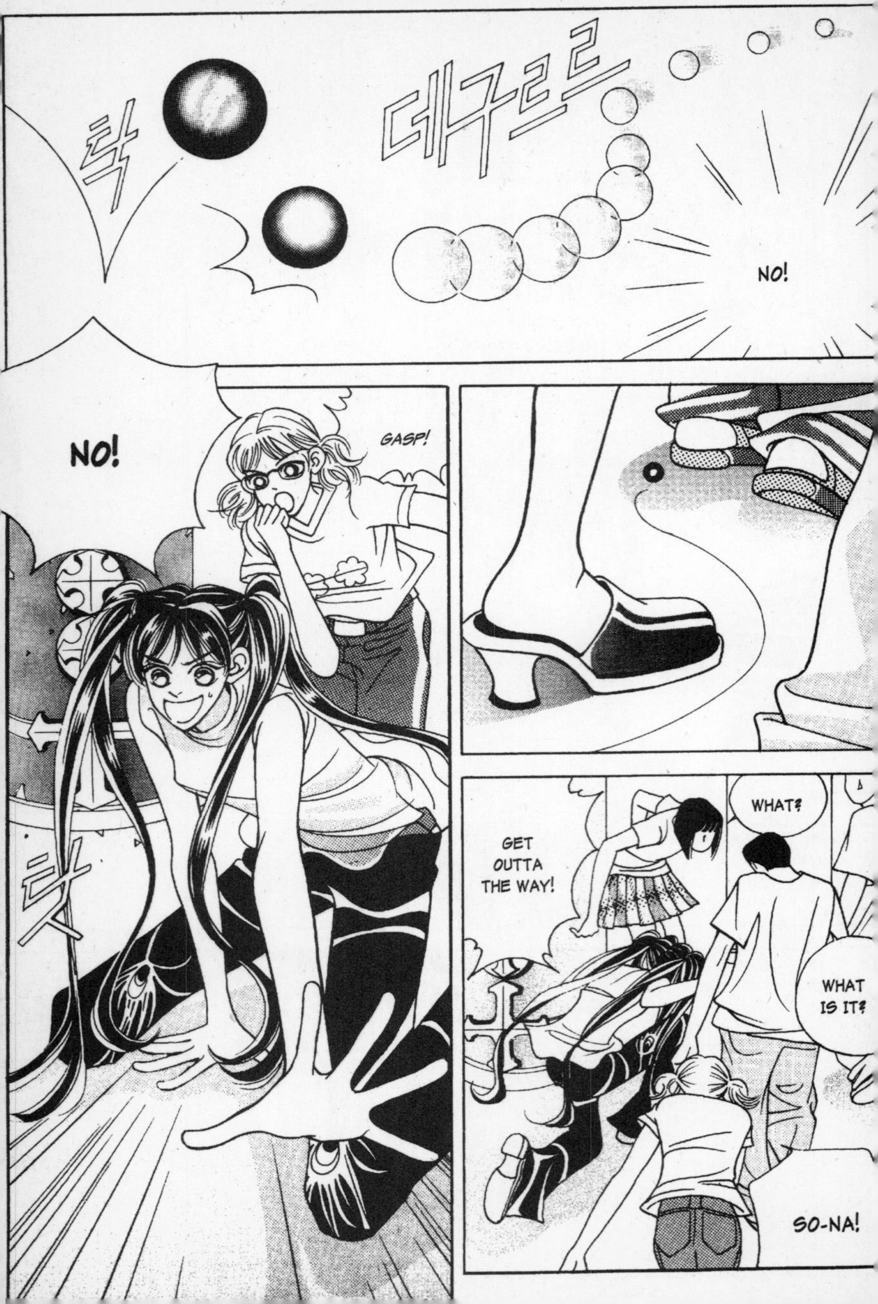
탁
데구르르
NO!
NO!
GASP!
탁
GET OUTTA THE WAY!
WHAT?
WHAT IS IT?
SO-NA!

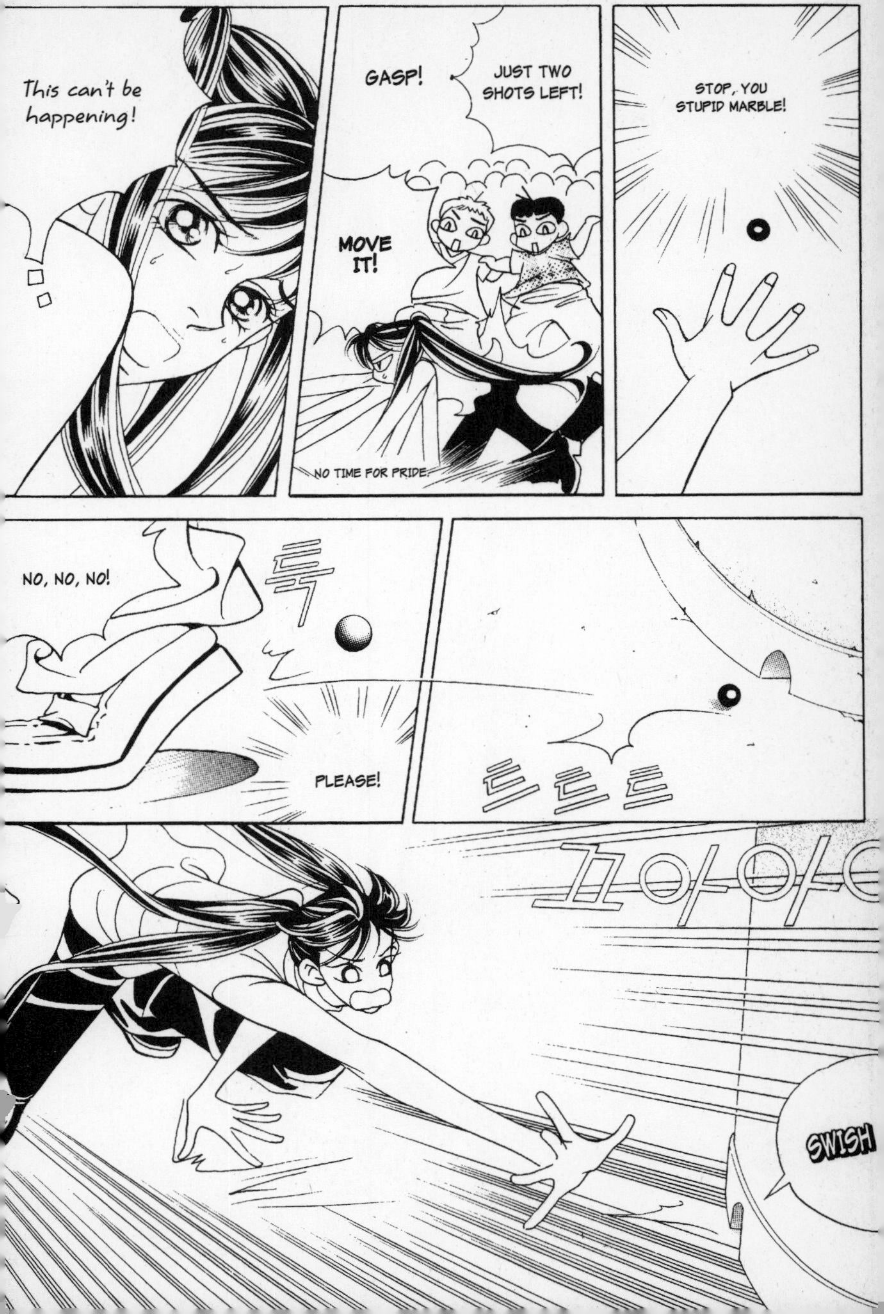
This can't be happening!
GASP!
JUST TWO SHOTS LEFT!
MOVE IT!
NO TIME FOR PRIDE.
STOP, YOU STUPID MARBLE!
NO, NO, NO!
PLEASE!
SWISH

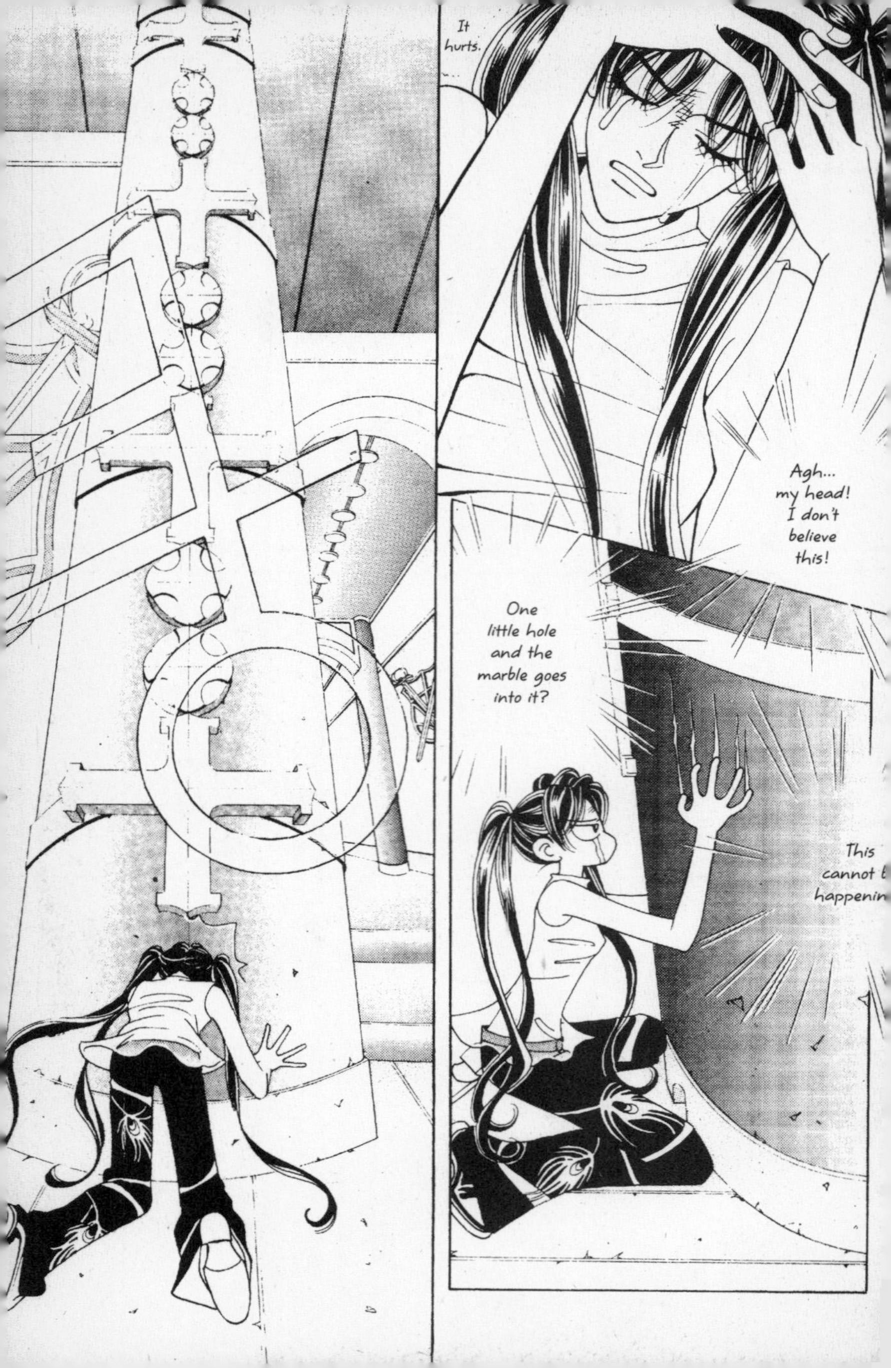
It hurts. ...
Agh... my head! I don't believe this!
One little hole and the marble goes into it?
This cannot b happenin

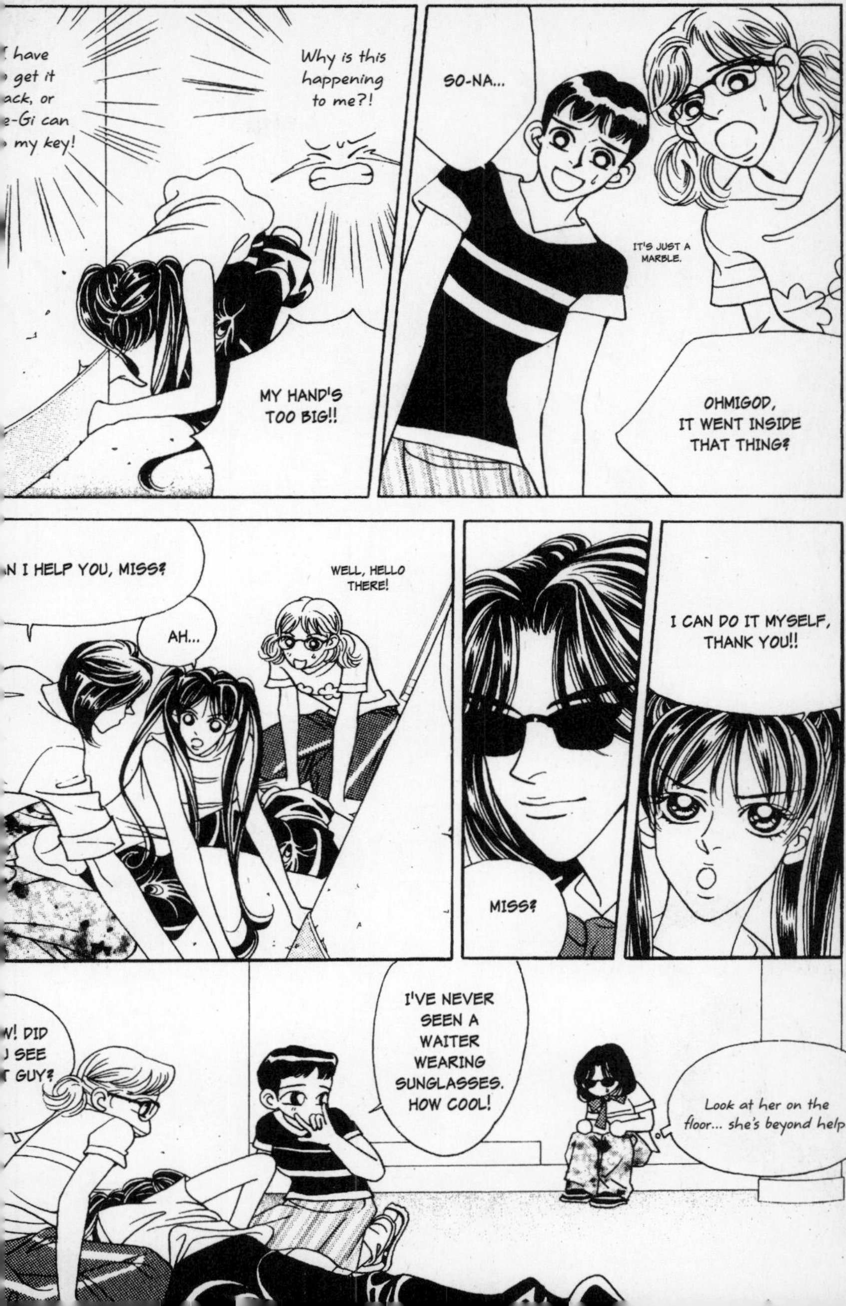

I have
get it
ack, or
e-Gi can
my key!
Why is this happening to me?!
MY HAND'S TOO BIG!!
SO-NA...
IT'S JUST A MARBLE.
OHMIGOD, IT WENT INSIDE THAT THING?
N I HELP YOU, MISS?
AH...
WELL, HELLO THERE!
MISS?
I CAN DO IT MYSELF, THANK YOU!!
W! DID
SEE
T GUY?
I'VE NEVER SEEN A WAITER WEARING SUNGLASSES. HOW COOL!
Look at her on the floor... she's beyond help.

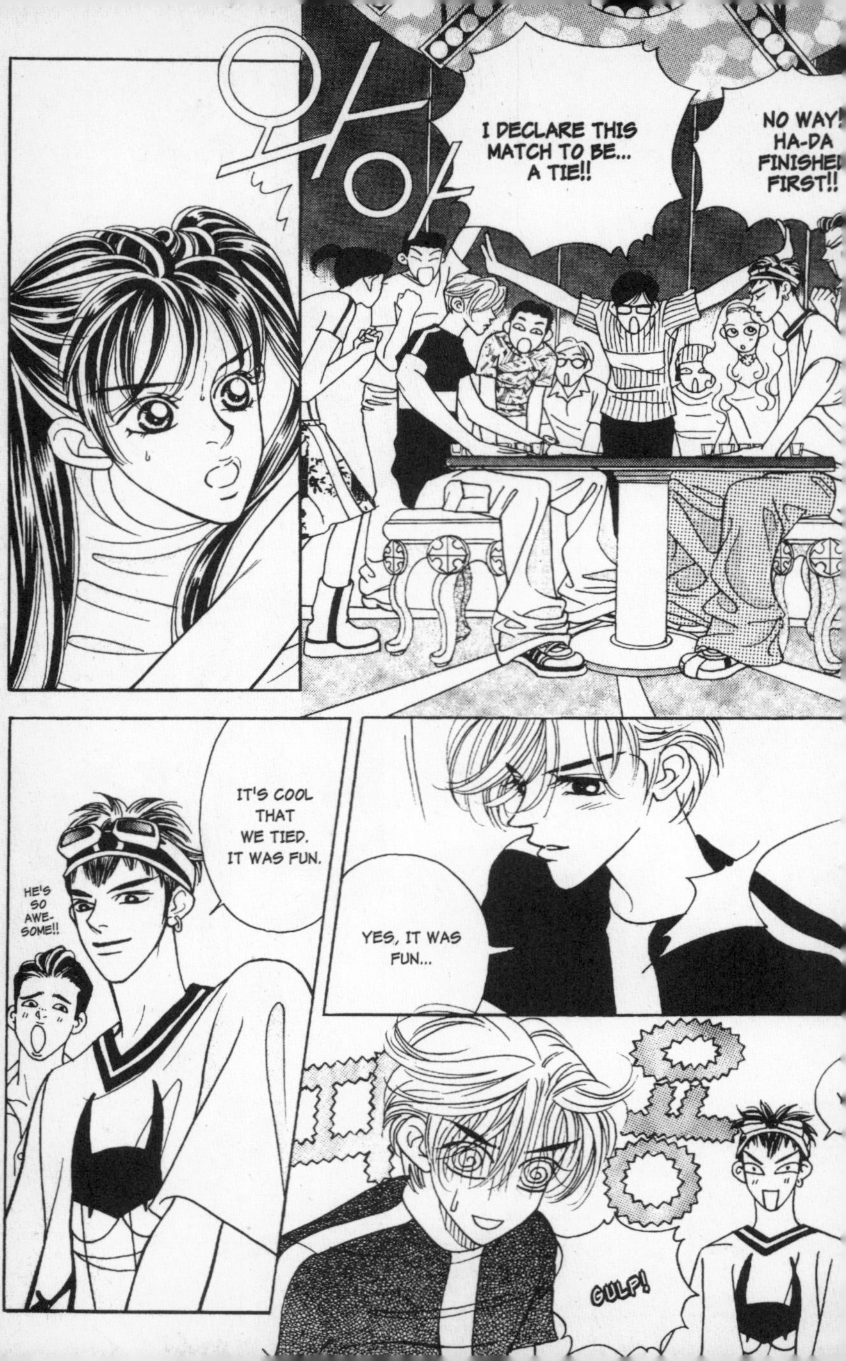
I DECLARE THIS MATCH TO BE... A TIE!!
NO WAY! HA-DA FINISHE FIRST!!
HE'S SO AWE-SOME!!
IT'S COOL THAT WE TIED. IT WAS FUN.
YES, IT WAS FUN...
GULP!

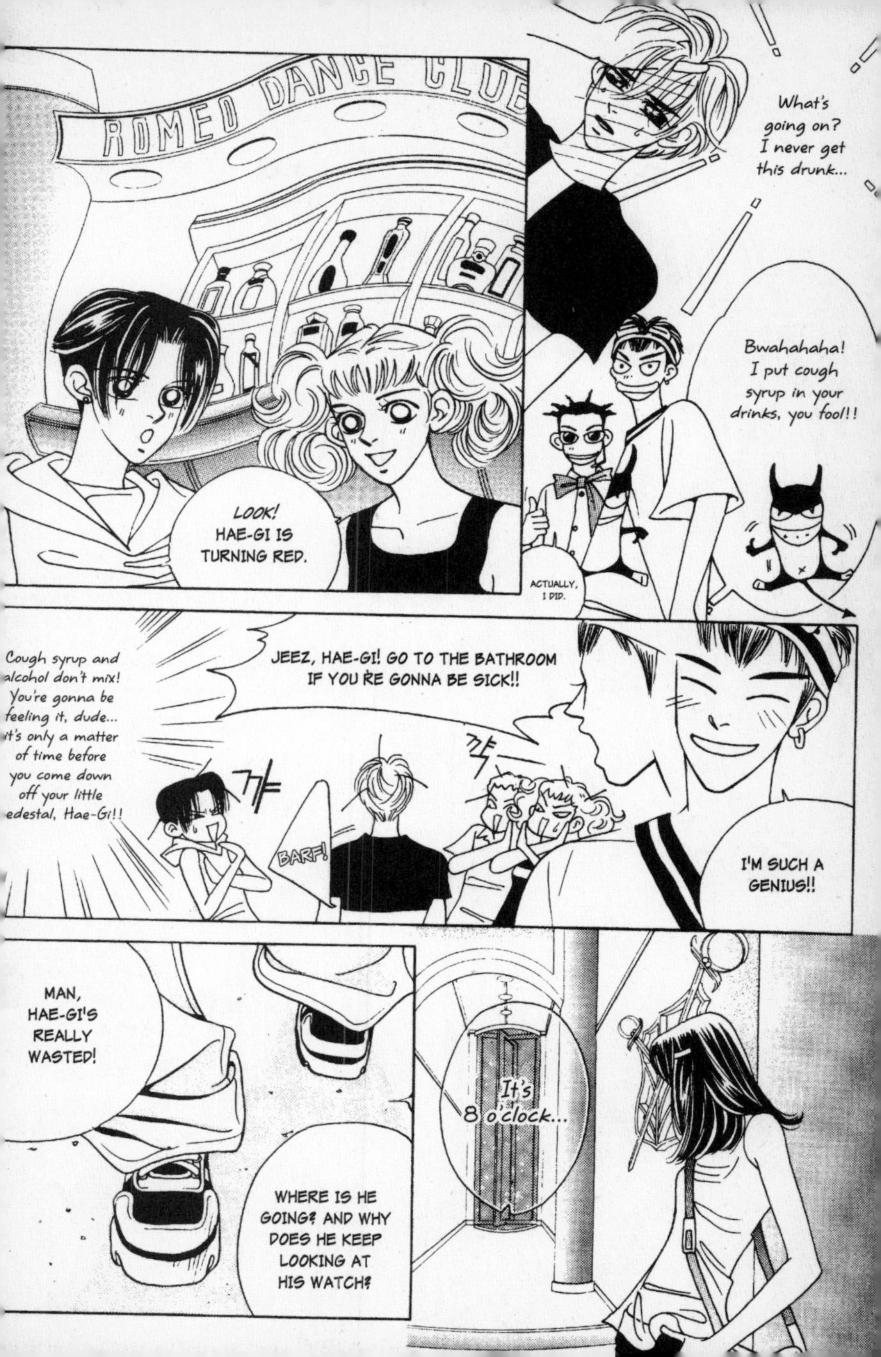
ROMEO DANCE CLUB
LOOK! HAE-GI IS TURNING RED.
What's going on? I never get this drunk...
Bwahahaha! I put cough syrup in your drinks, you fool!!
ACTUALLY, I DID.
Cough syrup and alcohol don't mix! You're gonna be feeling it, dude... it's only a matter of time before you come down off your little edestal, Hae-Gi!!
JEEZ, HAE-GI! GO TO THE BATHROOM IF YOU'RE GONNA BE SICK!!
BARF!
I'M SUCH A GENIUS!!
MAN, HAE-GI'S REALLY WASTED!
WHERE IS HE GOING? AND WHY DOES HE KEEP LOOKING AT HIS WATCH?
It's 8 o'clock...

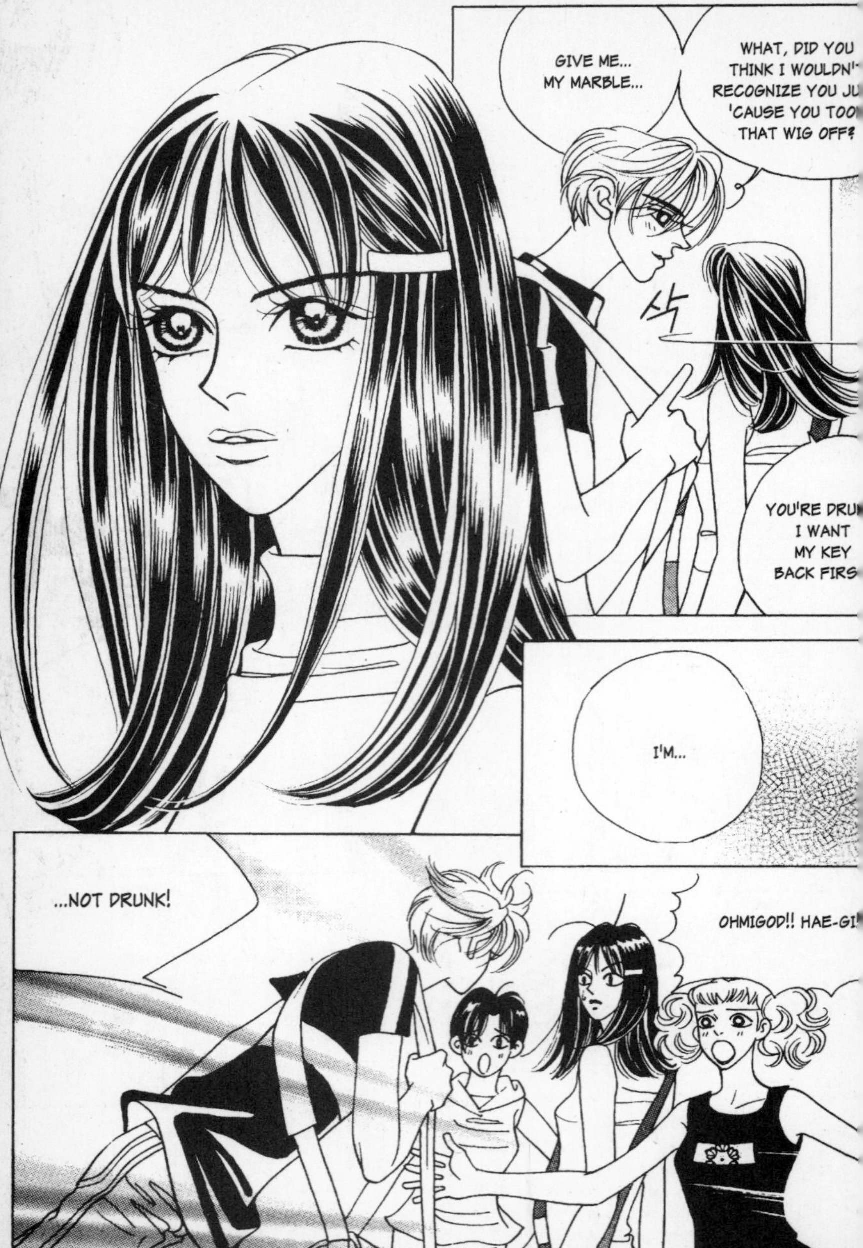
GIVE ME... MY MARBLE...
WHAT, DID YOU THINK I WOULDN' RECOGNIZE YOU JU 'CAUSE YOU TOO THAT WIG OFF?
쓱
YOU'RE DRU I WANT MY KEY BACK FIRS
I'M...
...NOT DRUNK!
OHMIGOD!! HAE-GI!

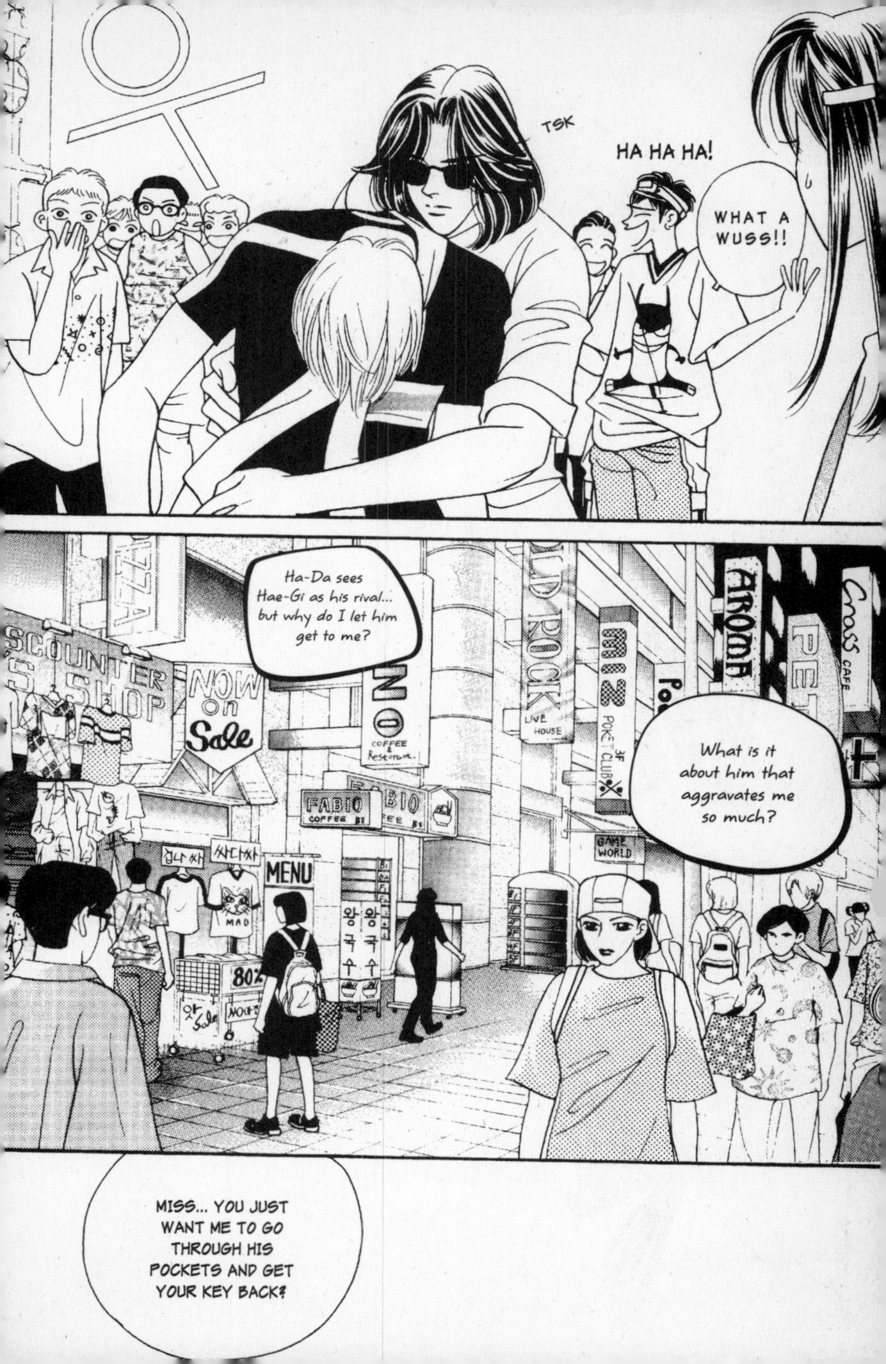

TSK
HA HA HA!
WHAT A WUSS!!
Ha-Da sees Hae-Gi as his rival... but why do I let him get to me?
NOW on Sale
FABIO COFFEE B1
MENU
LIVE HOUSE
POKET CLUB
GAME WORLD
AROMA
What is it about him that aggravates me so much?
MISS... YOU JUST WANT ME TO GO THROUGH HIS POCKETS AND GET YOUR KEY BACK?

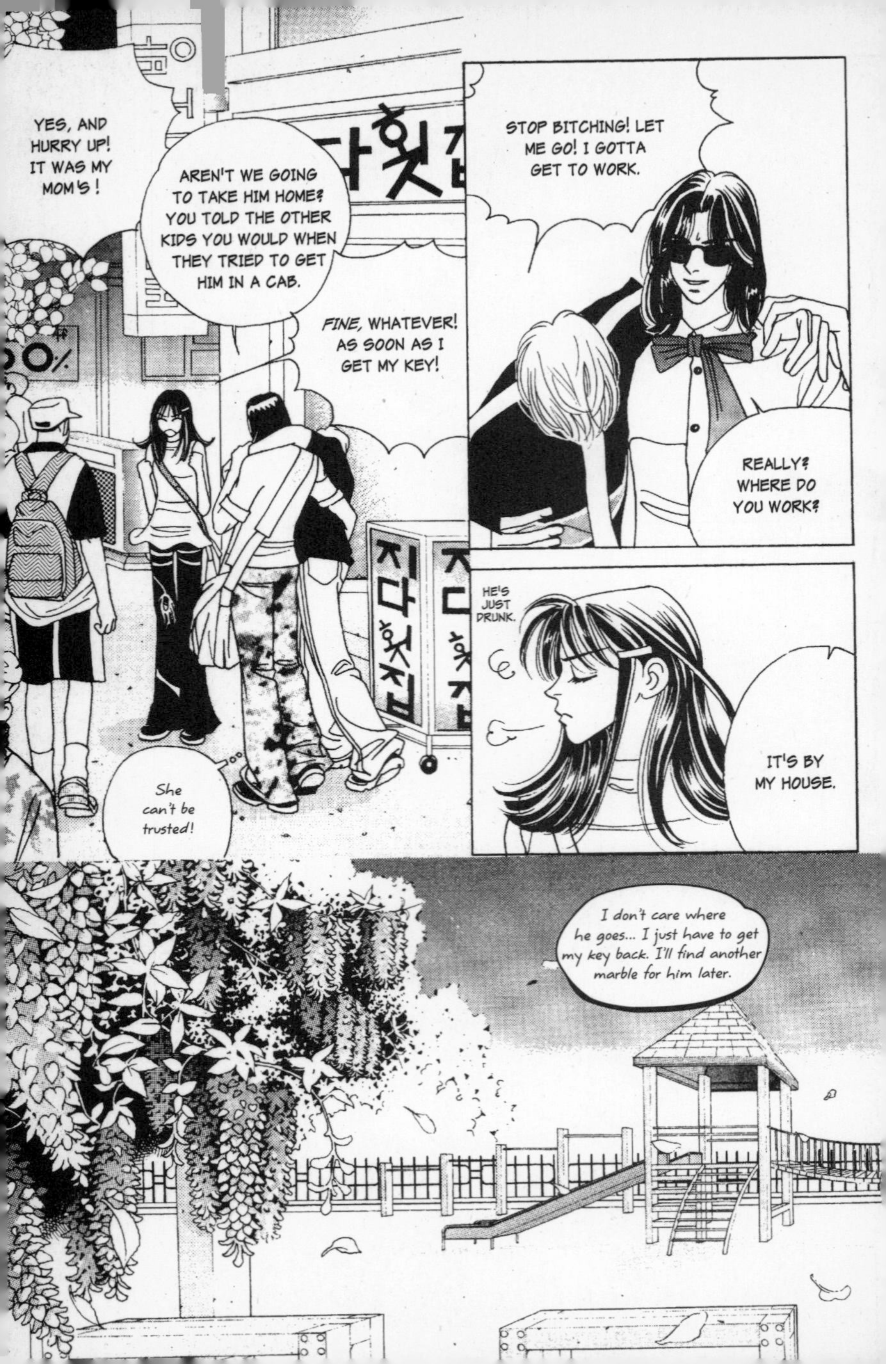
YES, AND HURRY UP! IT WAS MY MOM'S!
AREN'T WE GOING TO TAKE HIM HOME? YOU TOLD THE OTHER KIDS YOU WOULD WHEN THEY TRIED TO GET HIM IN A CAB.
FINE, WHATEVER! AS SOON AS I GET MY KEY!
She can't be trusted!
STOP BITCHING! LET ME GO! I GOTTA GET TO WORK.
REALLY? WHERE DO YOU WORK?
HE'S JUST DRUNK.
IT'S BY MY HOUSE.
I don't care where he goes... I just have to get my key back. I'll find another marble for him later.

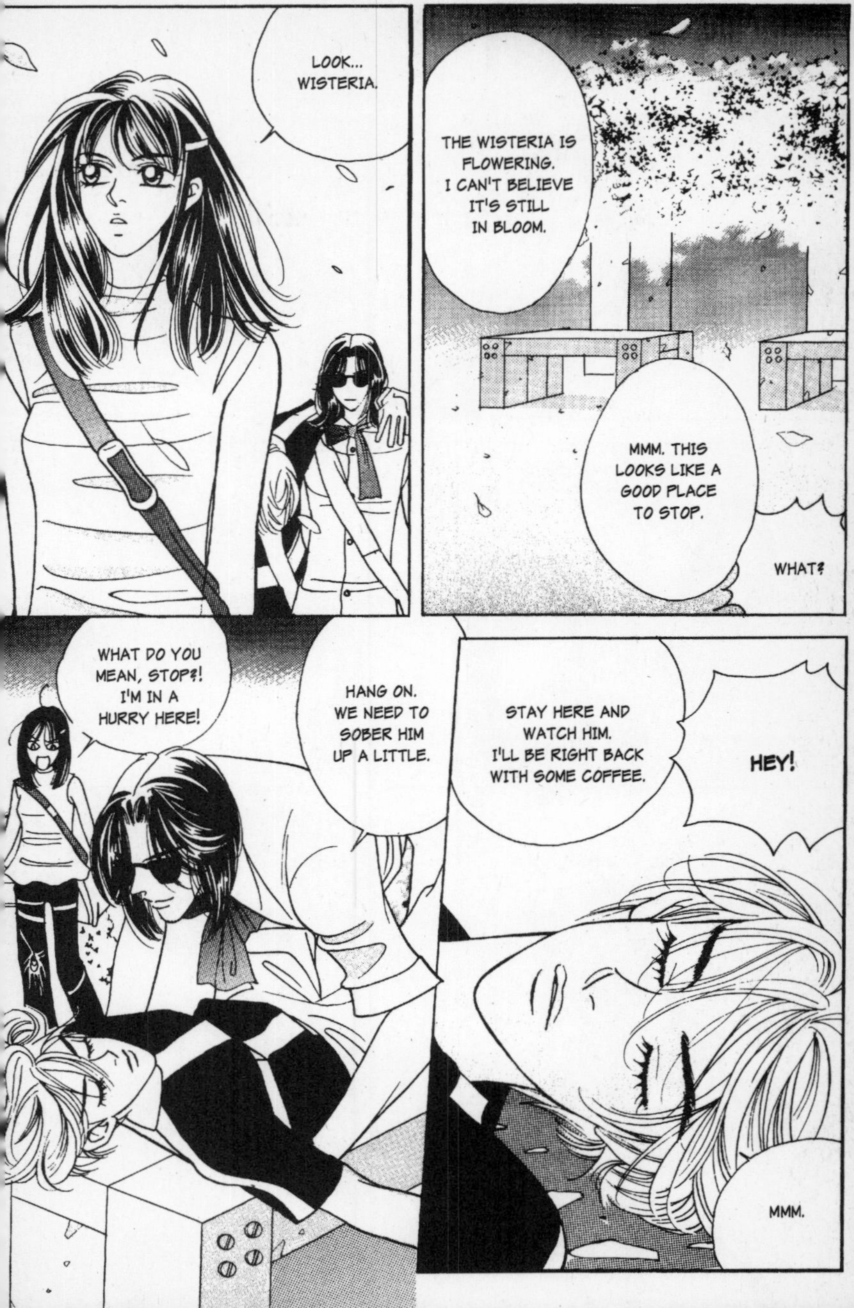
LOOK... WISTERIA.
THE WISTERIA IS FLOWERING. I CAN'T BELIEVE IT'S STILL IN BLOOM.
MMM. THIS LOOKS LIKE A GOOD PLACE TO STOP.
WHAT?
WHAT DO YOU MEAN, STOP?! I'M IN A HURRY HERE!
HANG ON. WE NEED TO SOBER HIM UP A LITTLE.
STAY HERE AND WATCH HIM. I'LL BE RIGHT BACK WITH SOME COFFEE.
HEY!
MMM.

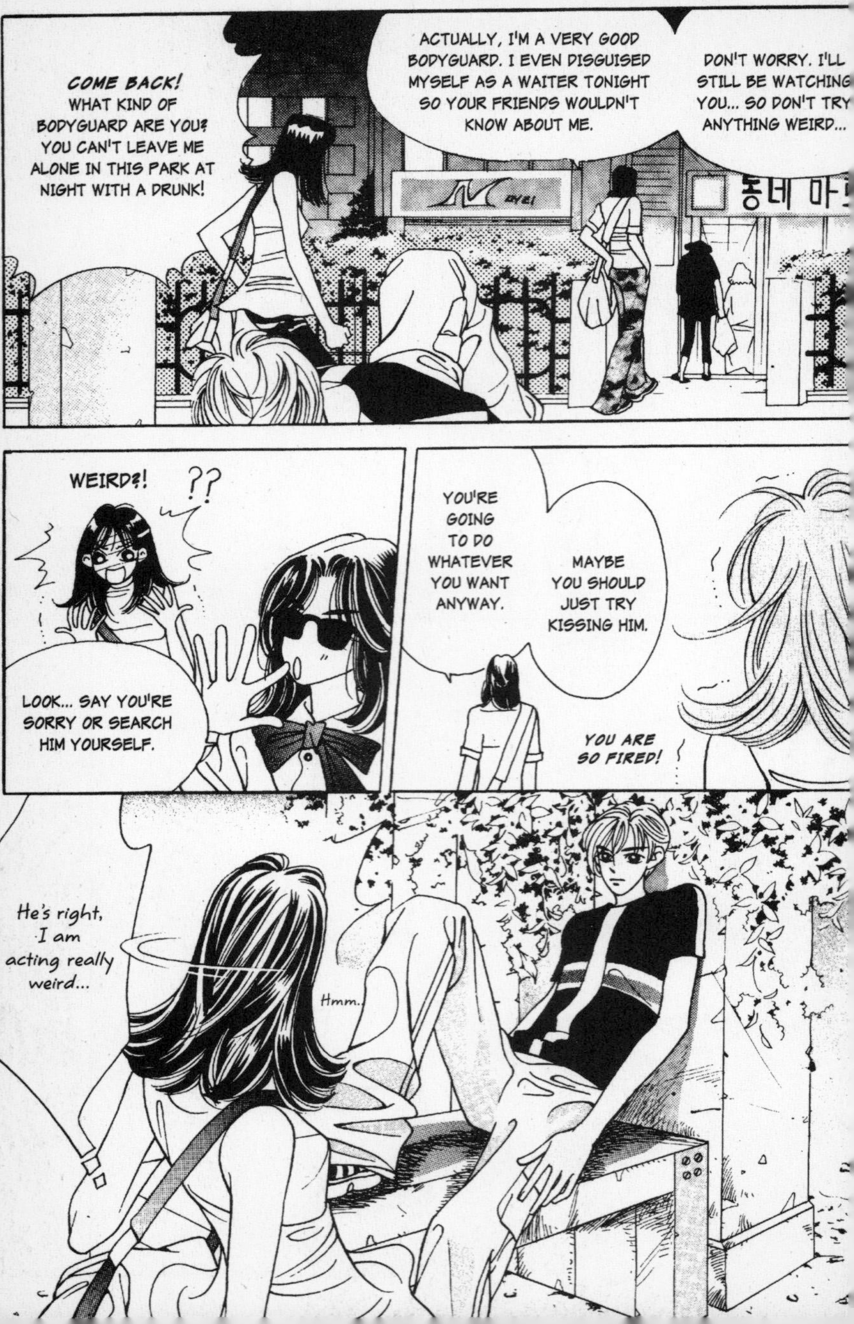
COME BACK! WHAT KIND OF BODYGUARD ARE YOU? YOU CAN'T LEAVE ME ALONE IN THIS PARK AT NIGHT WITH A DRUNK!
ACTUALLY, I'M A VERY GOOD BODYGUARD. I EVEN DISGUISED MYSELF AS A WAITER TONIGHT SO YOUR FRIENDS WOULDN'T KNOW ABOUT ME.
DON'T WORRY. I'LL STILL BE WATCHING YOU... SO DON'T TRY ANYTHING WEIRD...
동네 마
WEIRD?!
??
LOOK... SAY YOU'RE SORRY OR SEARCH HIM YOURSELF.
YOU'RE GOING TO DO WHATEVER YOU WANT ANYWAY.
MAYBE YOU SHOULD JUST TRY KISSING HIM.
YOU ARE SO FIRED!
He's right, I am acting really weird...
Hmm..

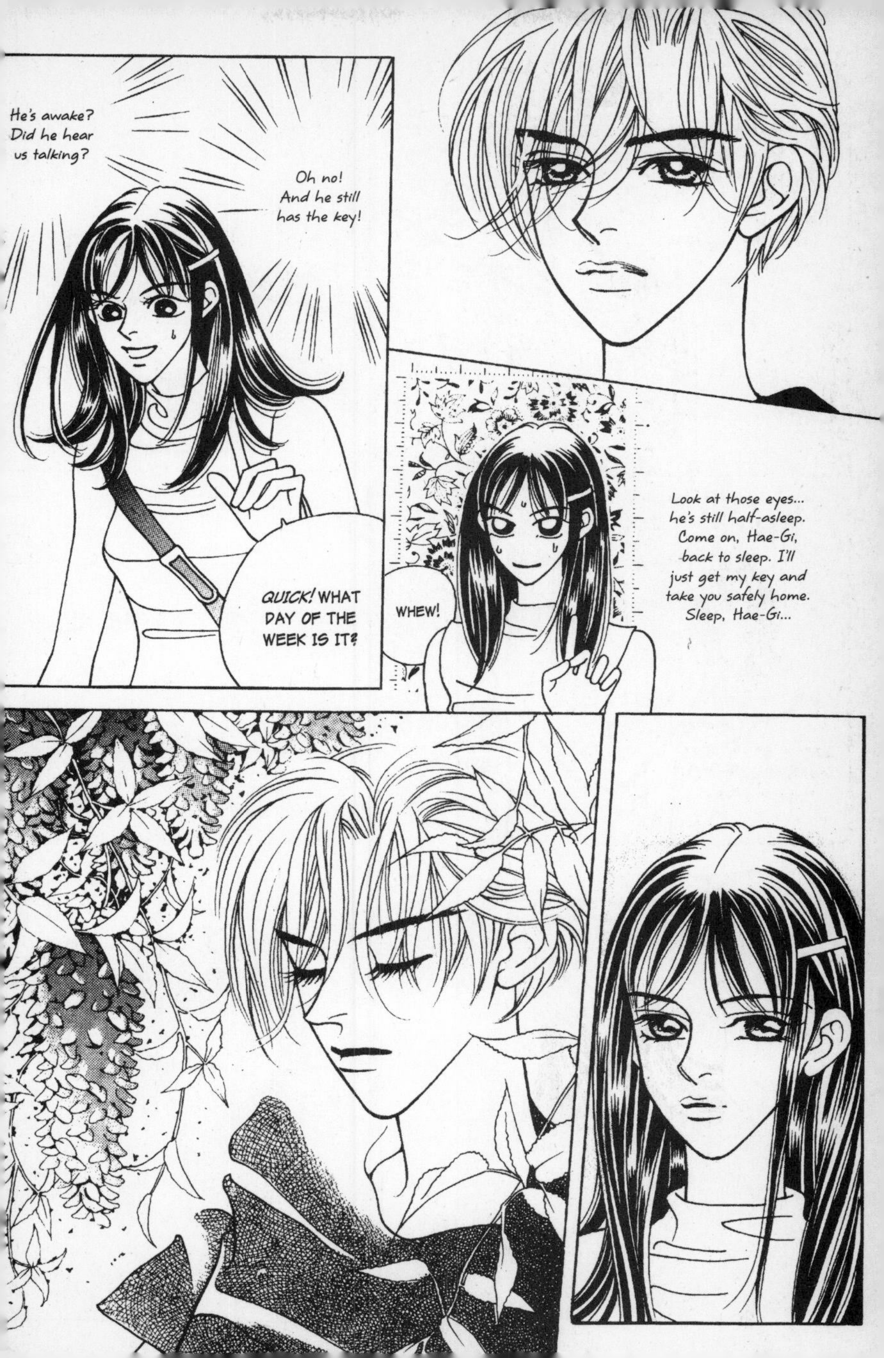
He's awake? Did he hear us talking?
Oh no! And he still has the key!
QUICK! WHAT DAY OF THE WEEK IS IT?
WHEW!
Look at those eyes... he's still half-asleep. Come on, Hae-Gi, back to sleep. I'll just get my key and take you safely home. Sleep, Hae-Gi...

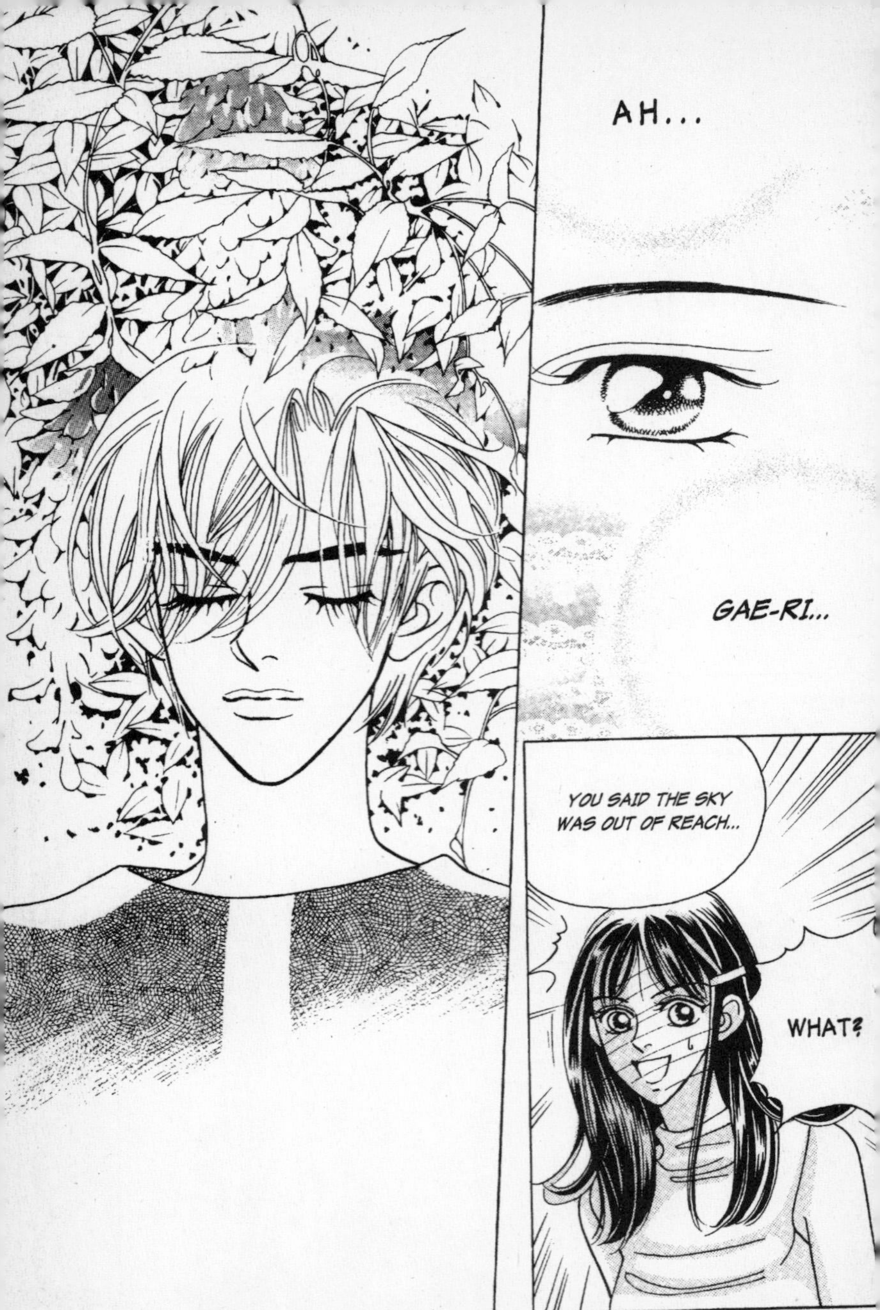
AH...
GAE-RI...
YOU SAID THE SKY WAS OUT OF REACH...
WHAT?

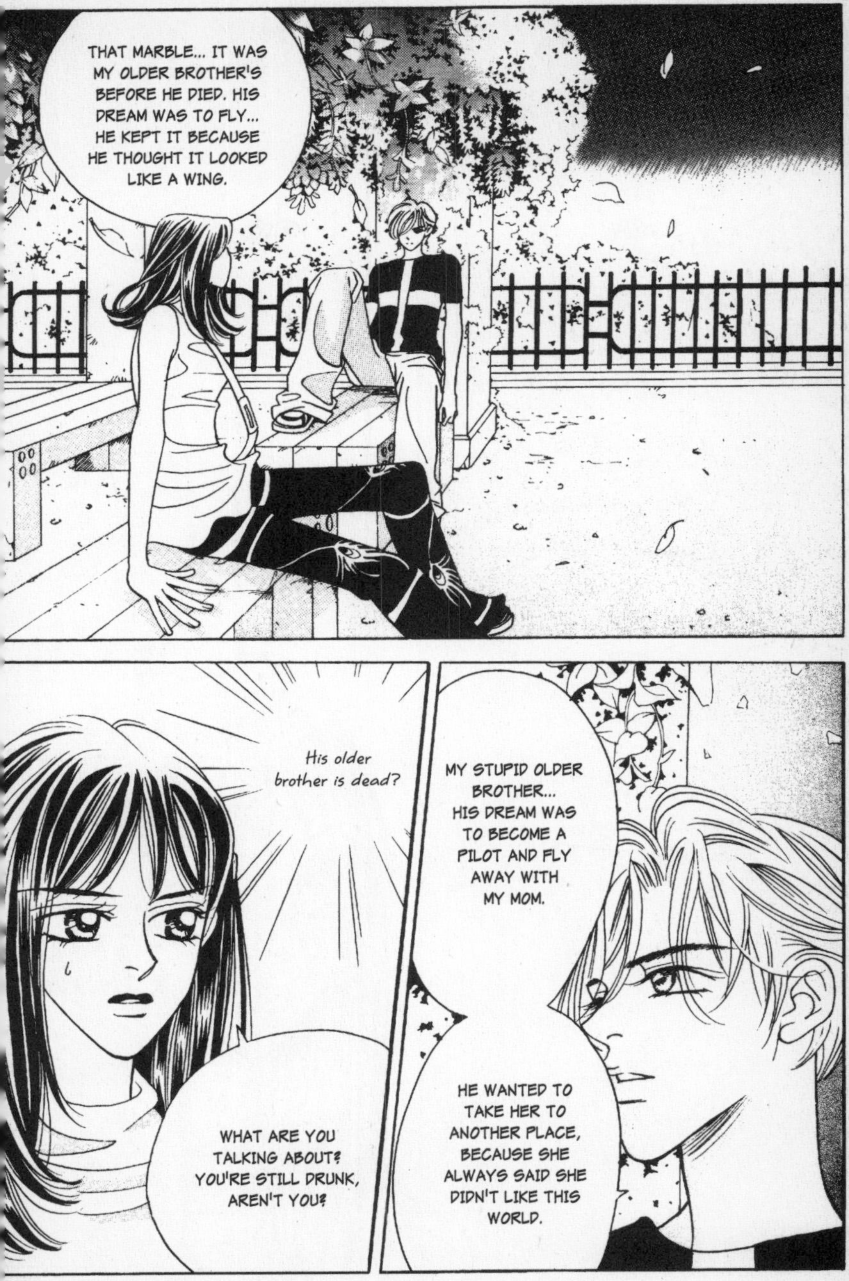
THAT MARBLE... IT WAS MY OLDER BROTHER'S BEFORE HE DIED. HIS DREAM WAS TO FLY... HE KEPT IT BECAUSE HE THOUGHT IT LOOKED LIKE A WING.
His older brother is dead?
WHAT ARE YOU TALKING ABOUT? YOU'RE STILL DRUNK, AREN'T YOU?
MY STUPID OLDER BROTHER... HIS DREAM WAS TO BECOME A PILOT AND FLY AWAY WITH MY MOM.
HE WANTED TO TAKE HER TO ANOTHER PLACE, BECAUSE SHE ALWAYS SAID SHE DIDN'T LIKE THIS WORLD.

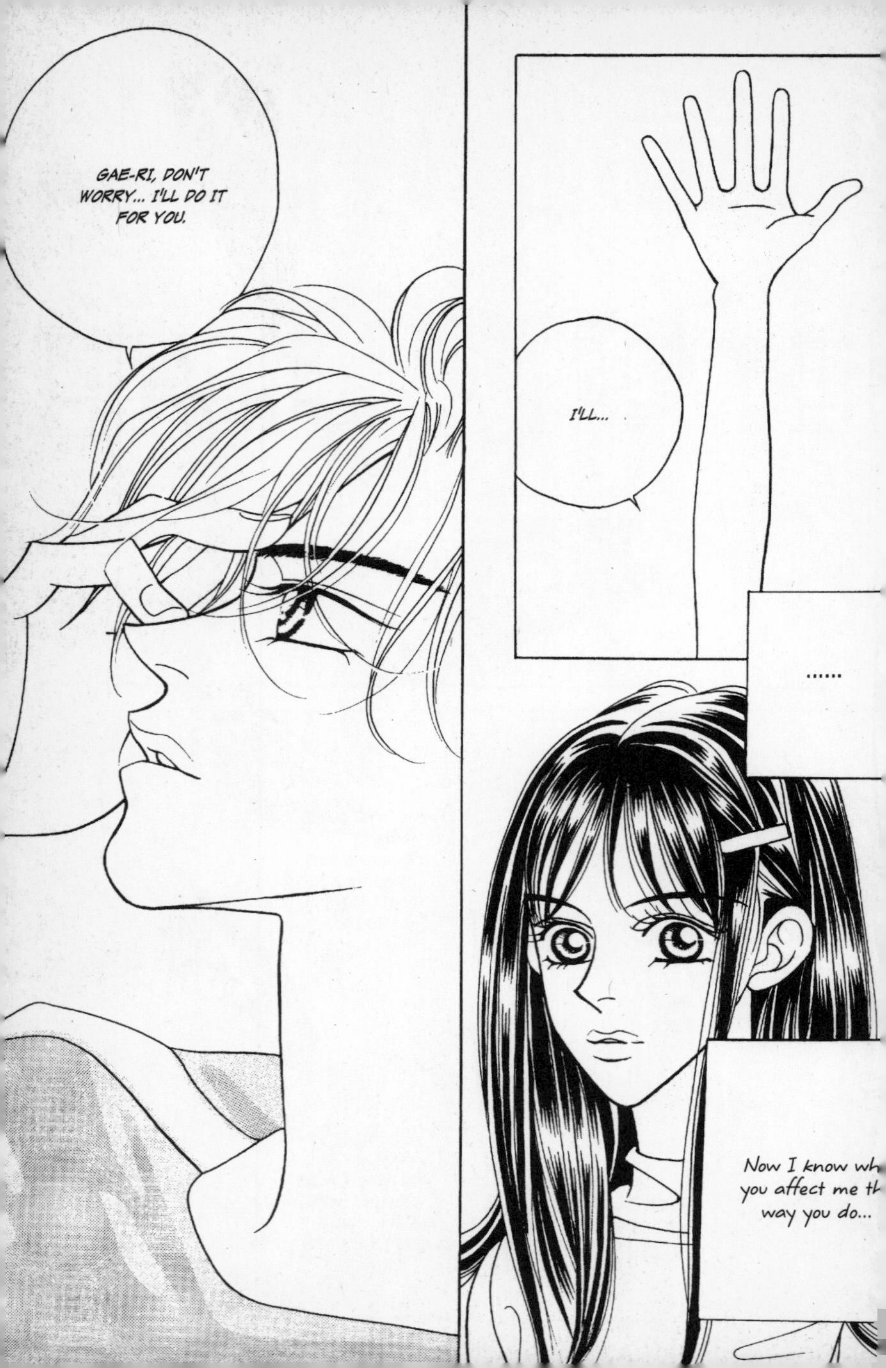
GAE-RI, DON'T WORRY... I'LL DO IT FOR YOU.
I'LL...
......
Now I know wh
you affect me th
way you do...

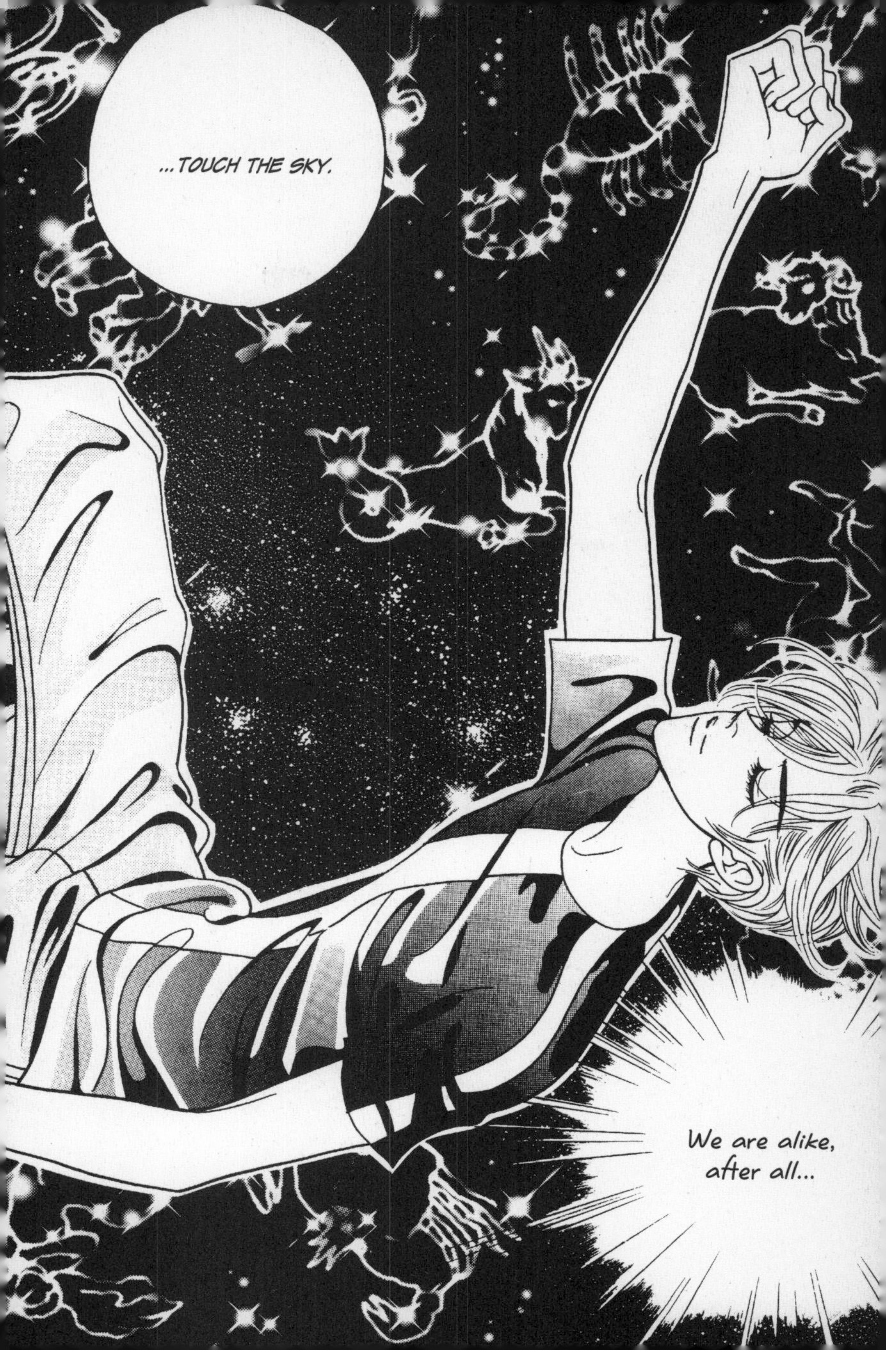
...TOUCH THE SKY.
We are alike, after all...

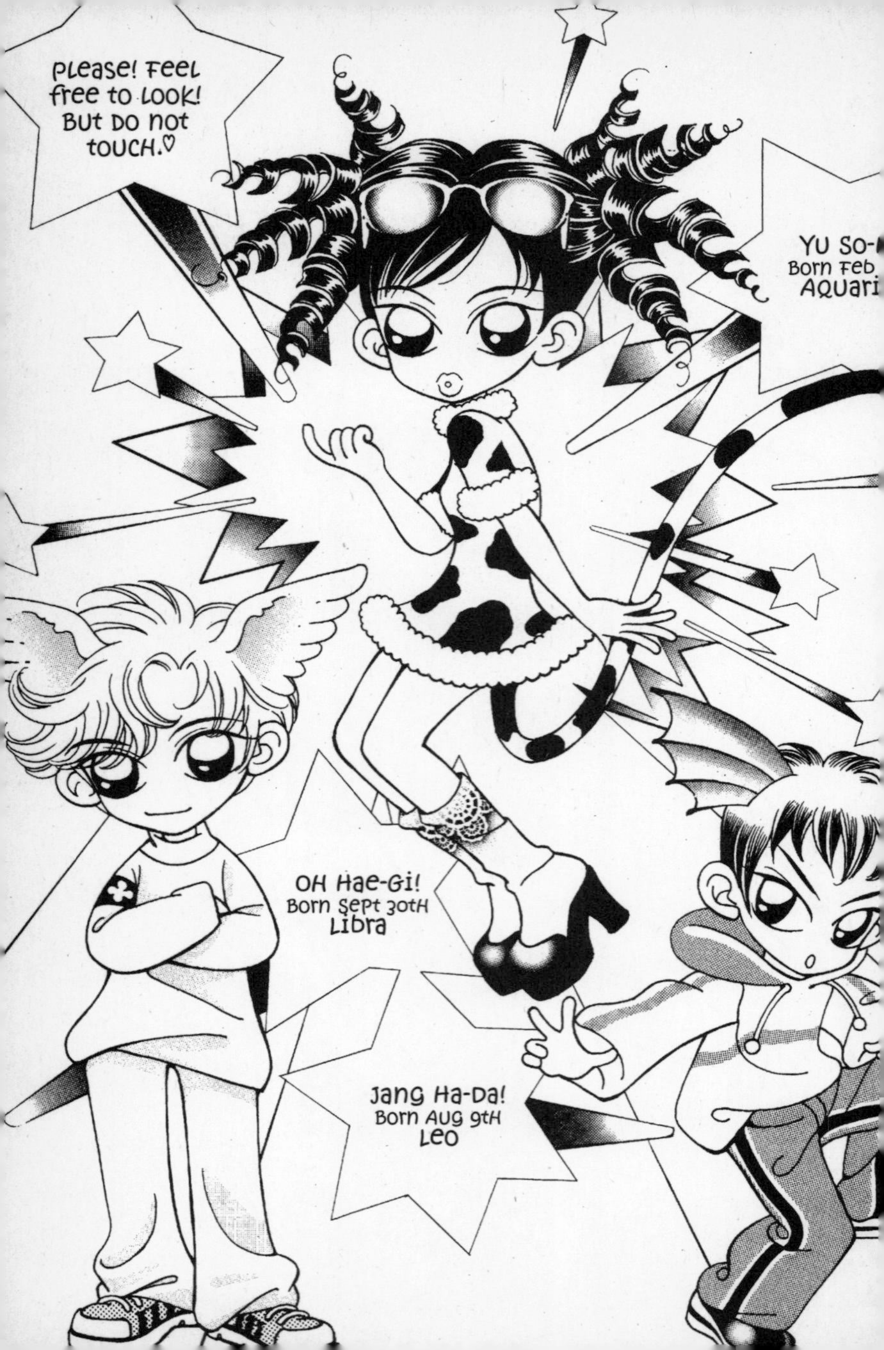
Please! Feel free to look! But do not touch.♡
Yu So-
Born Feb
Aquari
Oh Hae-Gi! Born Sept 30th Libra
Jang Ha-Da! Born Aug 9th Leo

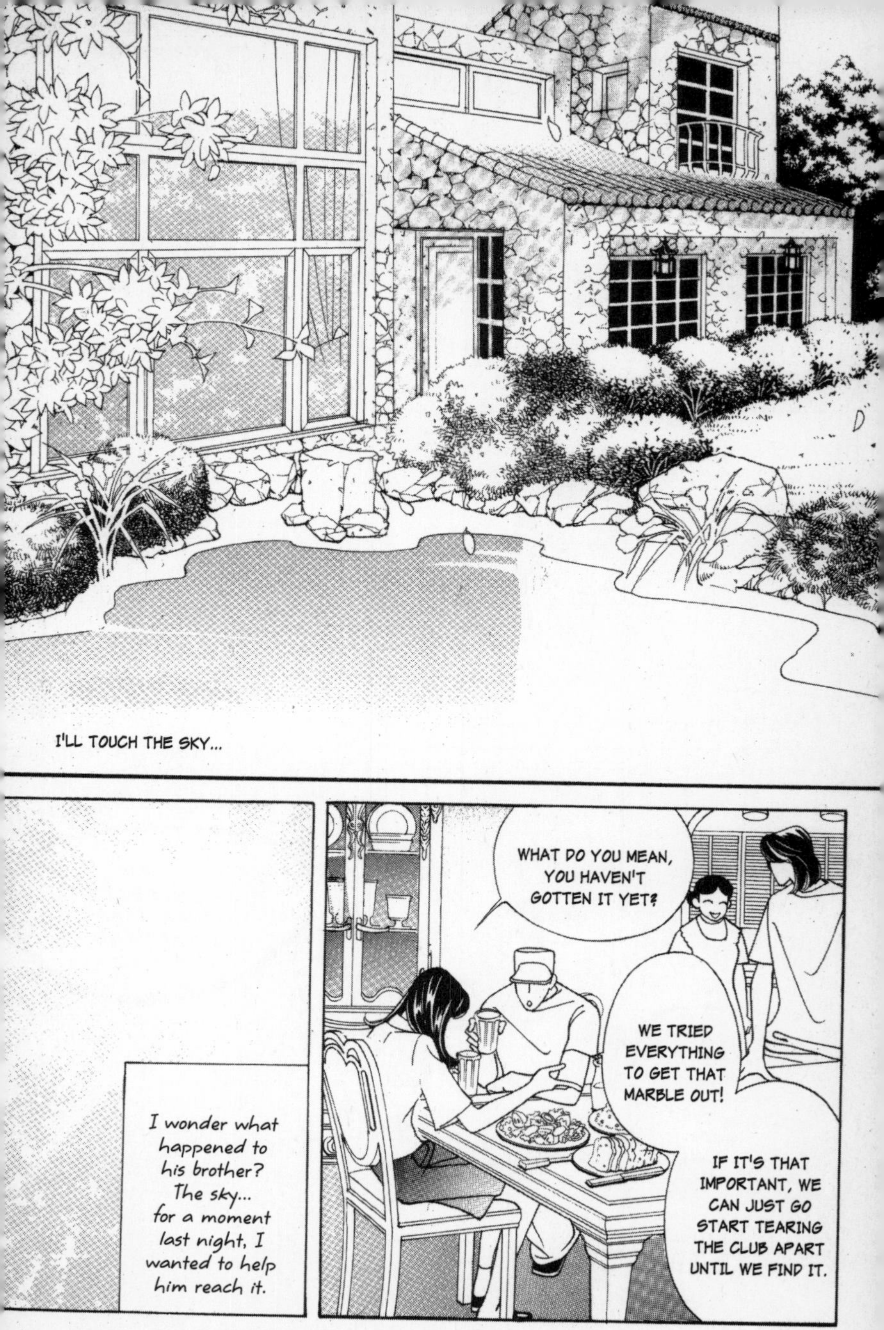
I'LL TOUCH THE SKY...
I wonder what happened to his brother? The sky... for a moment last night, I wanted to help him reach it.
WHAT DO YOU MEAN, YOU HAVEN'T GOTTEN IT YET?
WE TRIED EVERYTHING TO GET THAT MARBLE OUT!
IF IT'S THAT IMPORTANT, WE CAN JUST GO START TEARING THE CLUB APART UNTIL WE FIND IT.

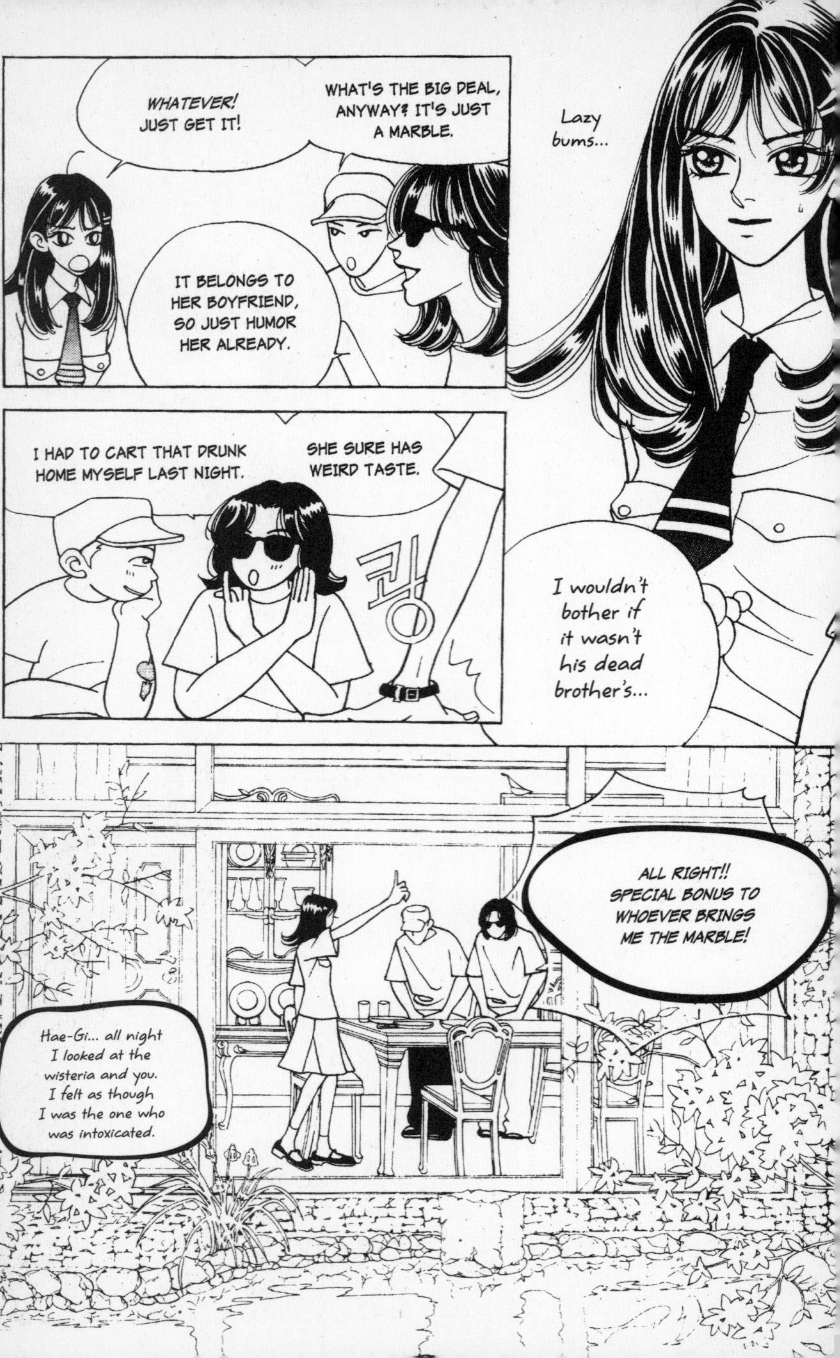
WHATEVER! JUST GET IT!
WHAT'S THE BIG DEAL, ANYWAY? IT'S JUST A MARBLE.
IT BELONGS TO HER BOYFRIEND, SO JUST HUMOR HER ALREADY.
I HAD TO CART THAT DRUNK HOME MYSELF LAST NIGHT.
SHE SURE HAS WEIRD TASTE.
Lazy bums...
I wouldn't bother if it wasn't his dead brother's...
Hae-Gi... all night I looked at the wisteria and you. I felt as though I was the one who was intoxicated.
ALL RIGHT!! SPECIAL BONUS TO WHOEVER BRINGS ME THE MARBLE!

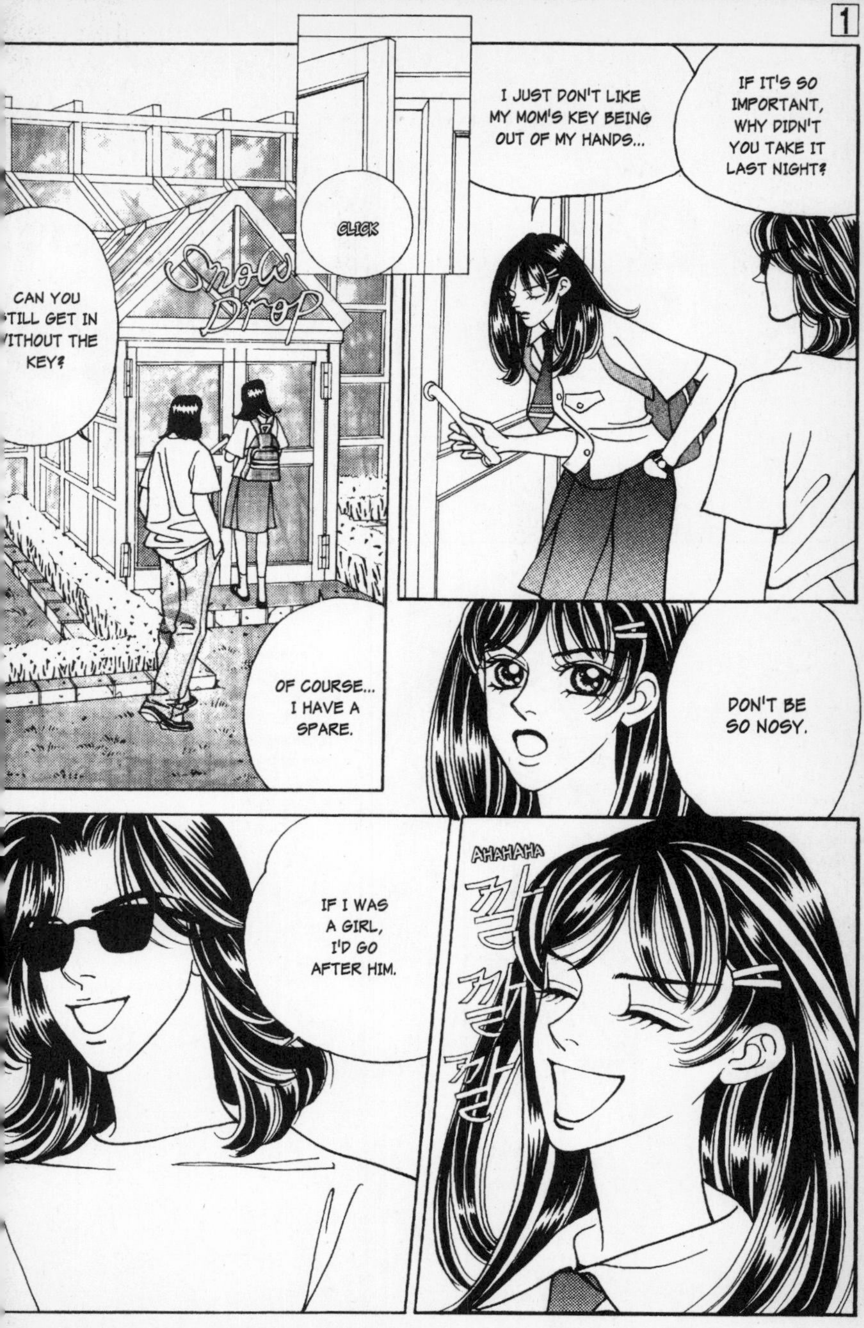
CAN YOU STILL GET IN WITHOUT THE KEY?
CLICK
OF COURSE... I HAVE A SPARE.
I JUST DON'T LIKE MY MOM'S KEY BEING OUT OF MY HANDS...
IF IT'S SO IMPORTANT, WHY DIDN'T YOU TAKE IT LAST NIGHT?
DON'T BE SO NOSY.
IF I WAS A GIRL, I'D GO AFTER HIM.
AHAHAHA

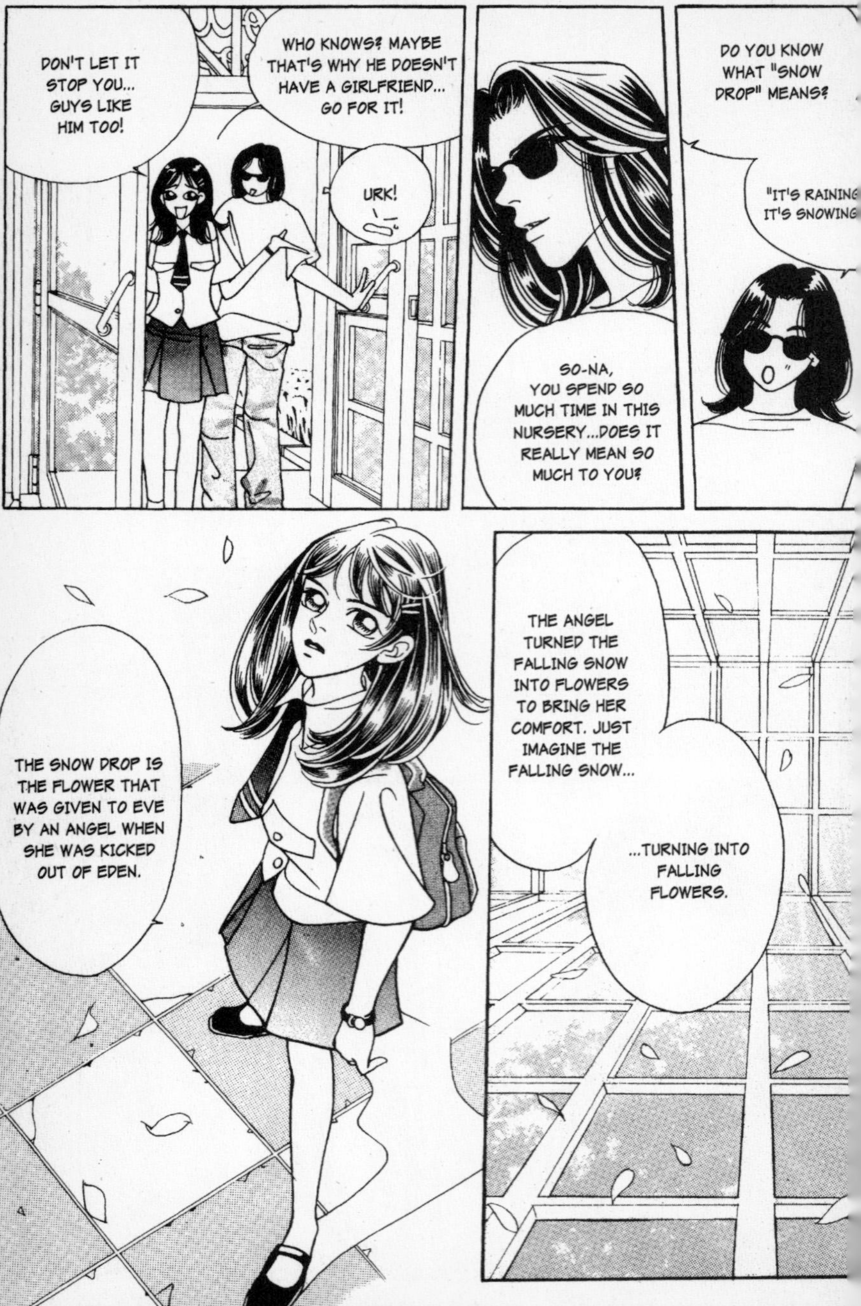
DON'T LET IT STOP YOU... GUYS LIKE HIM TOO!
WHO KNOWS? MAYBE THAT'S WHY HE DOESN'T HAVE A GIRLFRIEND... GO FOR IT!
URK!
SO-NA, YOU SPEND SO MUCH TIME IN THIS NURSERY...DOES IT REALLY MEAN SO MUCH TO YOU?
DO YOU KNOW WHAT "SNOW DROP" MEANS?
"IT'S RAINING IT'S SNOWING
THE SNOW DROP IS THE FLOWER THAT WAS GIVEN TO EVE BY AN ANGEL WHEN SHE WAS KICKED OUT OF EDEN.
THE ANGEL TURNED THE FALLING SNOW INTO FLOWERS TO BRING HER COMFORT. JUST IMAGINE THE FALLING SNOW...
...TURNING INTO FALLING FLOWERS.

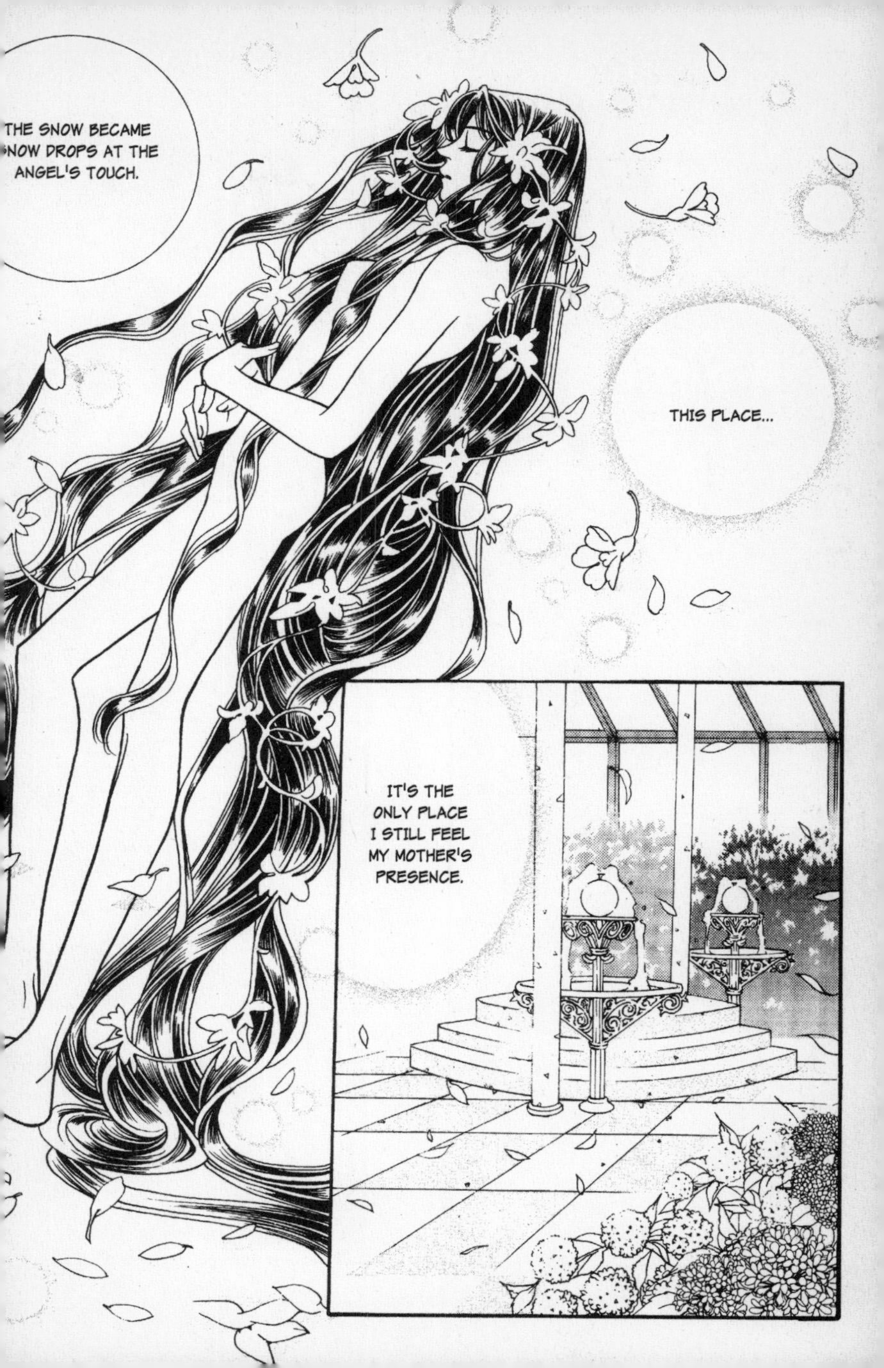
THE SNOW BECAME SNOW DROPS AT THE ANGEL'S TOUCH.
THIS PLACE...
IT'S THE ONLY PLACE I STILL FEEL MY MOTHER'S PRESENCE.

Snow Drop

Yu • So • Na

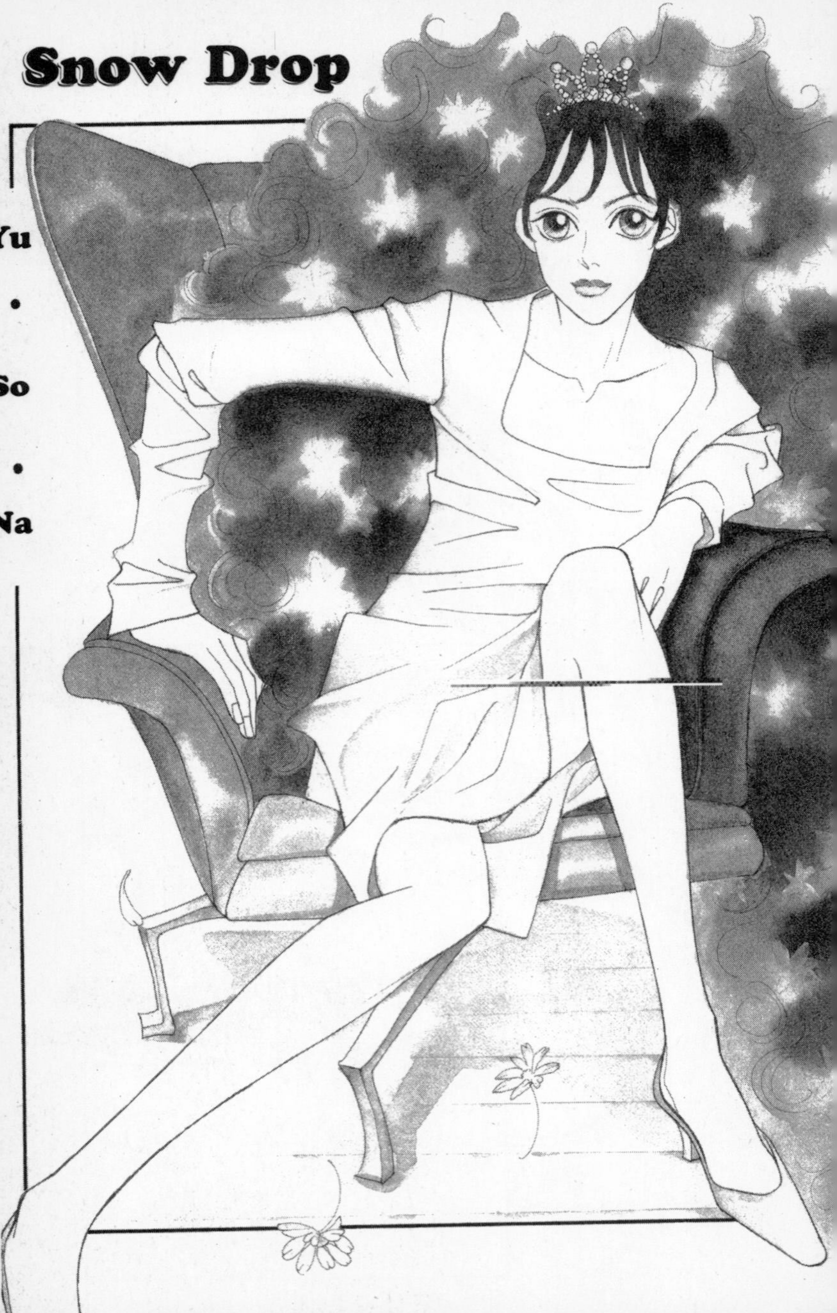

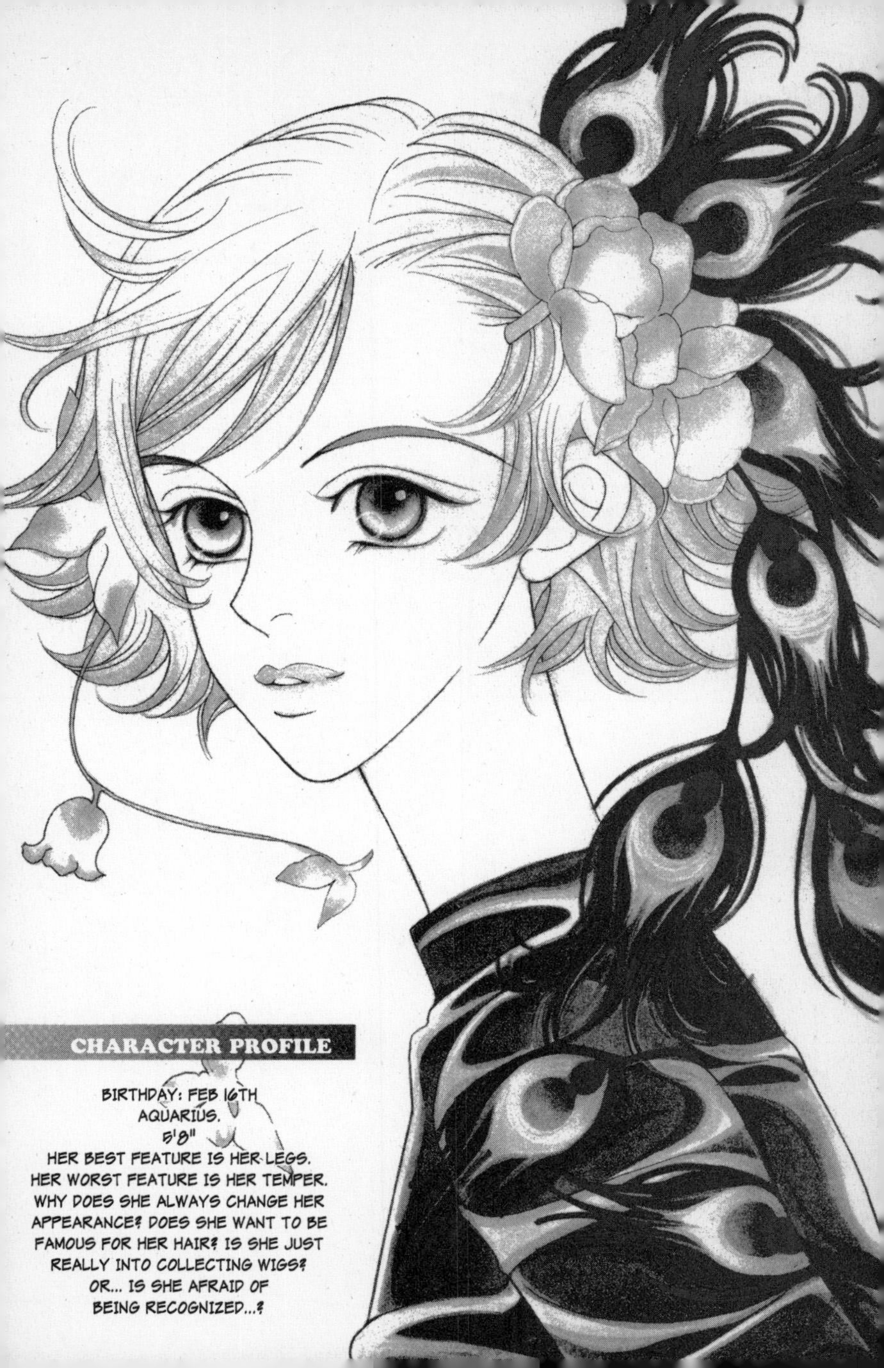

CHARACTER PROFILE

BIRTHDAY: FEB 16TH
AQUARIUS.
5'8"
HER BEST FEATURE IS HER LEGS.
HER WORST FEATURE IS HER TEMPER.
WHY DOES SHE ALWAYS CHANGE HER APPEARANCE? DOES SHE WANT TO BE FAMOUS FOR HER HAIR? IS SHE JUST REALLY INTO COLLECTING WIGS? OR... IS SHE AFRAID OF BEING RECOGNIZED...?

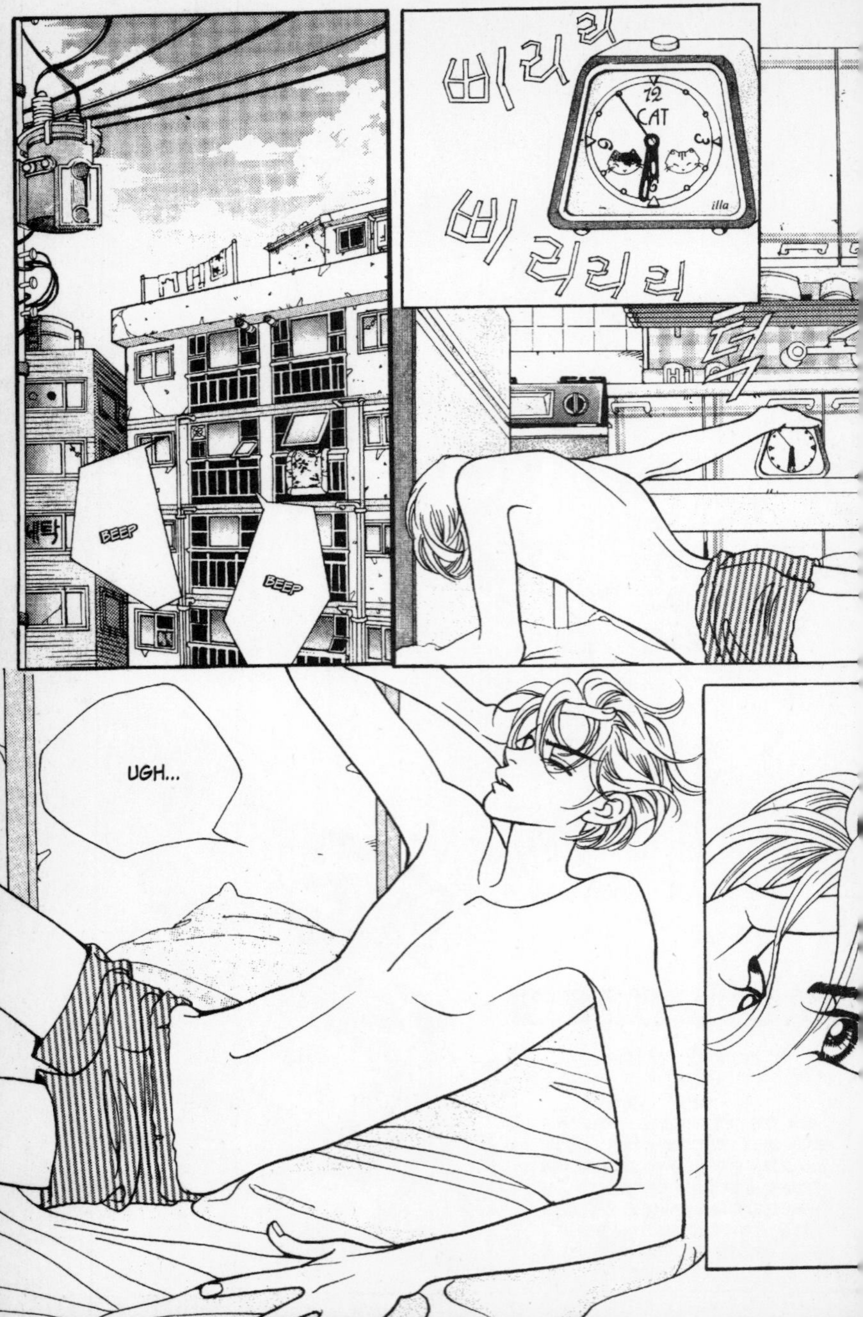
BEEP
BEEP
삐리릭
CAT
삐리리리
탁
UGH...

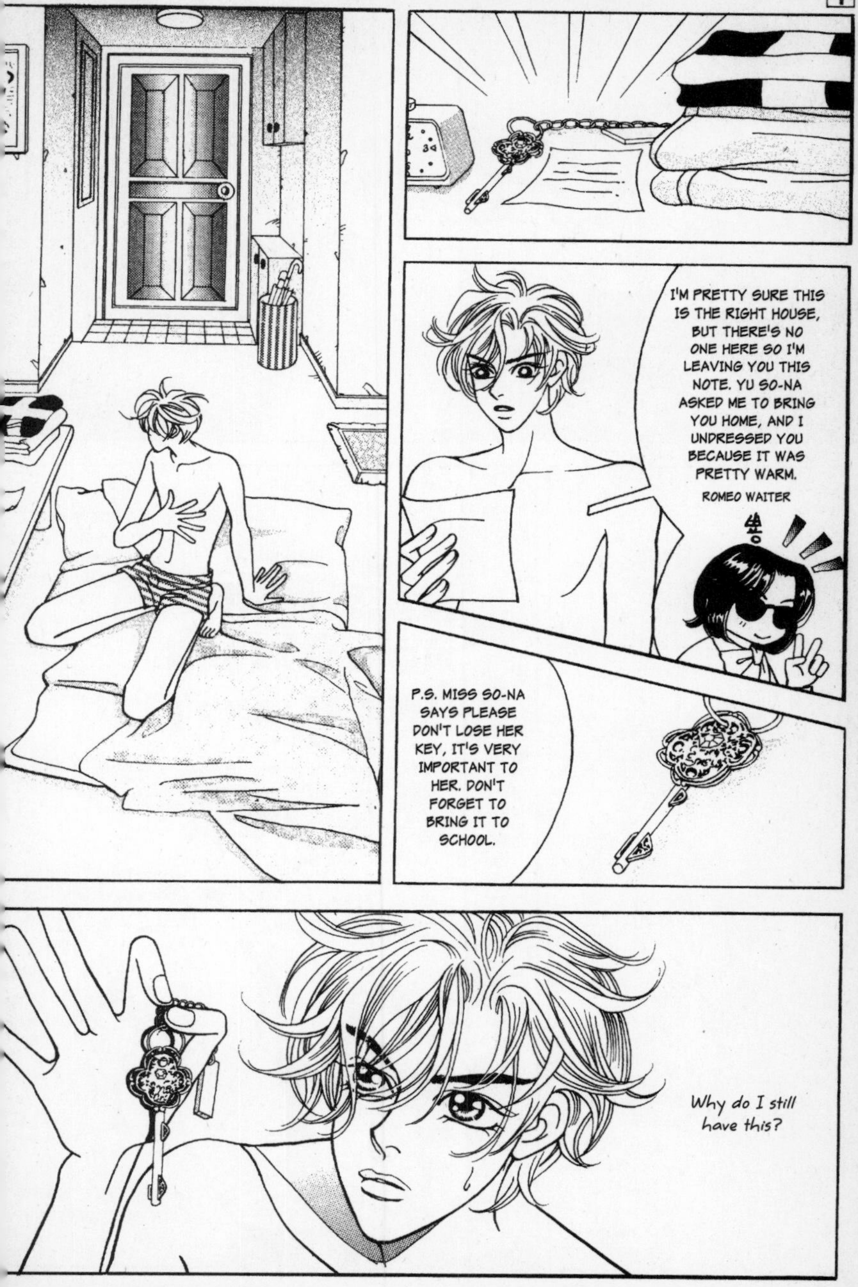
I'M PRETTY SURE THIS IS THE RIGHT HOUSE, BUT THERE'S NO ONE HERE SO I'M LEAVING YOU THIS NOTE. YU SO-NA ASKED ME TO BRING YOU HOME, AND I UNDRESSED YOU BECAUSE IT WAS PRETTY WARM.
ROMEO WAITER
P.S. MISS SO-NA SAYS PLEASE DON'T LOSE HER KEY, IT'S VERY IMPORTANT TO HER. DON'T FORGET TO BRING IT TO SCHOOL.
Why do I still have this?

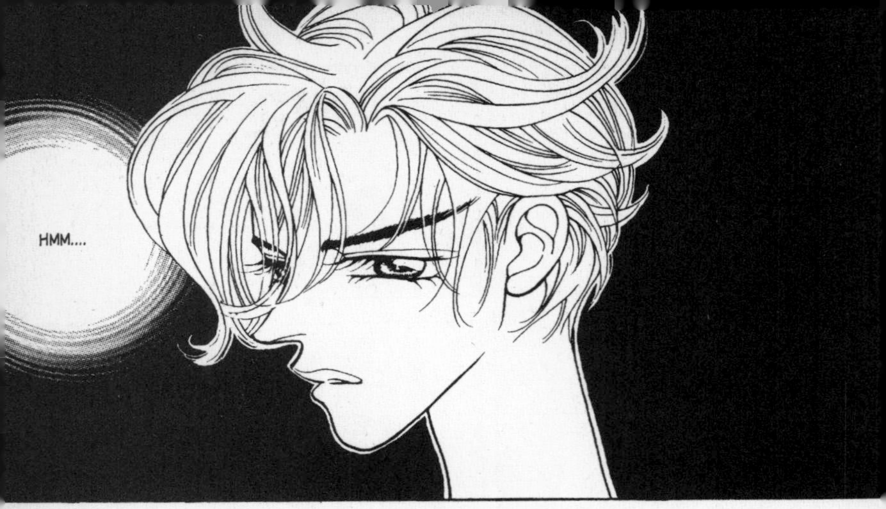
HMM....

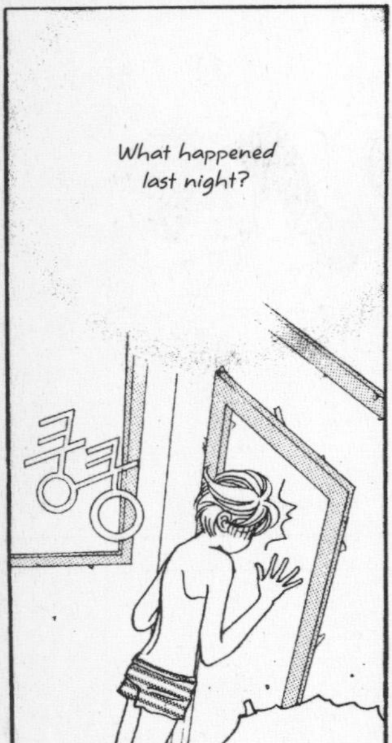
What happened last night?
How can you fall asleep and not even know someone took your clothes off? Hae-Gi, you're such an idiot!

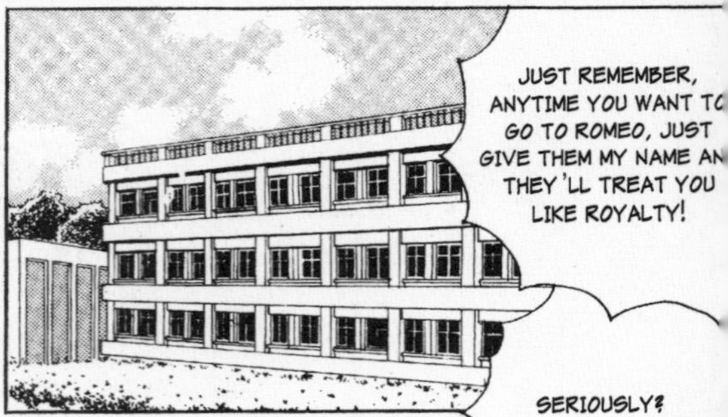
JUST REMEMBER, ANYTIME YOU WANT TO GO TO ROMEO, JUST GIVE THEM MY NAME AN THEY'LL TREAT YOU LIKE ROYALTY!

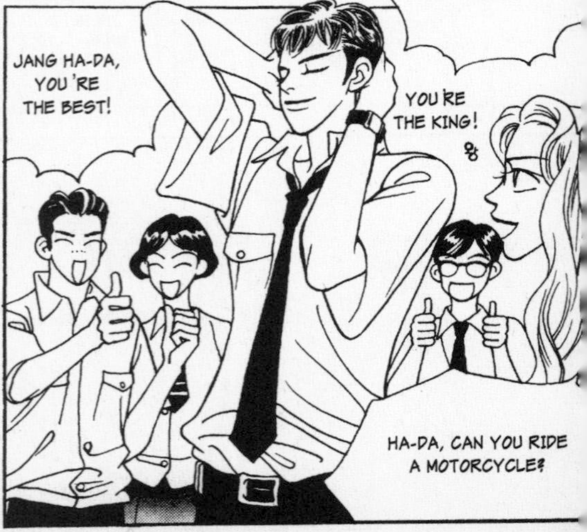
SERIOUSLY?
JANG HA-DA, YOU'RE THE BEST!
YOU'RE THE KING!
HA-DA, CAN YOU RIDE A MOTORCYCLE?

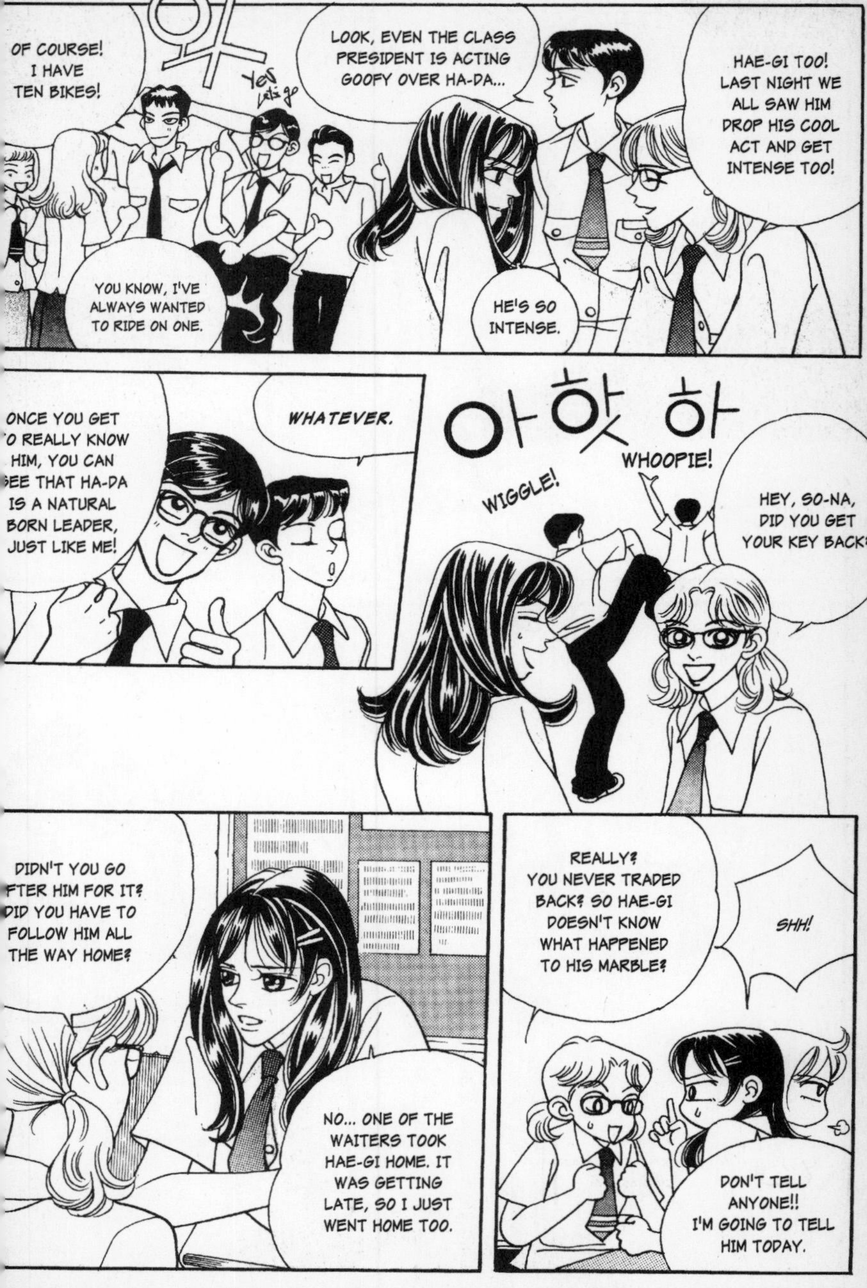

와
OF COURSE! I HAVE TEN BIKES!
YOU KNOW, I'VE ALWAYS WANTED TO RIDE ON ONE.
LOOK, EVEN THE CLASS PRESIDENT IS ACTING GOOFY OVER HA-DA...
HE'S SO INTENSE.
HAE-GI TOO! LAST NIGHT WE ALL SAW HIM DROP HIS COOL ACT AND GET INTENSE TOO!
ONCE YOU GET TO REALLY KNOW HIM, YOU CAN SEE THAT HA-DA IS A NATURAL BORN LEADER, JUST LIKE ME!
WHATEVER.
아핫 하
WHOOPIE!
WIGGLE!
HEY, SO-NA, DID YOU GET YOUR KEY BACK?
DIDN'T YOU GO AFTER HIM FOR IT? DID YOU HAVE TO FOLLOW HIM ALL THE WAY HOME?
NO... ONE OF THE WAITERS TOOK HAE-GI HOME. IT WAS GETTING LATE, SO I JUST WENT HOME TOO.
REALLY? YOU NEVER TRADED BACK? SO HAE-GI DOESN'T KNOW WHAT HAPPENED TO HIS MARBLE?
SHH!
DON'T TELL ANYONE!! I'M GOING TO TELL HIM TODAY.

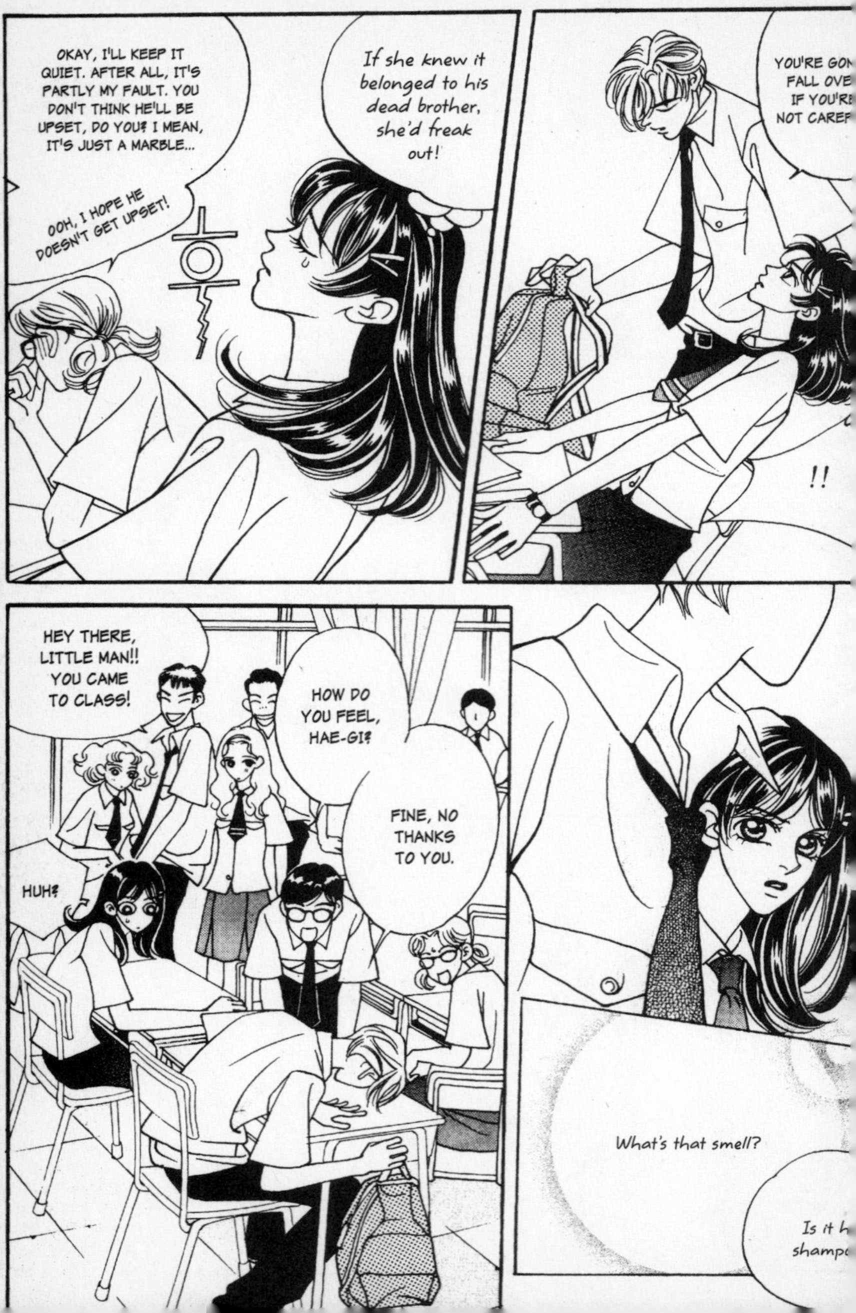

OKAY, I'LL KEEP IT QUIET. AFTER ALL, IT'S PARTLY MY FAULT. YOU DON'T THINK HE'LL BE UPSET, DO YOU? I MEAN, IT'S JUST A MARBLE...
OOH, I HOPE HE DOESN'T GET UPSET!
If she knew it belonged to his dead brother, she'd freak out!
YOU'RE GON FALL OVE IF YOU'RE NOT CAREF
!!
HEY THERE, LITTLE MAN!! YOU CAME TO CLASS!
HOW DO YOU FEEL, HAE-GI?
FINE, NO THANKS TO YOU.
HUH?
What's that smell?
Is it h shampo

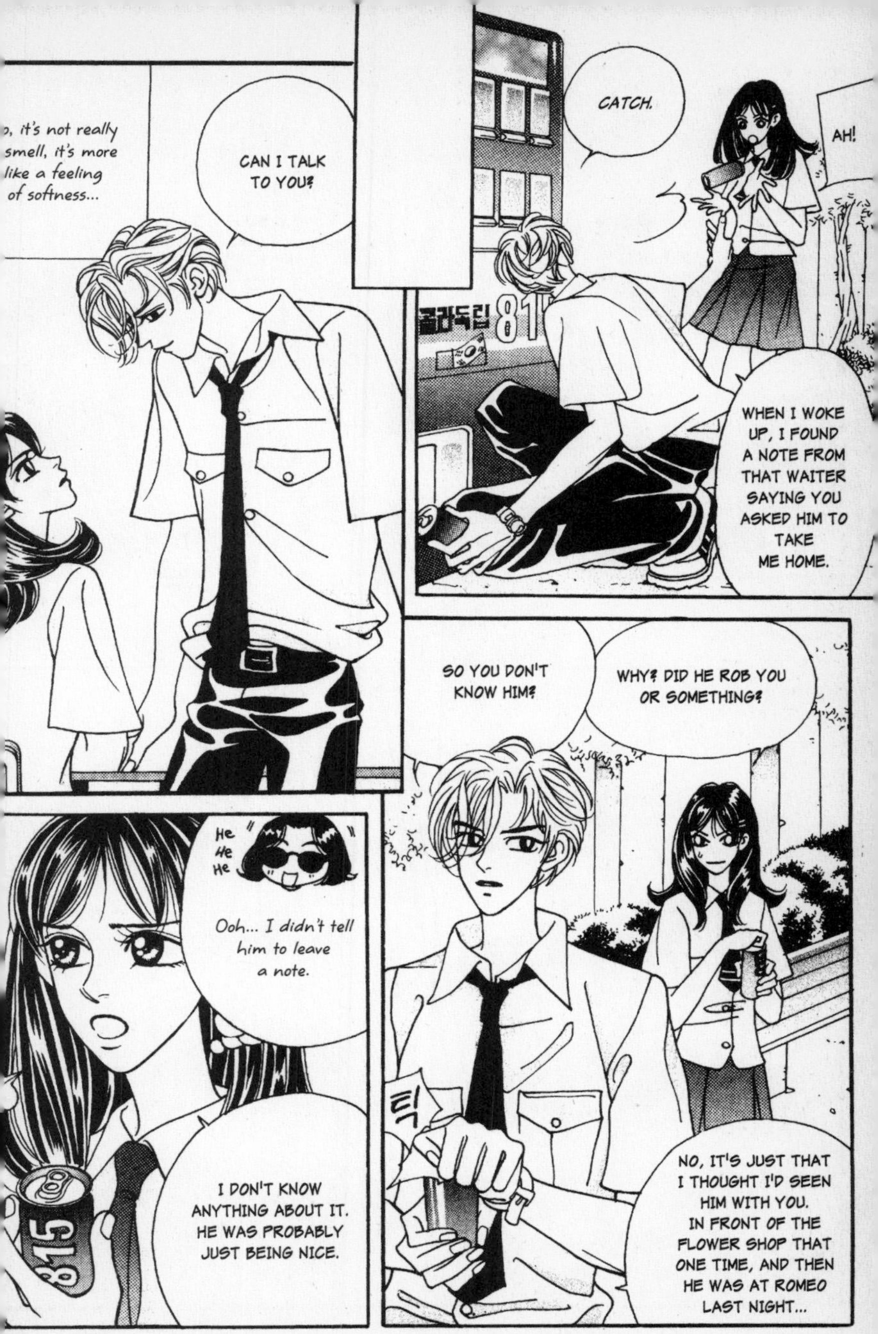
o, it's not really smell, it's more like a feeling of softness...
CAN I TALK TO YOU?
CATCH.
AH!
WHEN I WOKE UP, I FOUND A NOTE FROM THAT WAITER SAYING YOU ASKED HIM TO TAKE ME HOME.
He He He
Ooh... I didn't tell him to leave a note.
I DON'T KNOW ANYTHING ABOUT IT. HE WAS PROBABLY JUST BEING NICE.
SO YOU DON'T KNOW HIM?
WHY? DID HE ROB YOU OR SOMETHING?
틱
NO, IT'S JUST THAT I THOUGHT I'D SEEN HIM WITH YOU. IN FRONT OF THE FLOWER SHOP THAT ONE TIME, AND THEN HE WAS AT ROMEO LAST NIGHT...

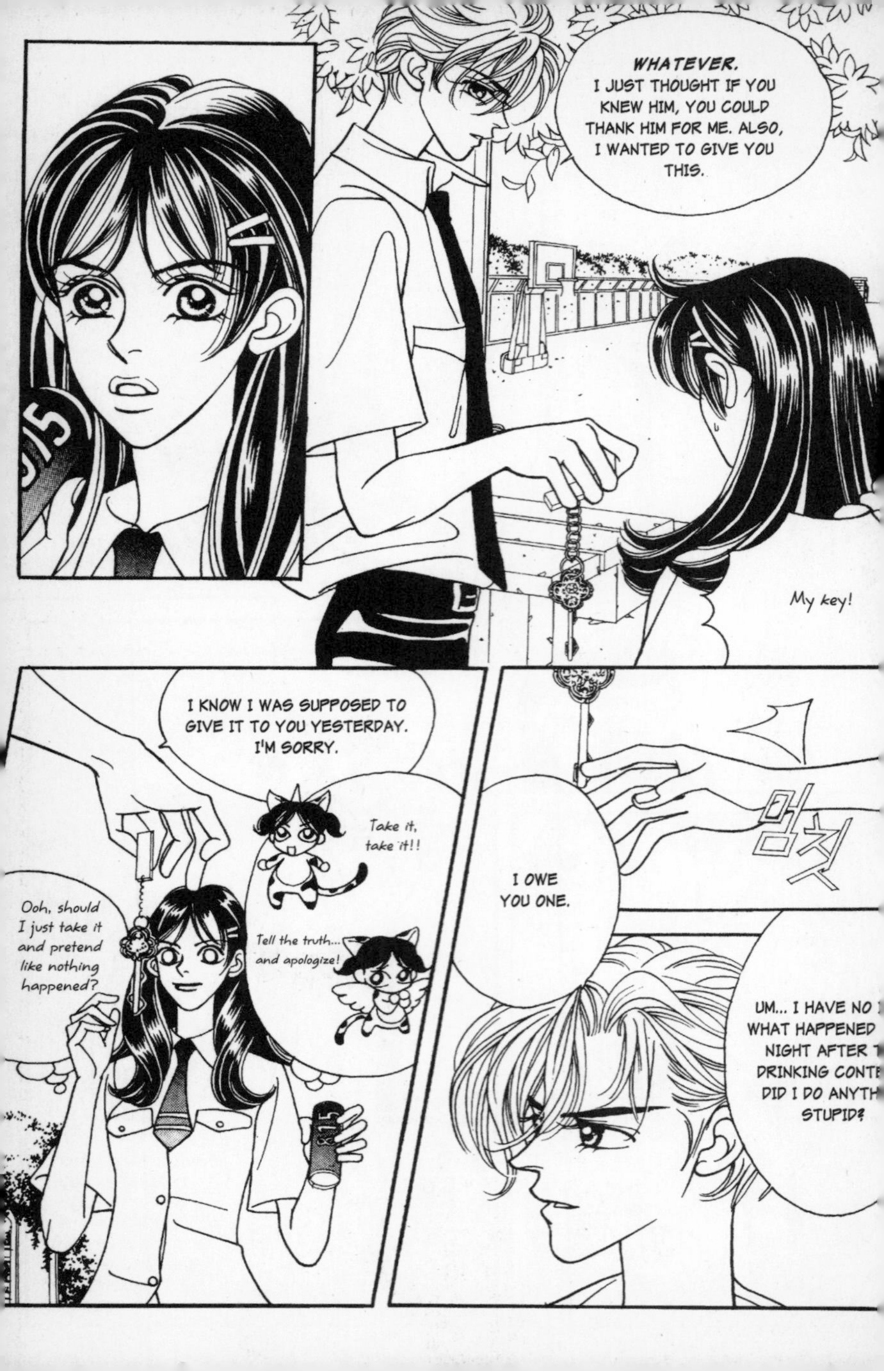
WHATEVER. I JUST THOUGHT IF YOU KNEW HIM, YOU COULD THANK HIM FOR ME. ALSO, I WANTED TO GIVE YOU THIS.
My key!
I KNOW I WAS SUPPOSED TO GIVE IT TO YOU YESTERDAY. I'M SORRY.
Ooh, should I just take it and pretend like nothing happened?
Take it, take it!!
Tell the truth... and apologize!
멈칫
I OWE YOU ONE.
UM... I HAVE NO
WHAT HAPPENED
NIGHT AFTER
DRINKING CONTE
DID I DO ANYTH
STUPID?

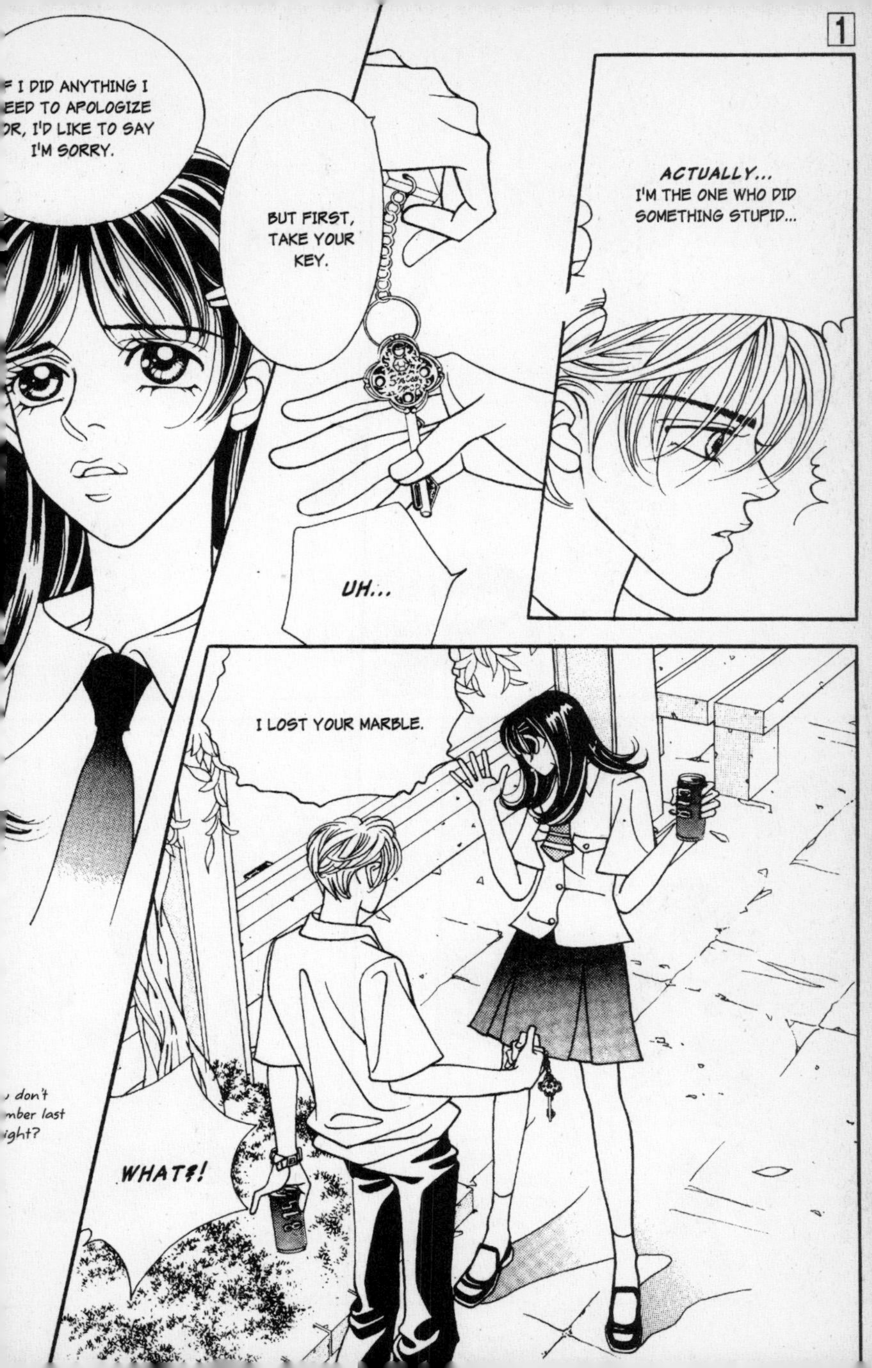
F I DID ANYTHING I
EED TO APOLOGIZE
OR, I'D LIKE TO SAY
I'M SORRY.
u don't
mber last
ight?
WHAT?!
BUT FIRST, TAKE YOUR KEY.
UH...
ACTUALLY... I'M THE ONE WHO DID SOMETHING STUPID...
I LOST YOUR MARBLE.

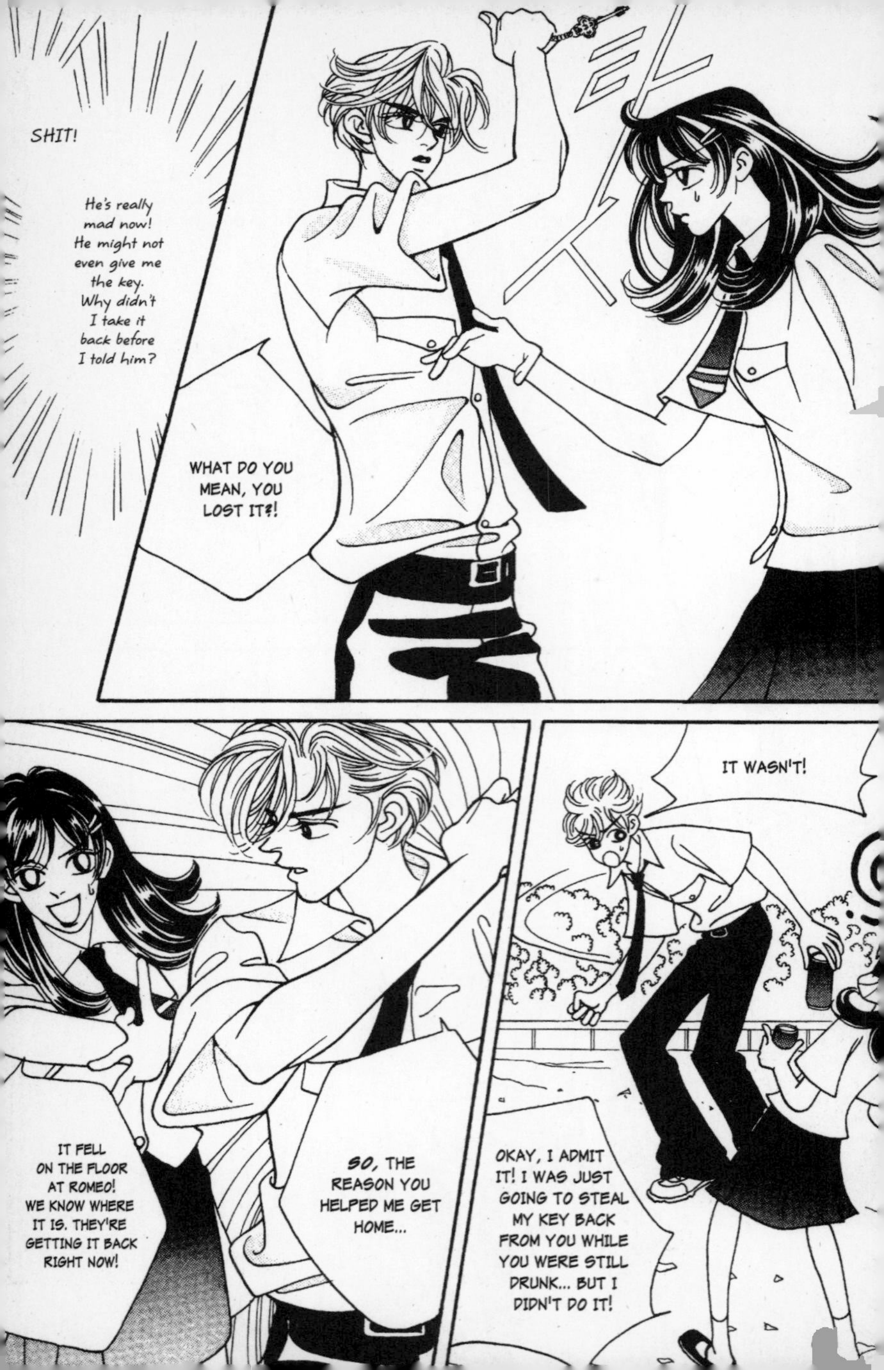
SHIT!
He's really mad now! He might not even give me the key. Why didn't I take it back before I told him?
WHAT DO YOU MEAN, YOU LOST IT?!
IT FELL ON THE FLOOR AT ROMEO! WE KNOW WHERE IT IS. THEY'RE GETTING IT BACK RIGHT NOW!
SO, THE REASON YOU HELPED ME GET HOME...
IT WASN'T!
OKAY, I ADMIT IT! I WAS JUST GOING TO STEAL MY KEY BACK FROM YOU WHILE YOU WERE STILL DRUNK... BUT I DIDN'T DO IT!

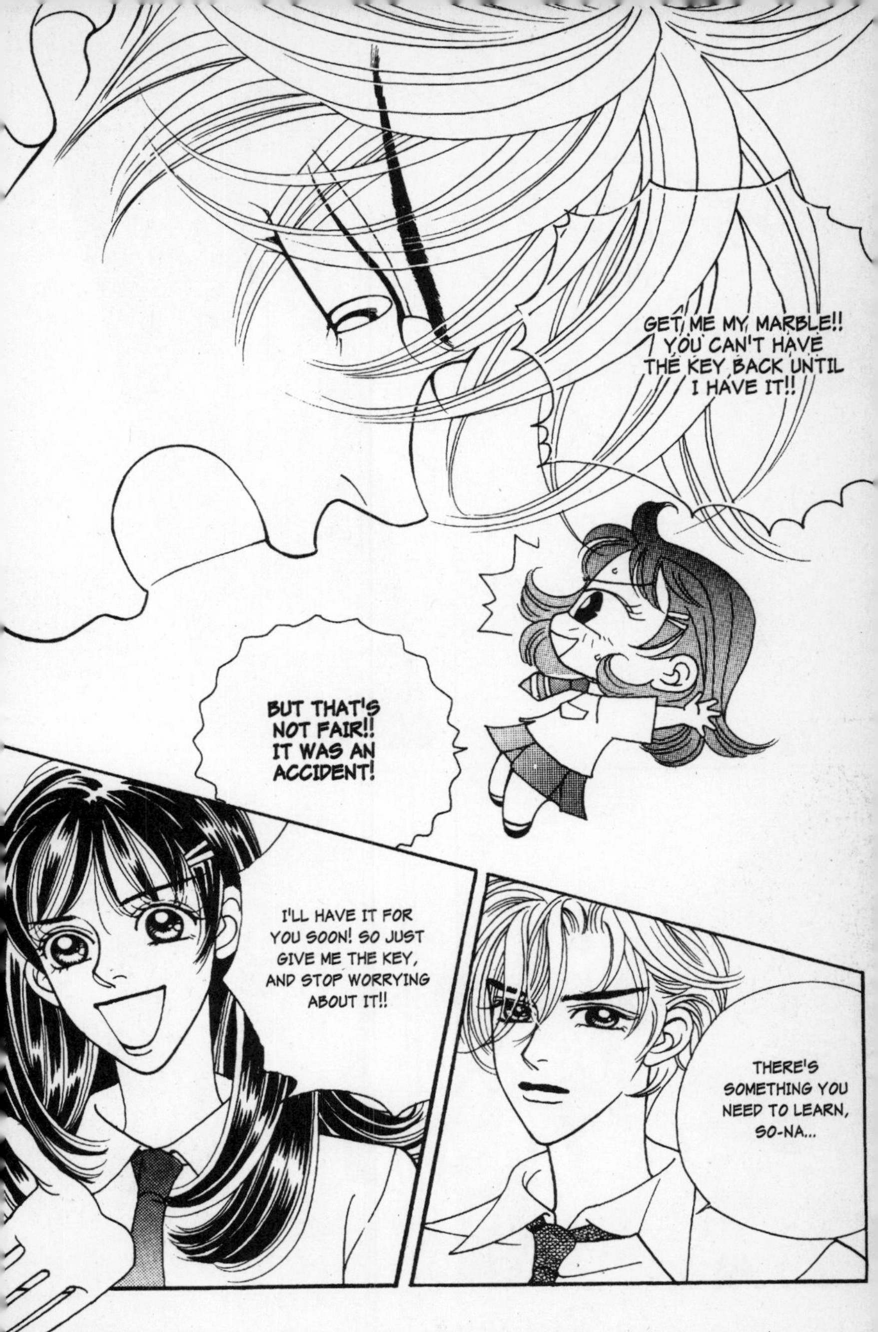
GET ME MY MARBLE!! YOU CAN'T HAVE THE KEY BACK UNTIL I HAVE IT!!
BUT THAT'S NOT FAIR!! IT WAS AN ACCIDENT!
I'LL HAVE IT FOR YOU SOON! SO JUST GIVE ME THE KEY, AND STOP WORRYING ABOUT IT!!
THERE'S SOMETHING YOU NEED TO LEARN, SO-NA...

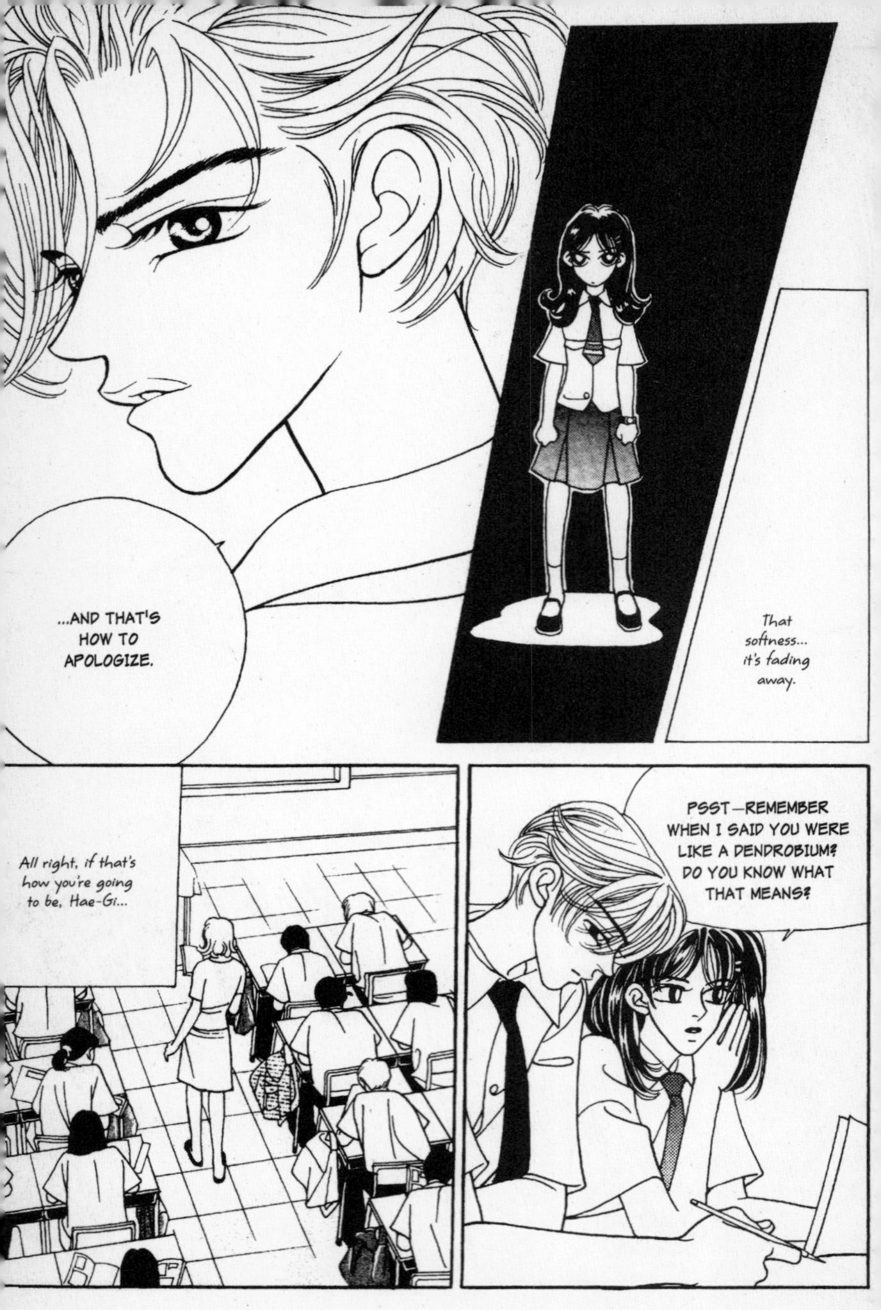
...AND THAT'S HOW TO APOLOGIZE.
That softness... it's fading away.
All right, if that's how you're going to be, Hae-Gi...
PSST—REMEMBER WHEN I SAID YOU WERE LIKE A DENDROBIUM? DO YOU KNOW WHAT THAT MEANS?

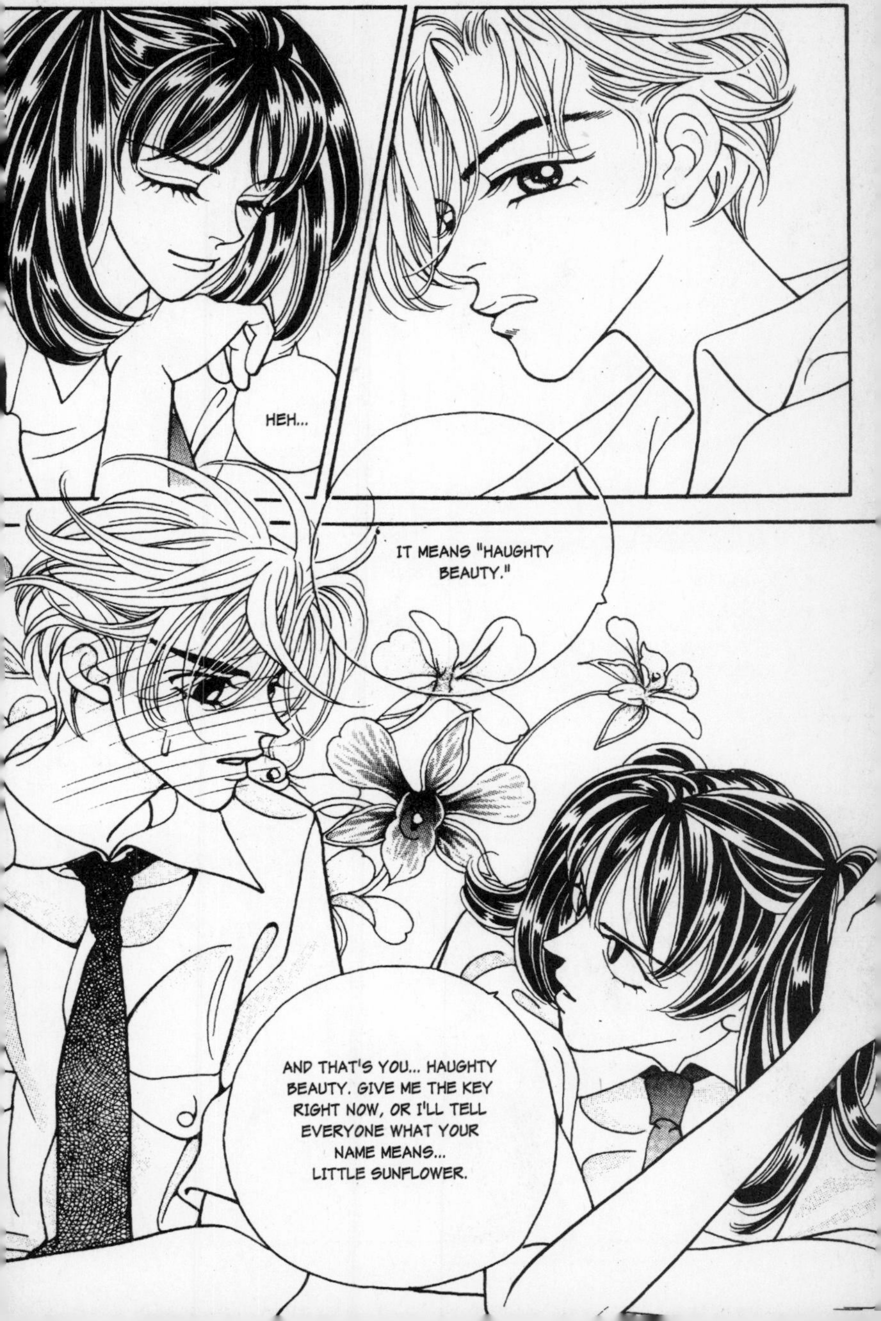
HEH...
IT MEANS "HAUGHTY BEAUTY."
AND THAT'S YOU... HAUGHTY BEAUTY. GIVE ME THE KEY RIGHT NOW, OR I'LL TELL EVERYONE WHAT YOUR NAME MEANS... LITTLE SUNFLOWER.

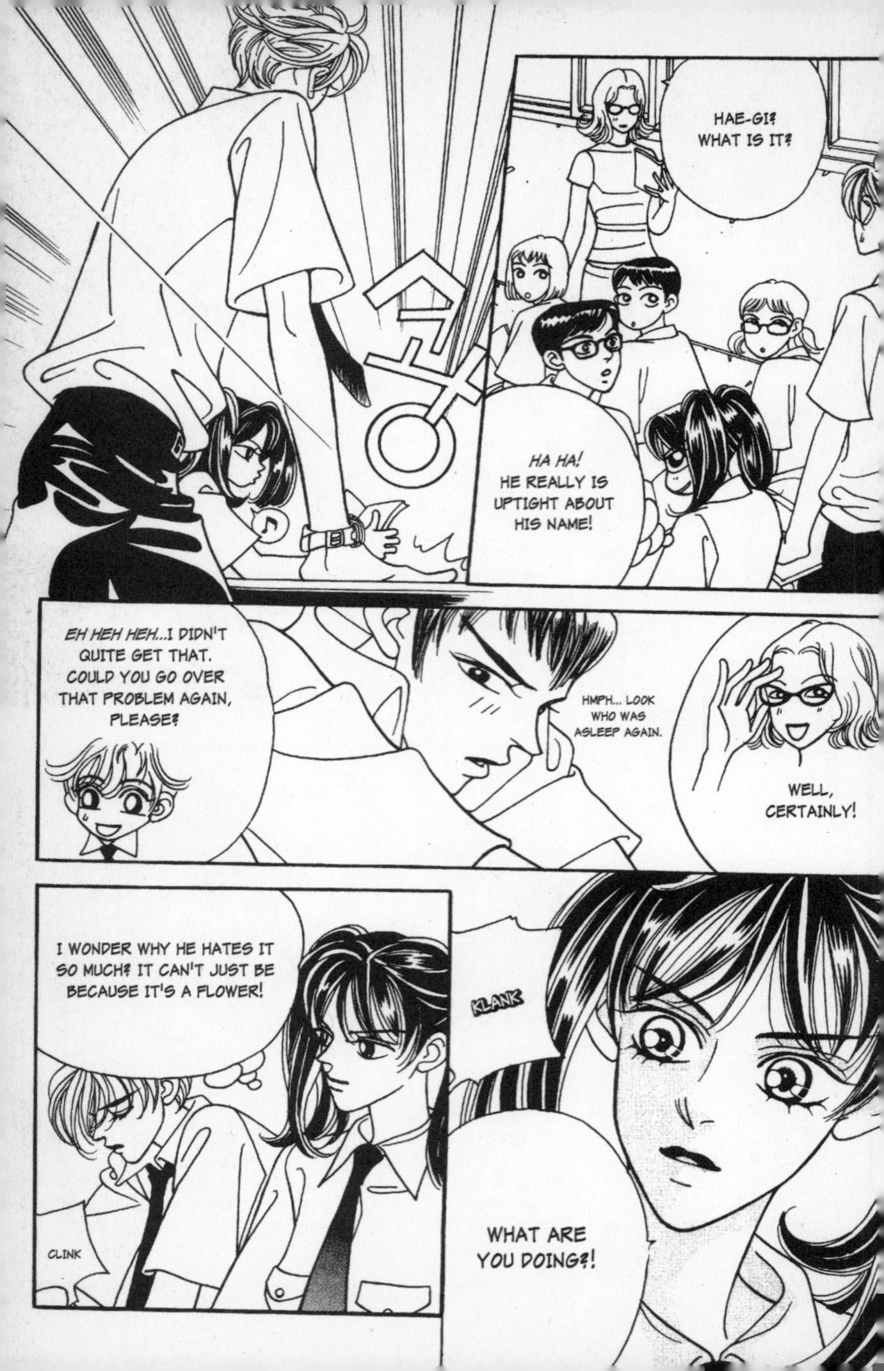
HAE-GI? WHAT IS IT?
HA HA! HE REALLY IS UPTIGHT ABOUT HIS NAME!
EH HEH HEH...I DIDN'T QUITE GET THAT. COULD YOU GO OVER THAT PROBLEM AGAIN, PLEASE?
HMPH... LOOK WHO WAS ASLEEP AGAIN.
WELL, CERTAINLY!
I WONDER WHY HE HATES IT SO MUCH? IT CAN'T JUST BE BECAUSE IT'S A FLOWER!
CLINK
KLANK
WHAT ARE YOU DOING?!

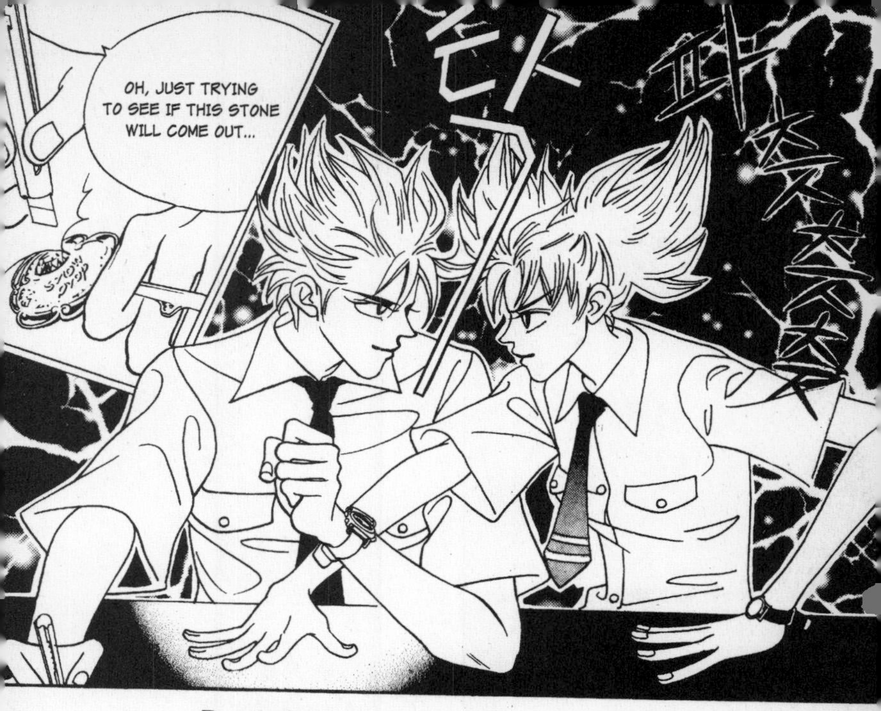
OH, JUST TRYING TO SEE IF THIS STONE WILL COME OUT...

Part 3. White Birch - I Waited For You.

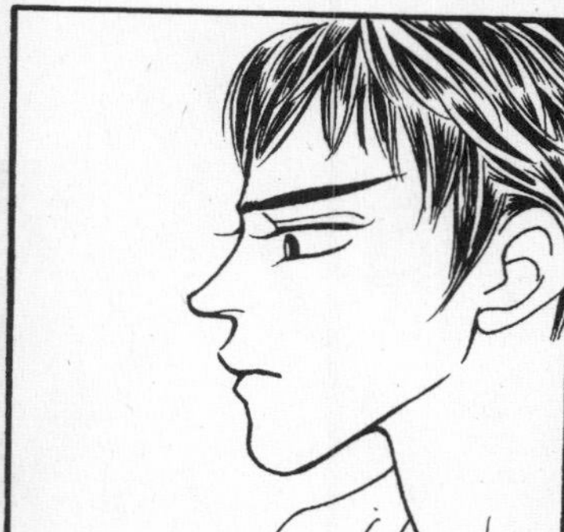

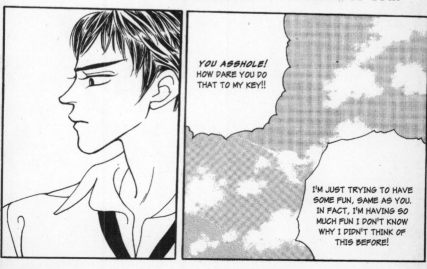

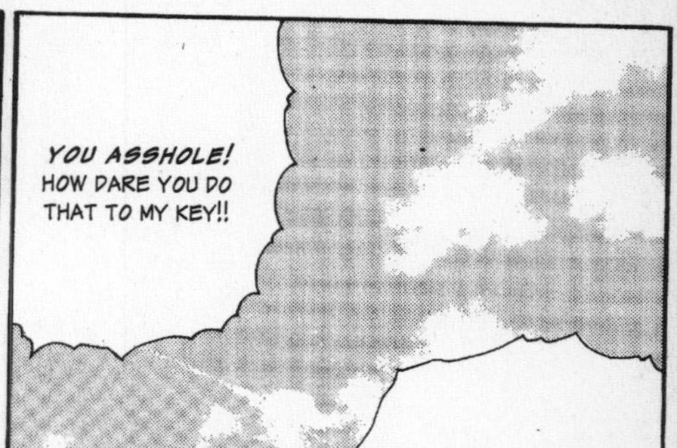
YOU ASSHOLE! HOW DARE YOU DO THAT TO MY KEY!!
I'M JUST TRYING TO HAVE SOME FUN, SAME AS YOU. IN FACT, I'M HAVING SO MUCH FUN I DON'T KNOW WHY I DIDN'T THINK OF THIS BEFORE!

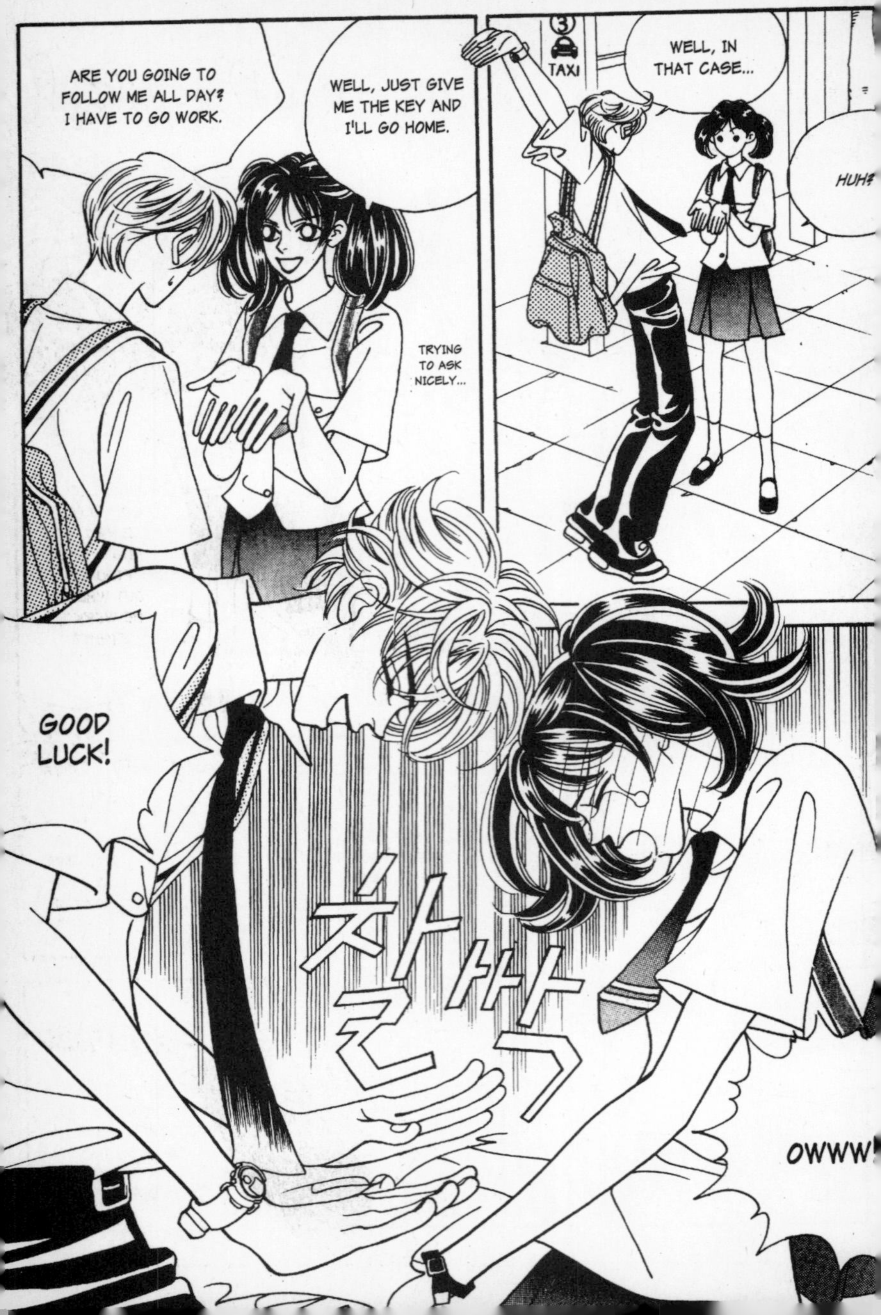
ARE YOU GOING TO FOLLOW ME ALL DAY? I HAVE TO GO WORK.
WELL, JUST GIVE ME THE KEY AND I'LL GO HOME.
TRYING TO ASK NICELY...
TAXI
WELL, IN THAT CASE...
HUH?
GOOD LUCK!
OWWW!

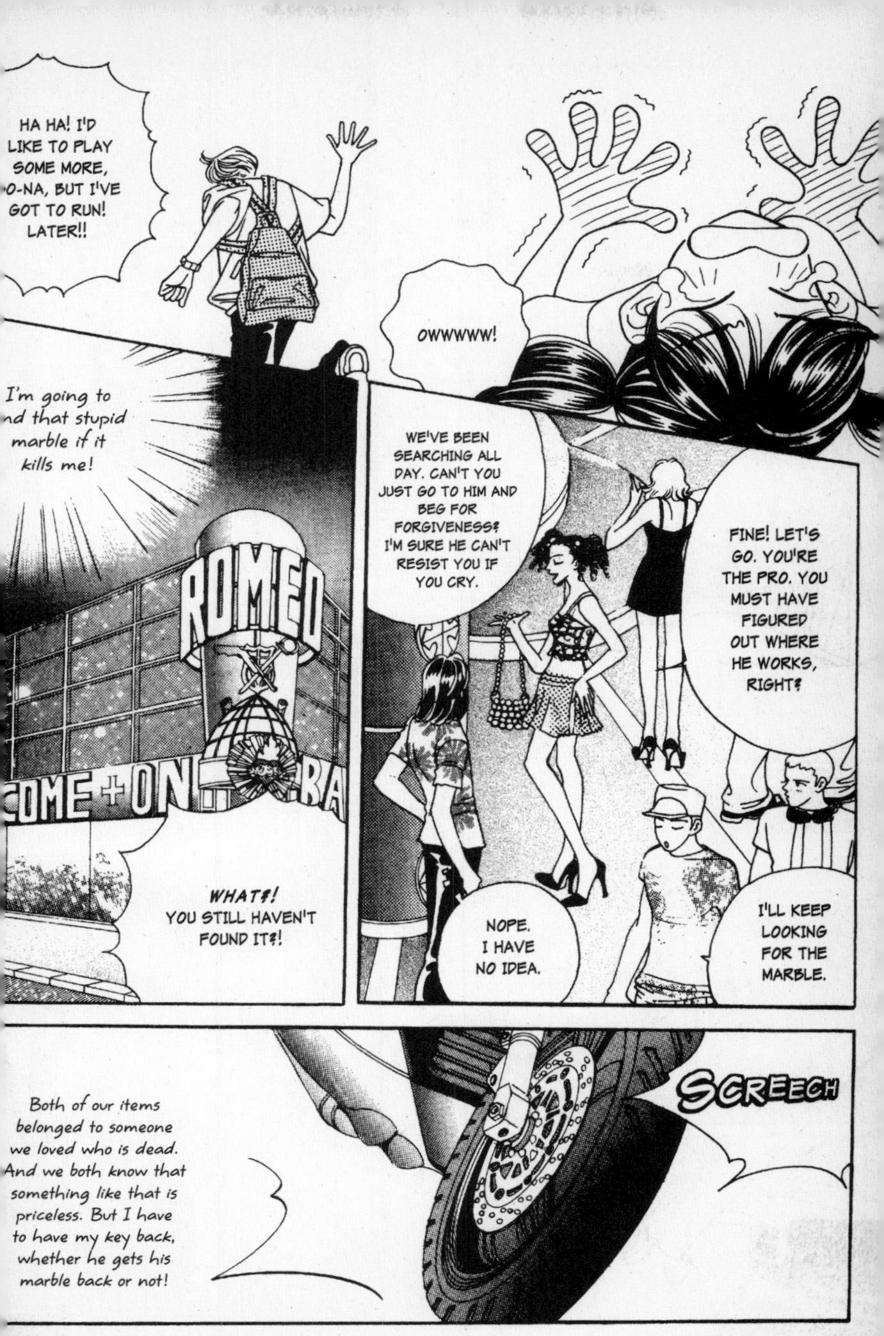
HA HA! I'D LIKE TO PLAY SOME MORE, O-NA, BUT I'VE GOT TO RUN! LATER!!
OWWWWW!
I'm going to nd that stupid marble if it kills me!
WHAT?! YOU STILL HAVEN'T FOUND IT?!
ROMEO
COME+ON BA
WE'VE BEEN SEARCHING ALL DAY. CAN'T YOU JUST GO TO HIM AND BEG FOR FORGIVENESS? I'M SURE HE CAN'T RESIST YOU IF YOU CRY.
FINE! LET'S GO. YOU'RE THE PRO. YOU MUST HAVE FIGURED OUT WHERE HE WORKS, RIGHT?
NOPE. I HAVE NO IDEA.
I'LL KEEP LOOKING FOR THE MARBLE.
Both of our items belonged to someone we loved who is dead. And we both know that something like that is priceless. But I have to have my key back, whether he gets his marble back or not!
SCREECH

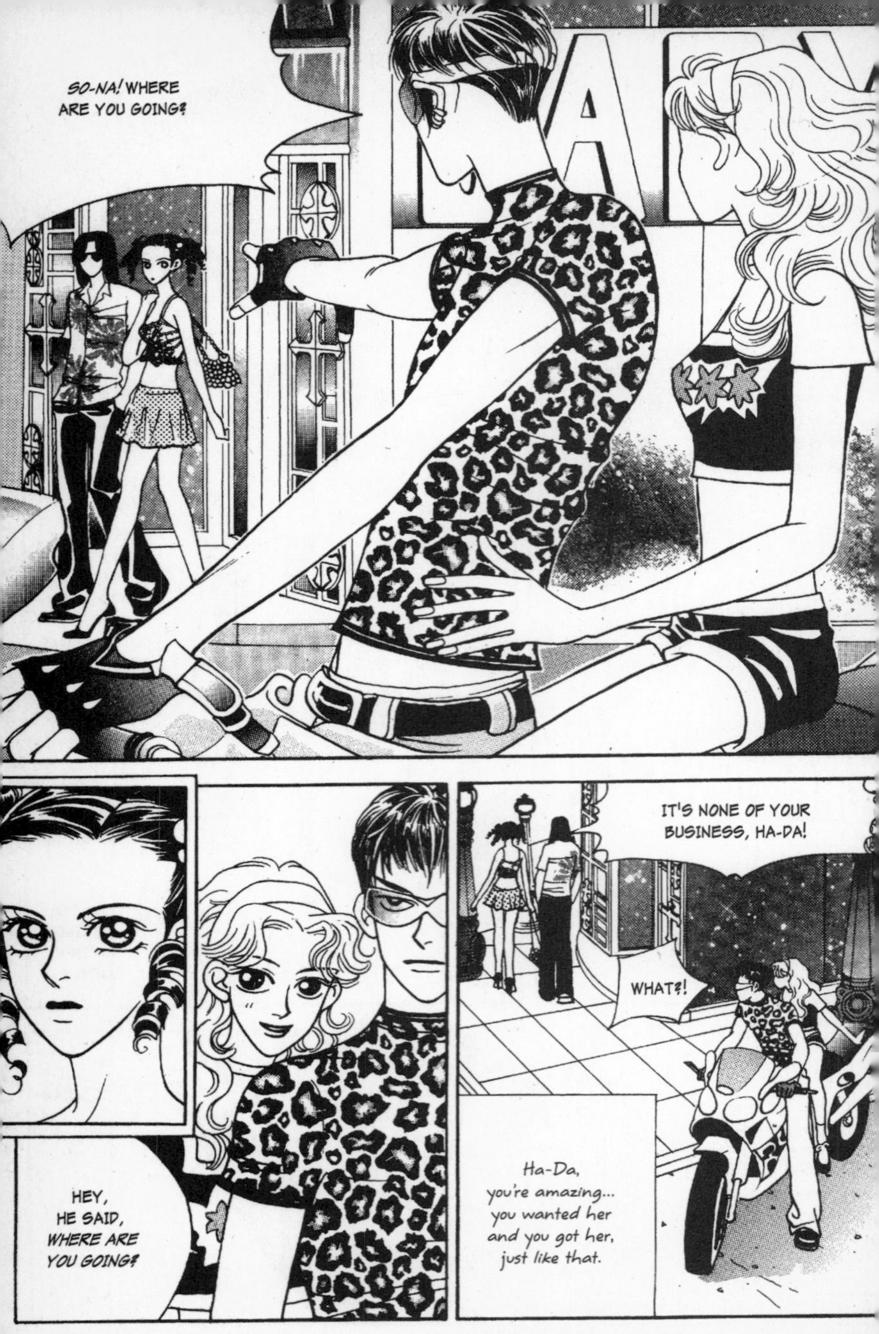
SO-NA! WHERE ARE YOU GOING?
HEY, HE SAID, WHERE ARE YOU GOING?
IT'S NONE OF YOUR BUSINESS, HA-DA!
WHAT?!
Ha-Da, you're amazing... you wanted her and you got her, just like that.

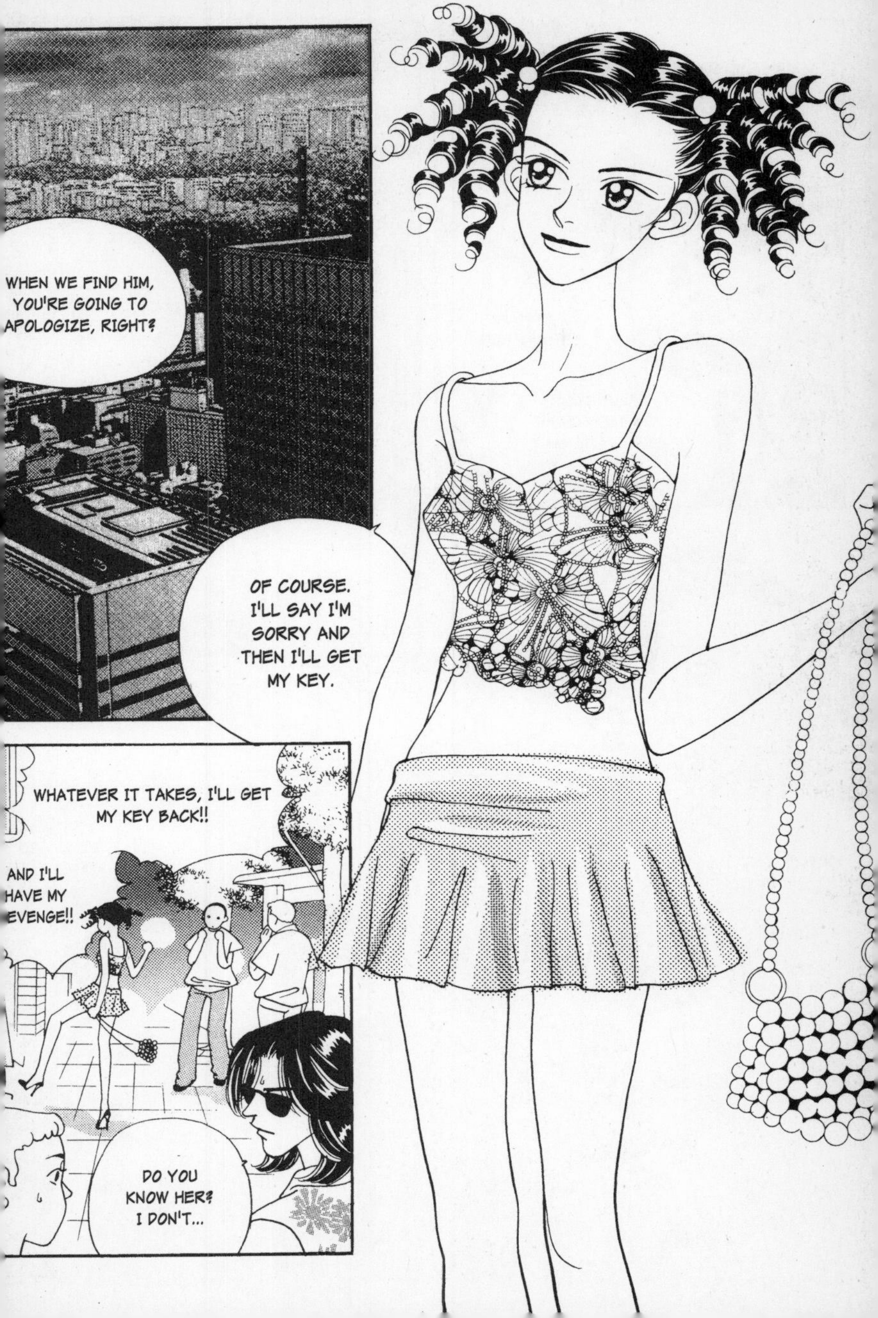
WHEN WE FIND HIM, YOU'RE GOING TO APOLOGIZE, RIGHT?
OF COURSE. I'LL SAY I'M SORRY AND THEN I'LL GET MY KEY.
WHATEVER IT TAKES, I'LL GET MY KEY BACK!!
AND I'LL HAVE MY EVENGE!!
DO YOU KNOW HER? I DON'T...

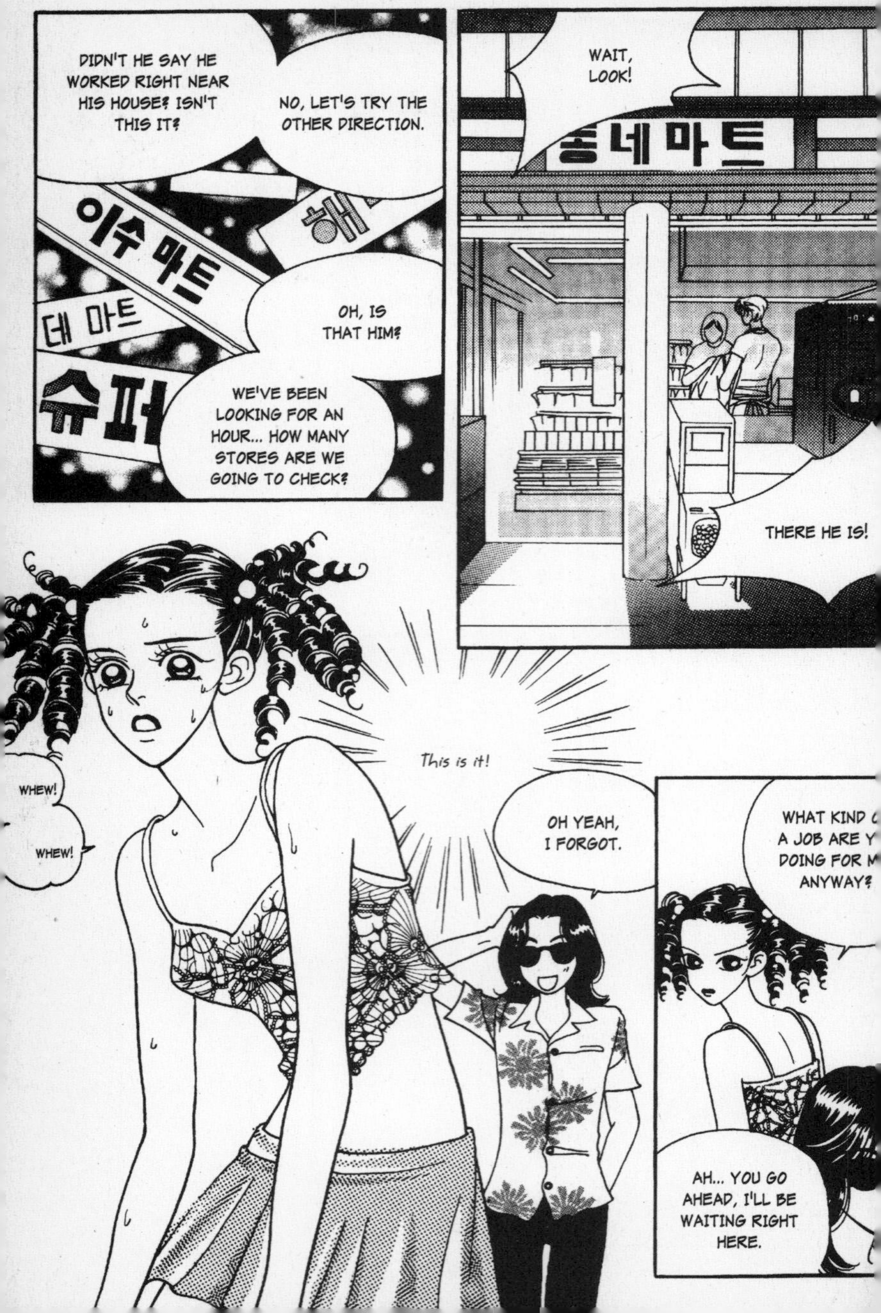
DIDN'T HE SAY HE WORKED RIGHT NEAR HIS HOUSE? ISN'T THIS IT?
NO, LET'S TRY THE OTHER DIRECTION.
이슈 마트
데 마트
슈퍼
OH, IS THAT HIM?
WE'VE BEEN LOOKING FOR AN HOUR... HOW MANY STORES ARE WE GOING TO CHECK?
WAIT, LOOK!
네 마트
THERE HE IS!
WHEW!
WHEW!
This is it!
OH YEAH, I FORGOT.
WHAT KIND C A JOB ARE Y DOING FOR M ANYWAY?
AH... YOU GO AHEAD, I'LL BE WAITING RIGHT HERE.

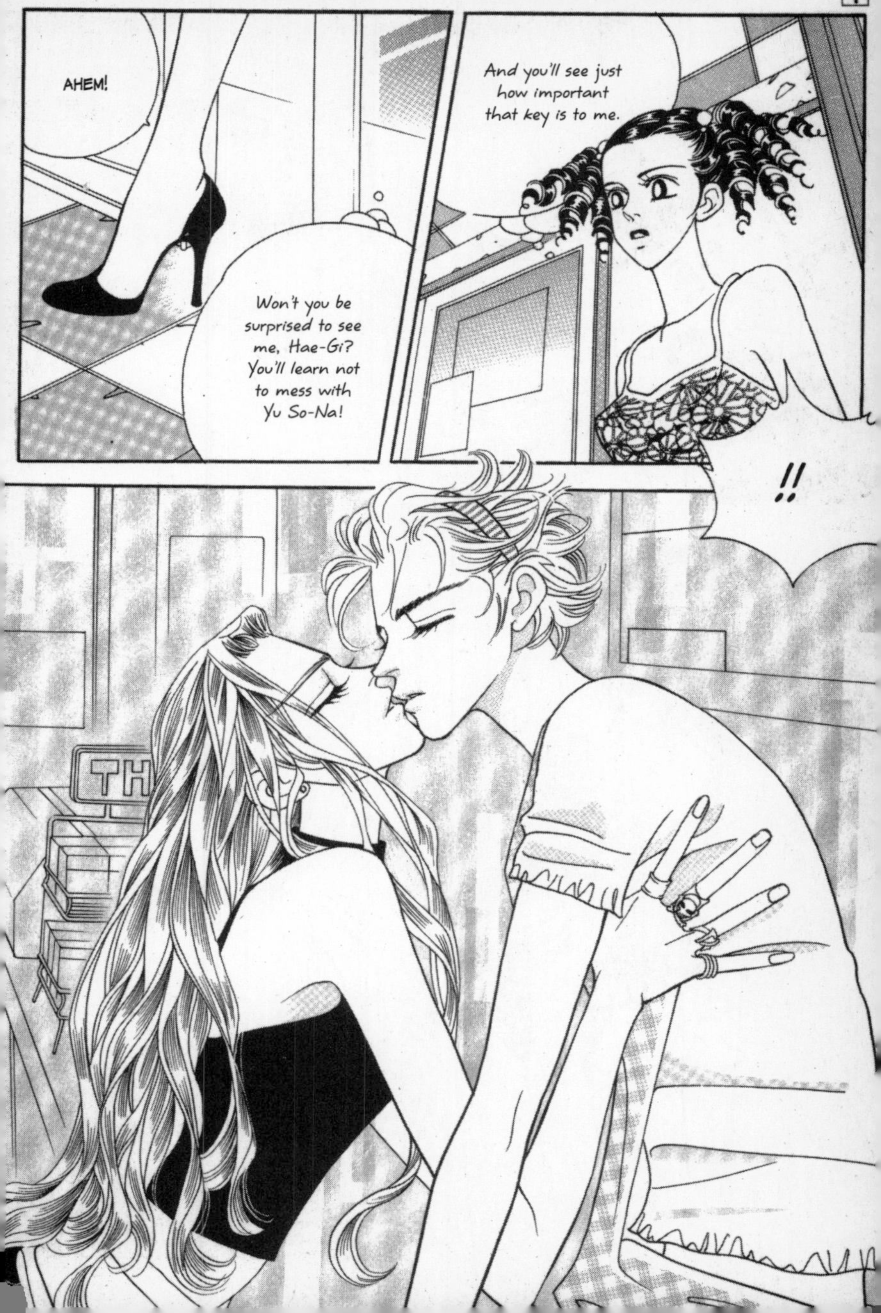
AHEM!
Won't you be surprised to see me, Hae-Gi? You'll learn not to mess with Yu So-Na!
And you'll see just how important that key is to me.
!!

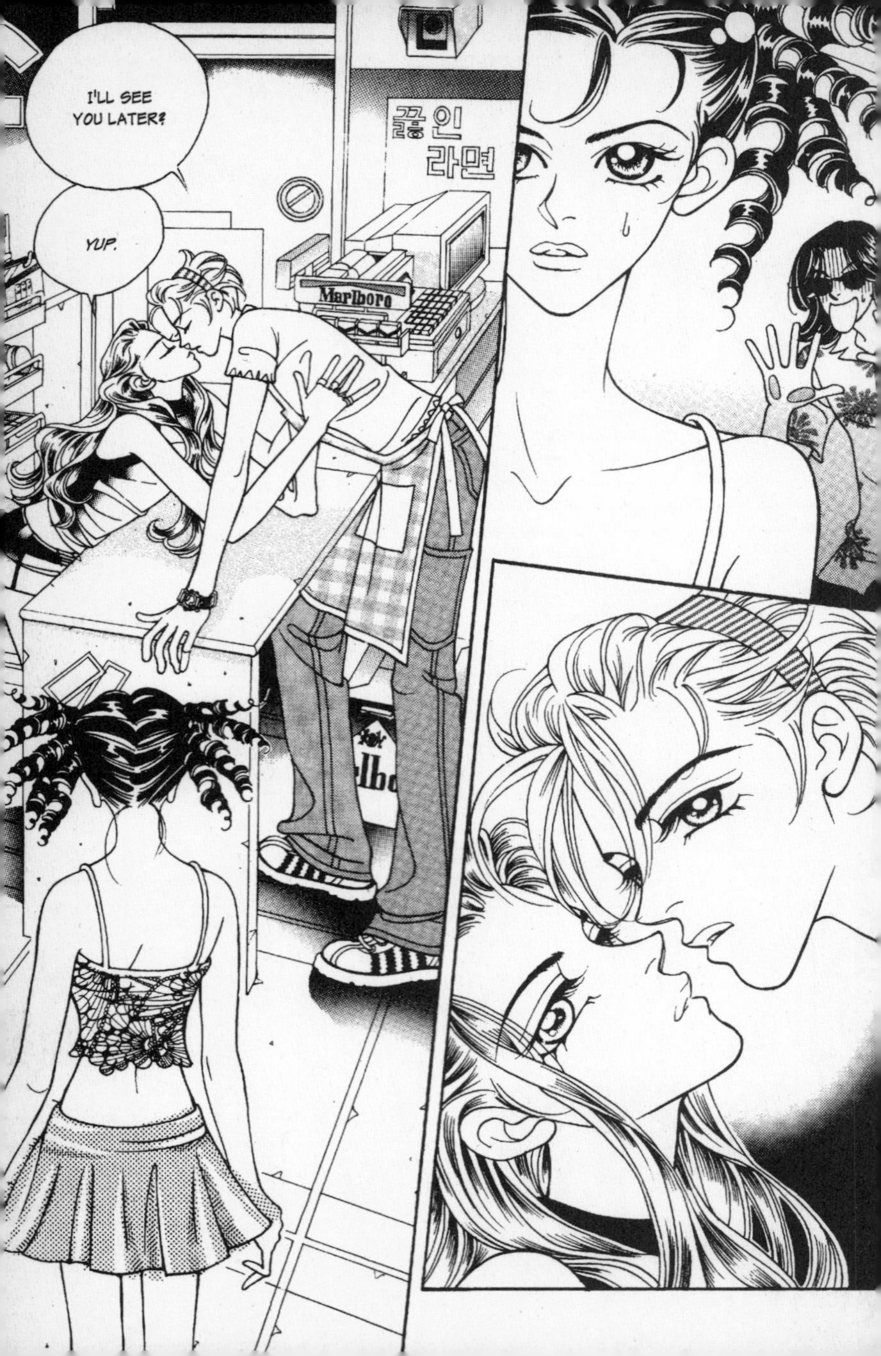
I'LL SEE YOU LATER?
YUP.
끓인
라면
Marlboro

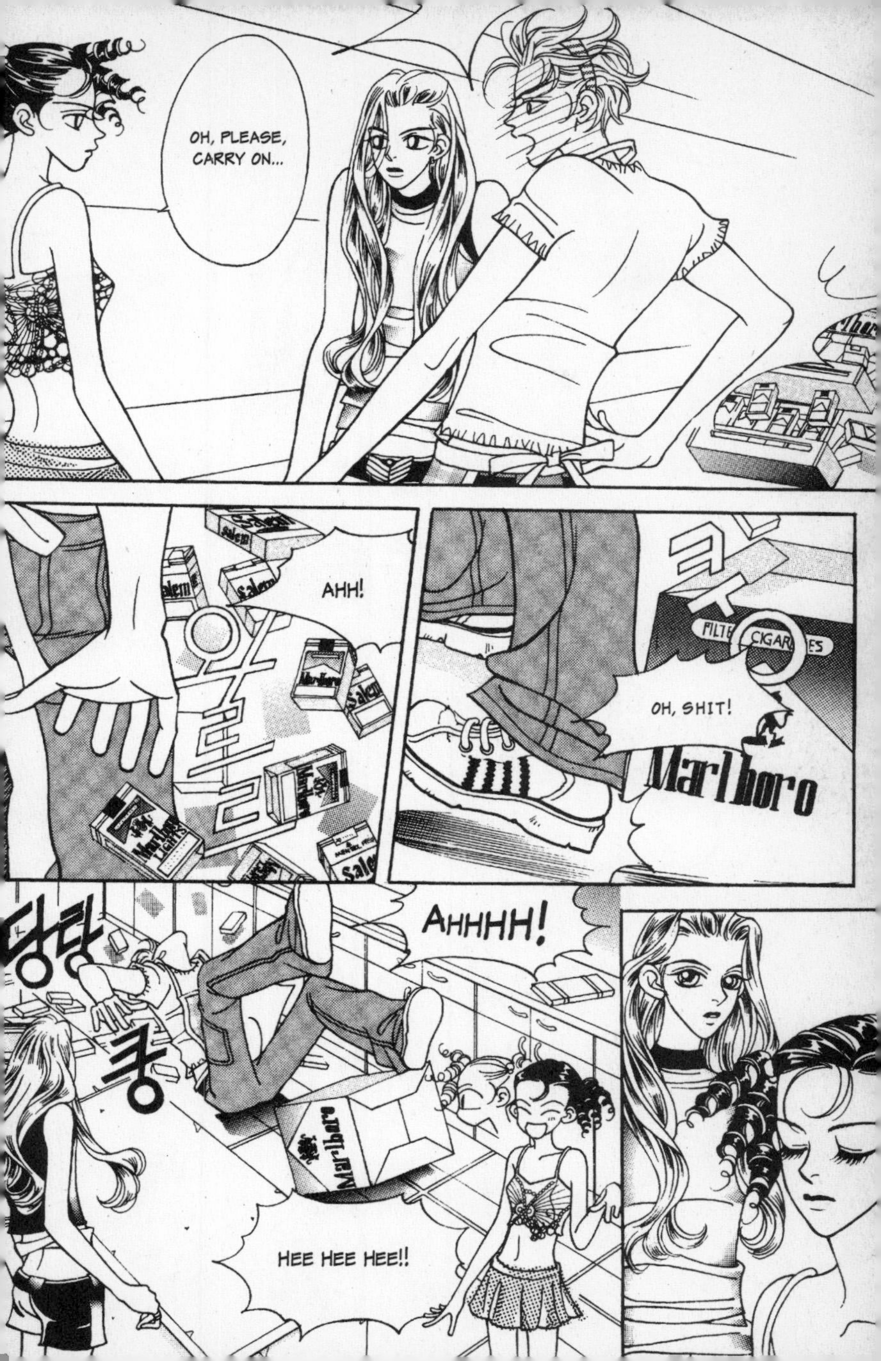
OH, PLEASE, CARRY ON...
AHH!
OH, SHIT!
Marlboro
AHHHH!
쿵
HEE HEE HEE!!

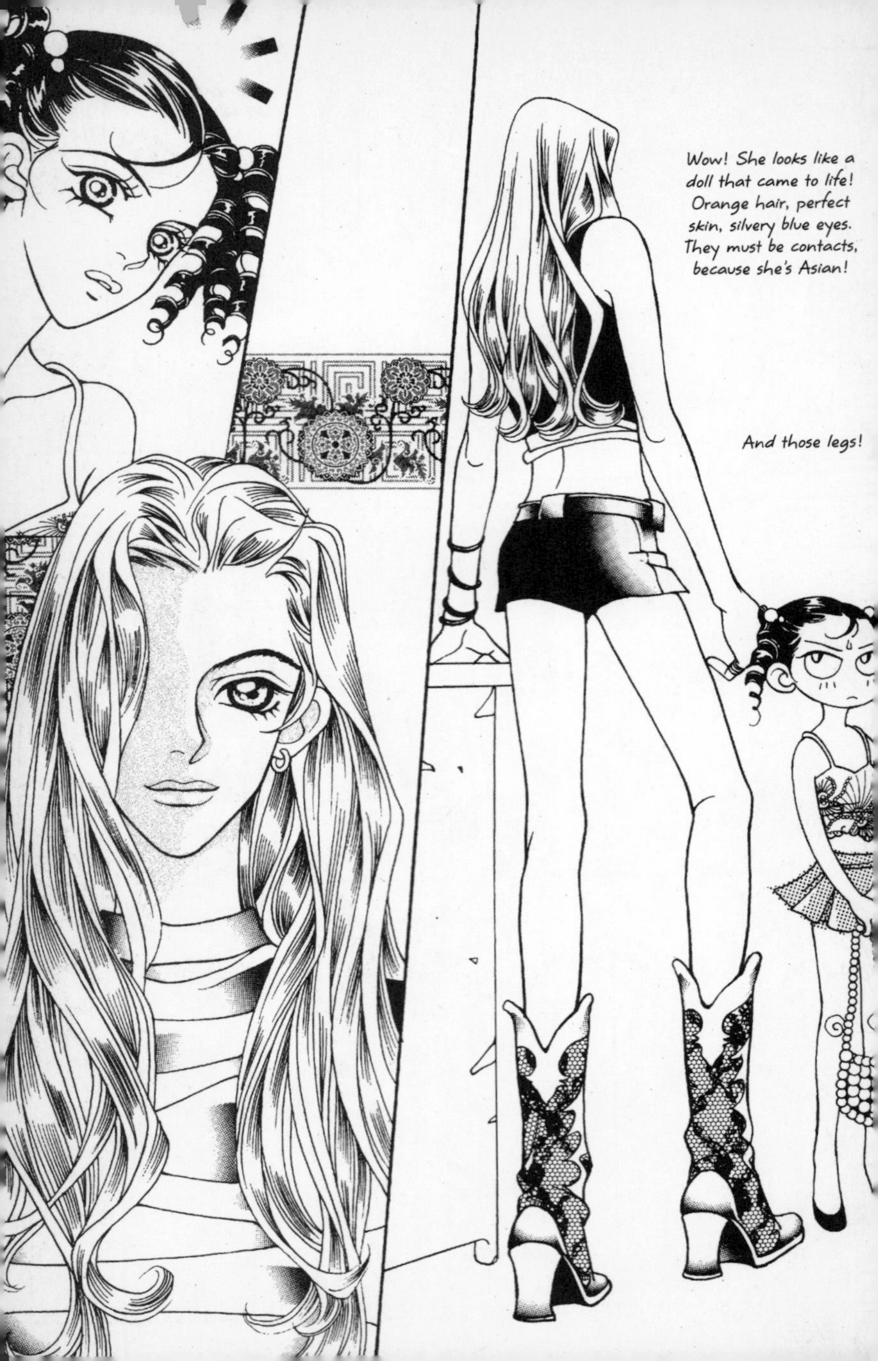
Wow! She looks like a doll that came to life! Orange hair, perfect skin, silvery blue eyes. They must be contacts, because she's Asian!
And those legs!

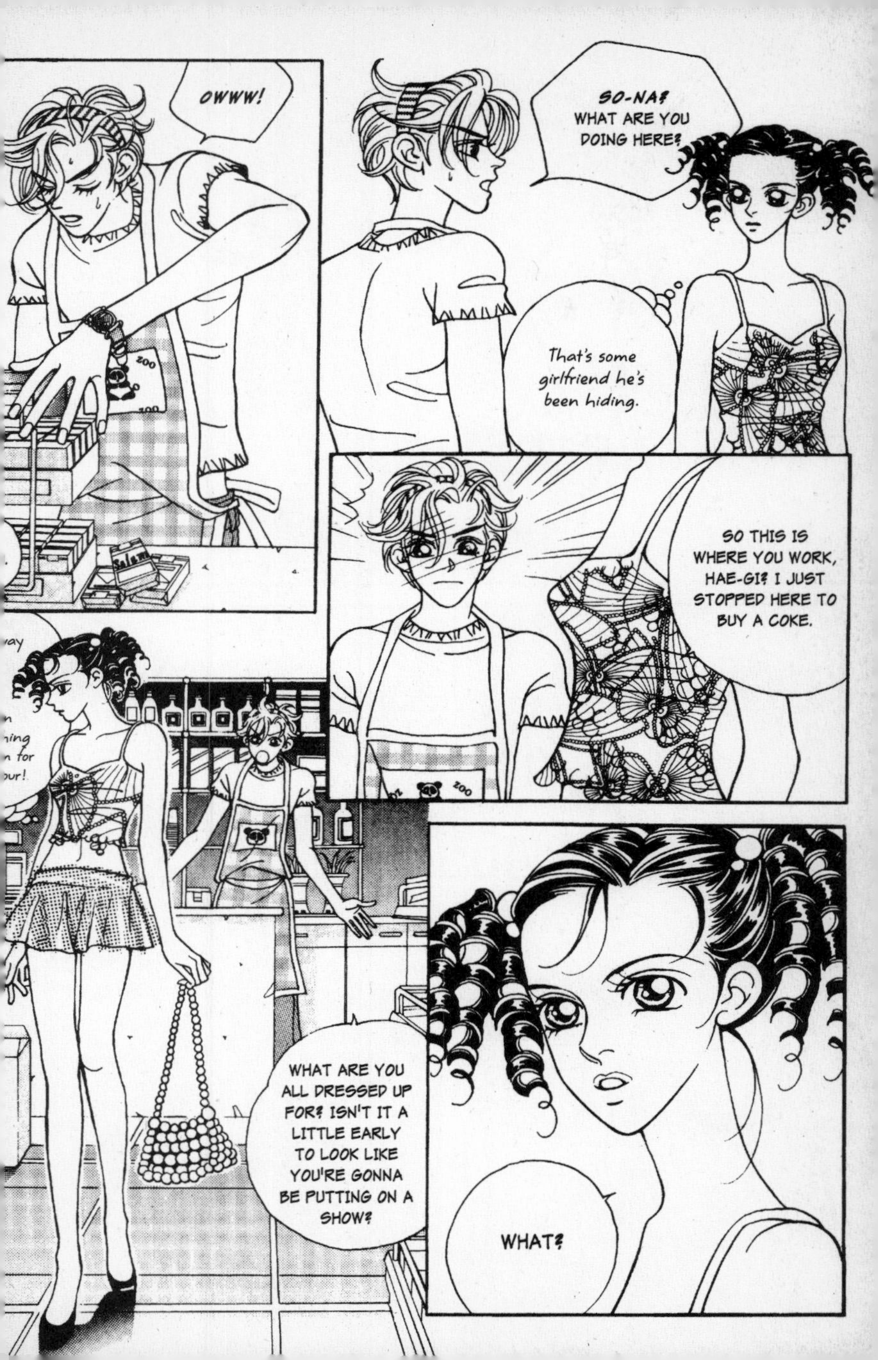
OWWW!
SO-NA? WHAT ARE YOU DOING HERE?
That's some girlfriend he's been hiding.
SO THIS IS WHERE YOU WORK, HAE-GI? I JUST STOPPED HERE TO BUY A COKE.
WHAT ARE YOU ALL DRESSED UP FOR? ISN'T IT A LITTLE EARLY TO LOOK LIKE YOU'RE GONNA BE PUTTING ON A SHOW?
WHAT?

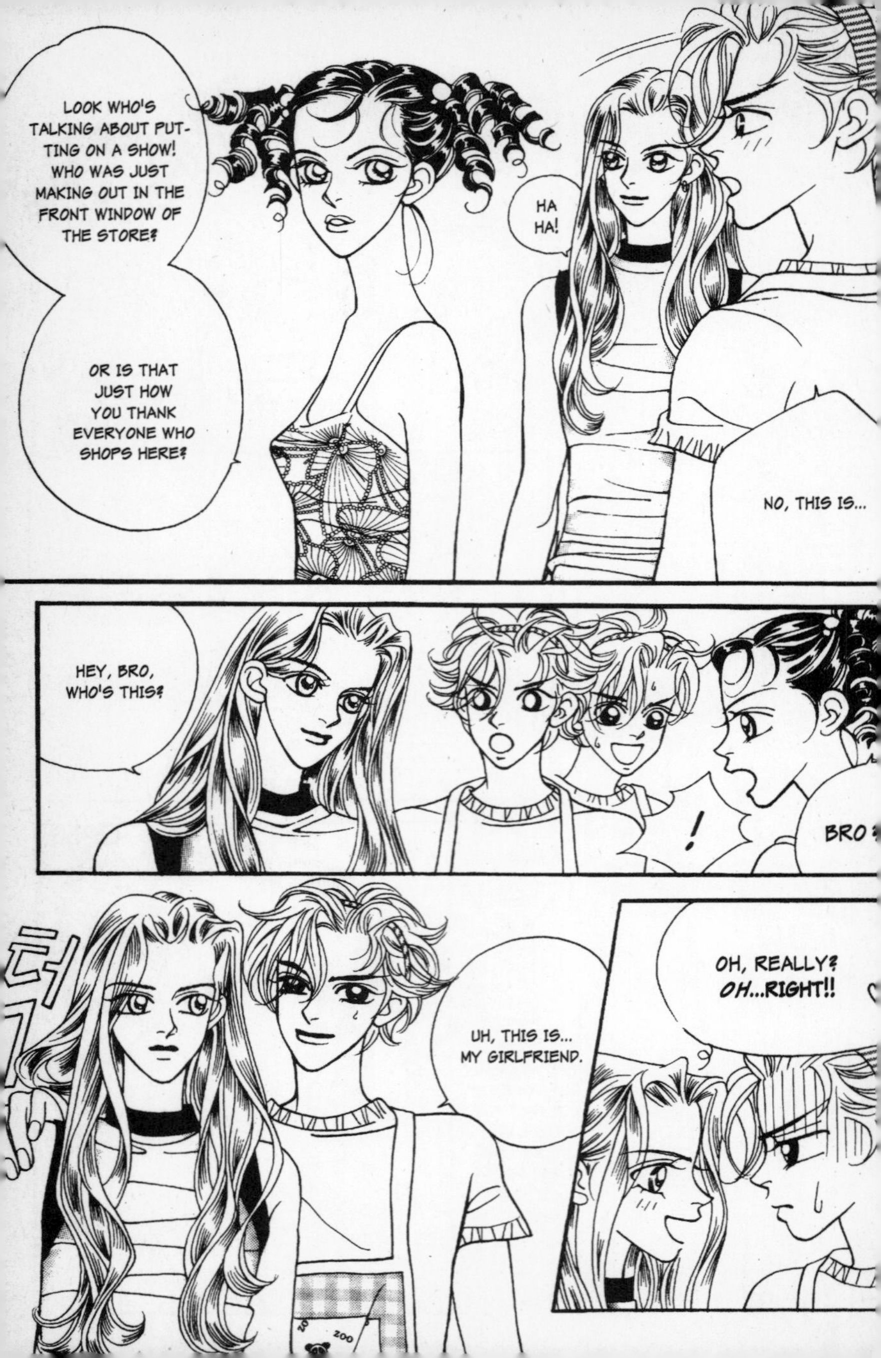
LOOK WHO'S TALKING ABOUT PUT-TING ON A SHOW! WHO WAS JUST MAKING OUT IN THE FRONT WINDOW OF THE STORE?
OR IS THAT JUST HOW YOU THANK EVERYONE WHO SHOPS HERE?
HA HA!
NO, THIS IS...
HEY, BRO, WHO'S THIS?
!
BRO?
UH, THIS IS... MY GIRLFRIEND.
OH, REALLY? *OH*...RIGHT!!

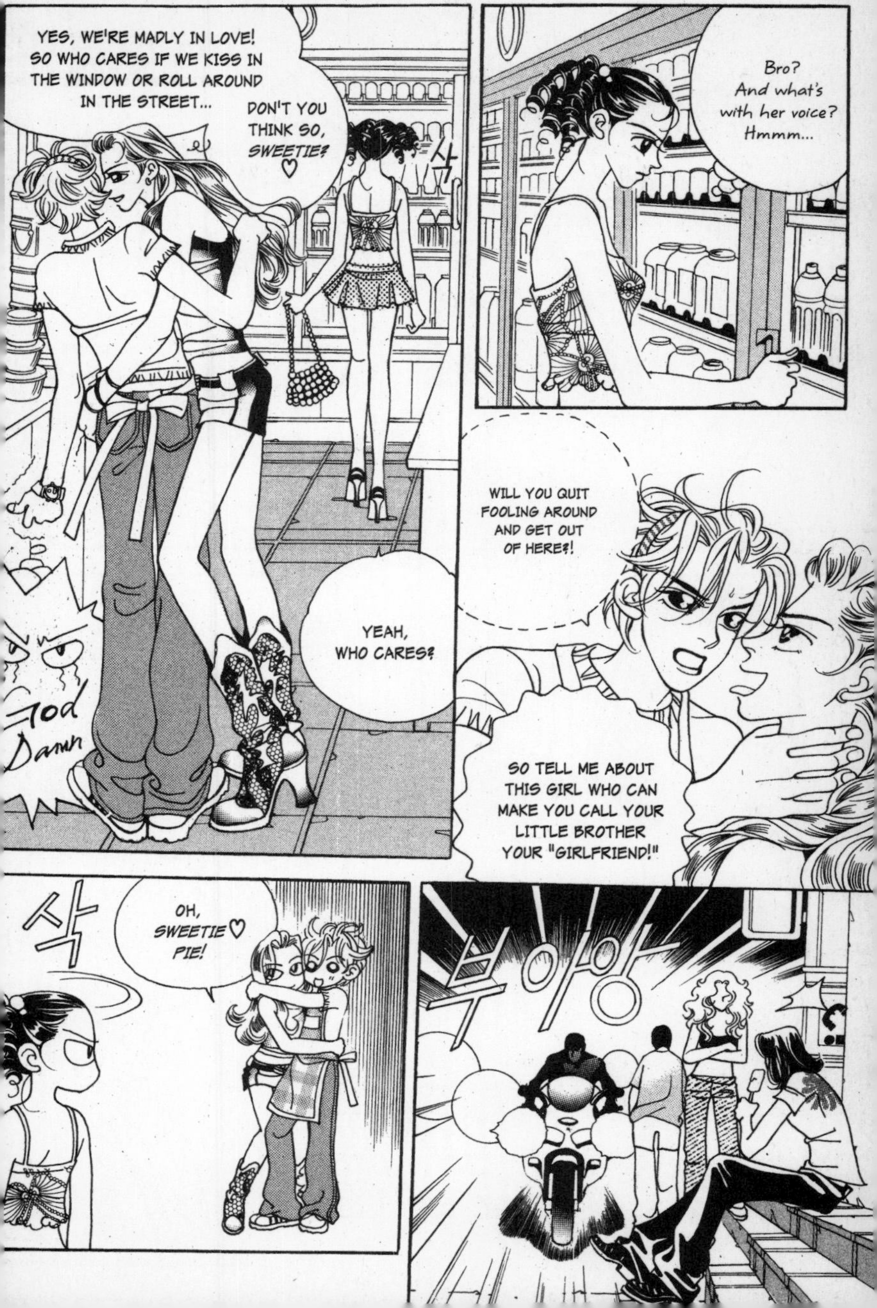
YES, WE'RE MADLY IN LOVE! SO WHO CARES IF WE KISS IN THE WINDOW OR ROLL AROUND IN THE STREET...
DON'T YOU THINK SO, SWEETIE? ♡
삭
YEAH, WHO CARES?
God Damn
Bro? And what's with her voice? Hmmm...
WILL YOU QUIT FOOLING AROUND AND GET OUT OF HERE?!
SO TELL ME ABOUT THIS GIRL WHO CAN MAKE YOU CALL YOUR LITTLE BROTHER YOUR "GIRLFRIEND!"
삭
OH, SWEETIE ♡ PIE!
부아앙

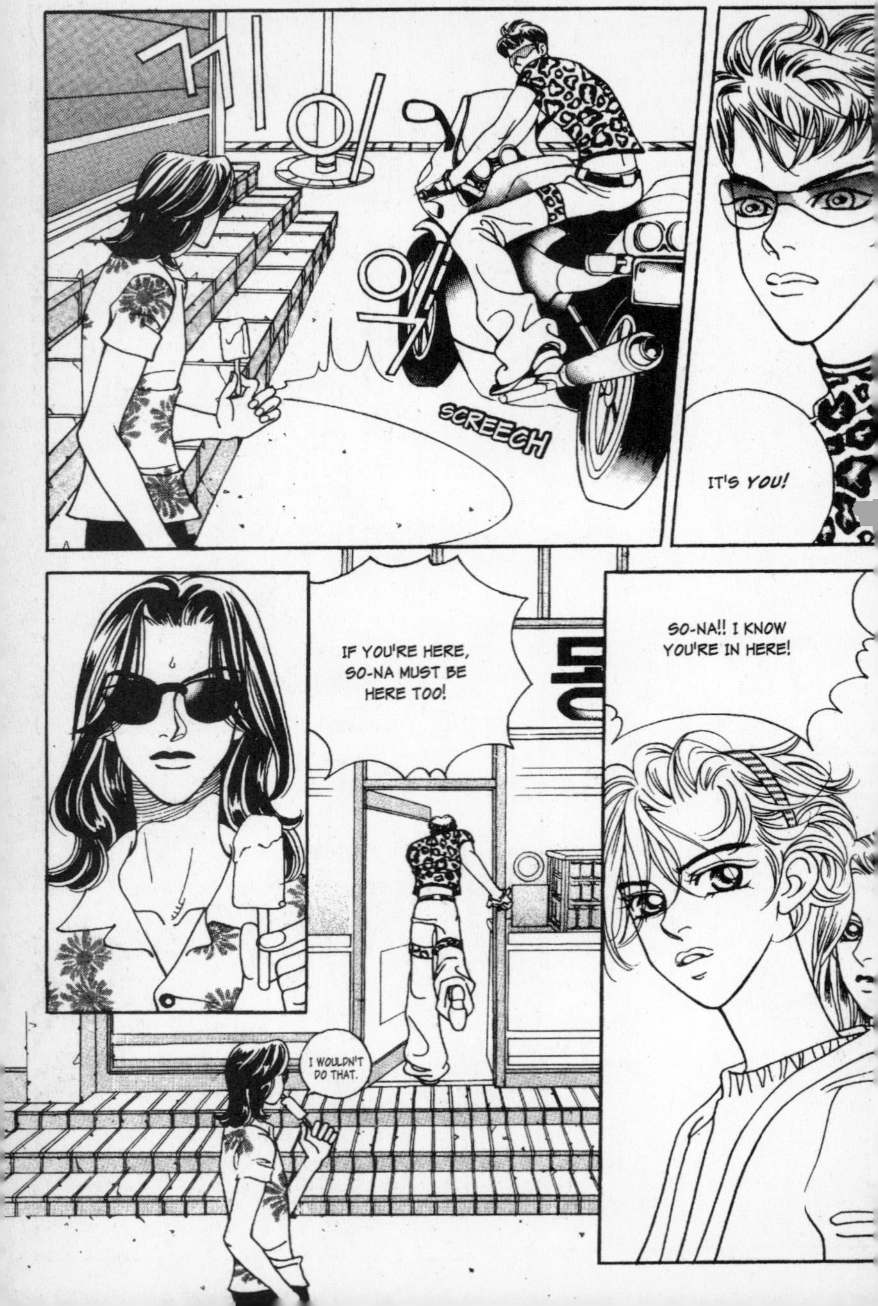

SCREECH
IT'S *YOU!*
IF YOU'RE HERE, SO-NA MUST BE HERE TOO!
I WOULDN'T DO THAT.
SO-NA!! I KNOW YOU'RE IN HERE!

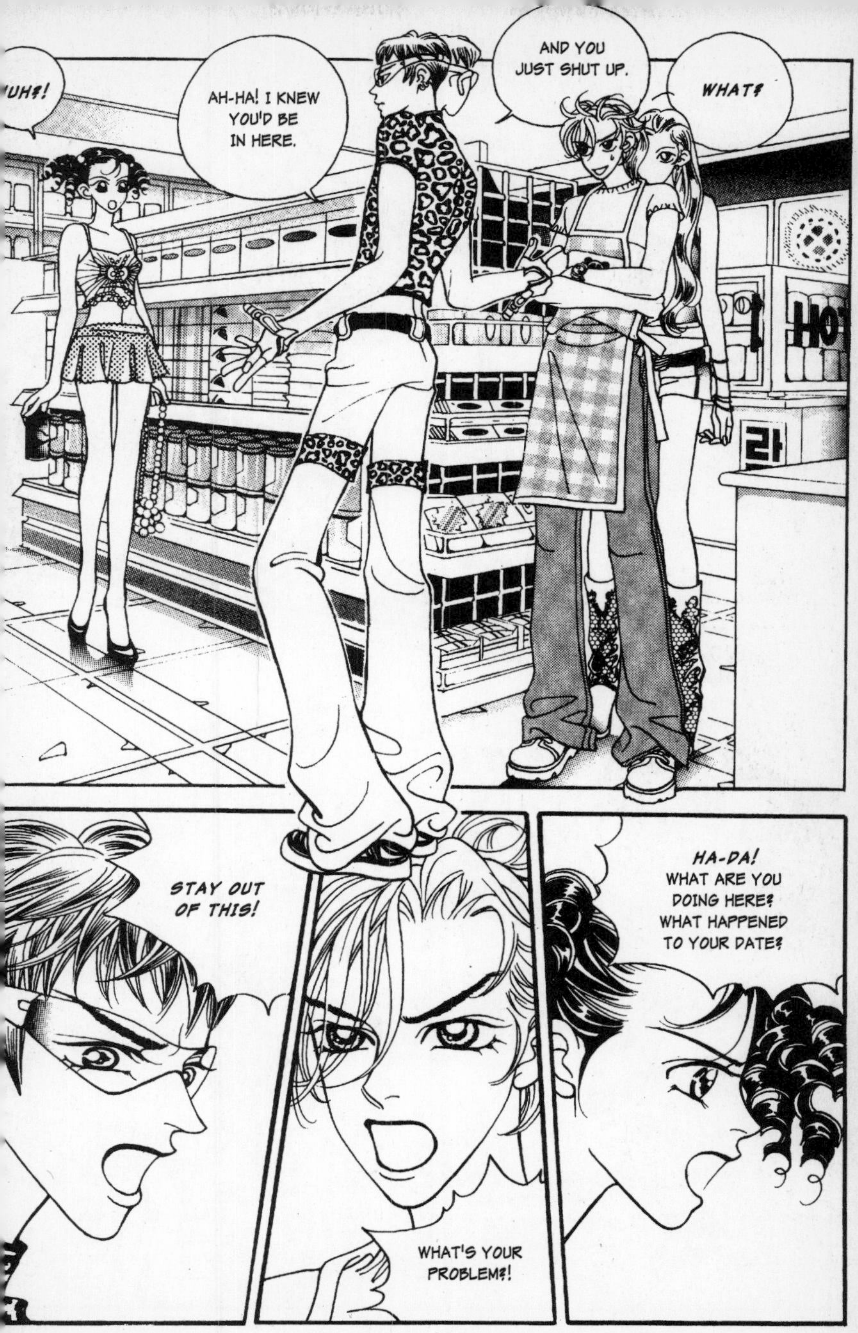
UH?!
AH-HA! I KNEW YOU'D BE IN HERE.
AND YOU JUST SHUT UP.
WHAT?
STAY OUT OF THIS!
WHAT'S YOUR PROBLEM?!
HA-DA! WHAT ARE YOU DOING HERE? WHAT HAPPENED TO YOUR DATE?

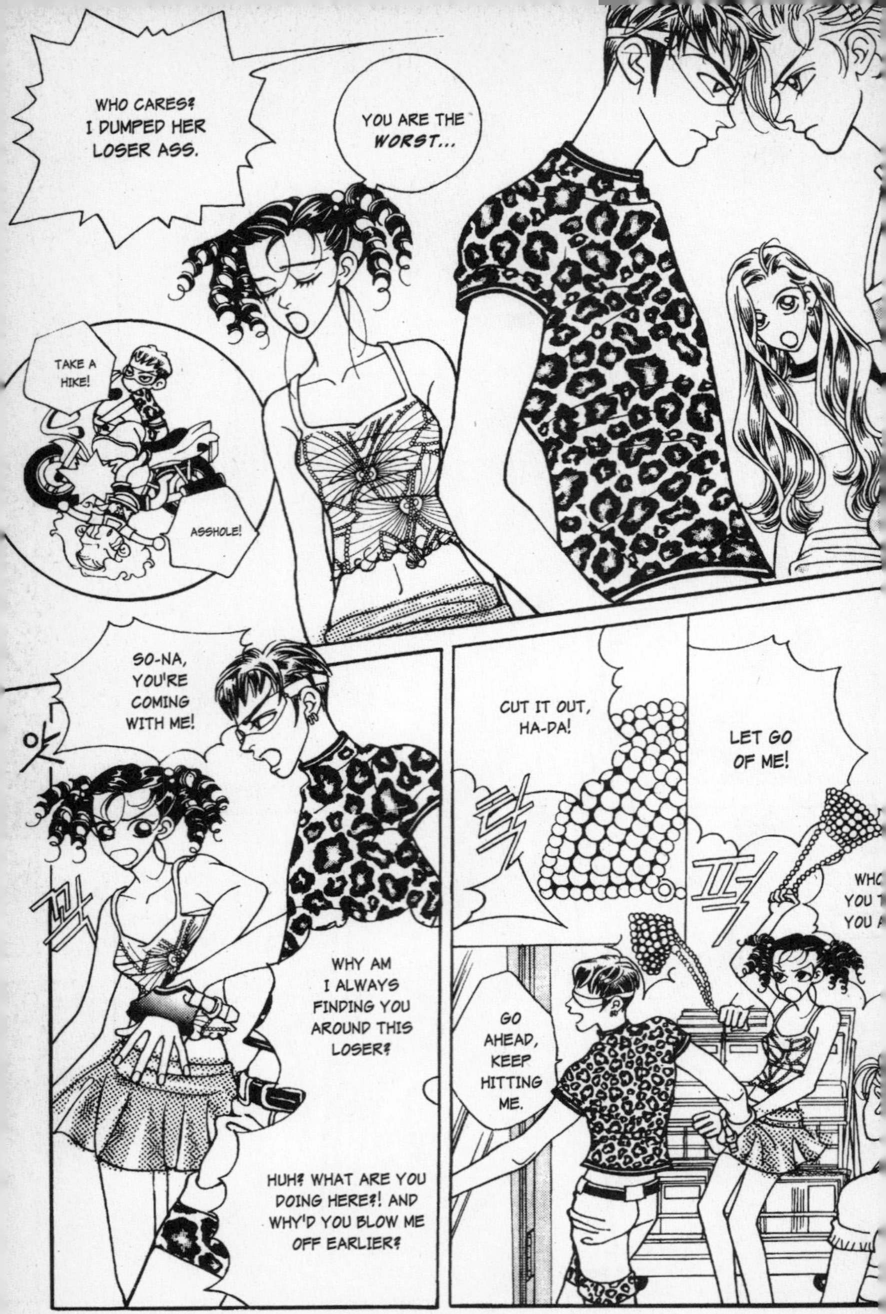
WHO CARES? I DUMPED HER LOSER ASS.
YOU ARE THE *WORST*...
TAKE A HIKE!
ASSHOLE!
SO-NA, YOU'RE COMING WITH ME!
WHY AM I ALWAYS FINDING YOU AROUND THIS LOSER?
HUH? WHAT ARE YOU DOING HERE?! AND WHY'D YOU BLOW ME OFF EARLIER?
CUT IT OUT, HA-DA!
LET GO OF ME!
GO AHEAD, KEEP HITTING ME.

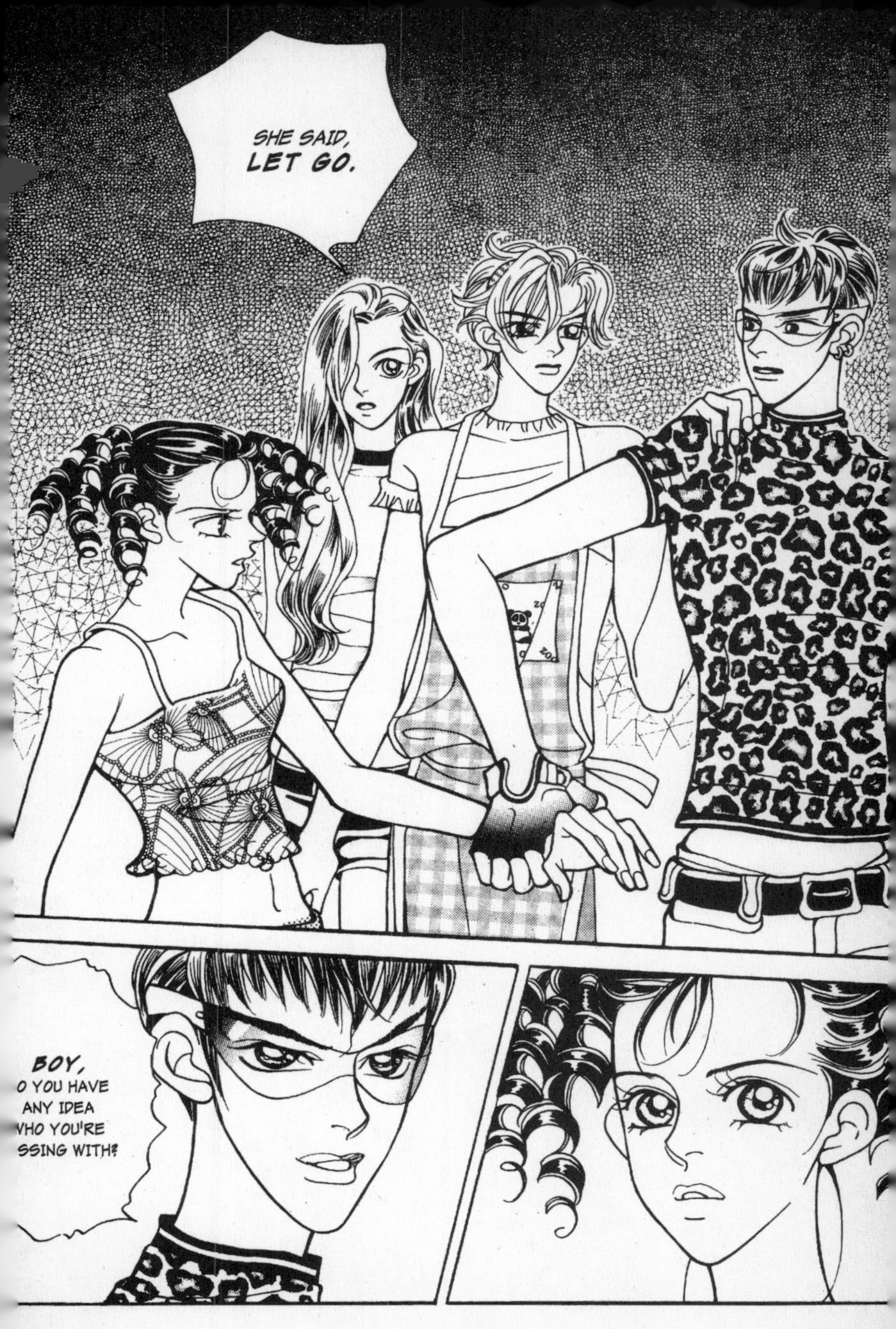
SHE SAID, LET GO.
BOY, O YOU HAVE ANY IDEA VHO YOU'RE SSING WITH?

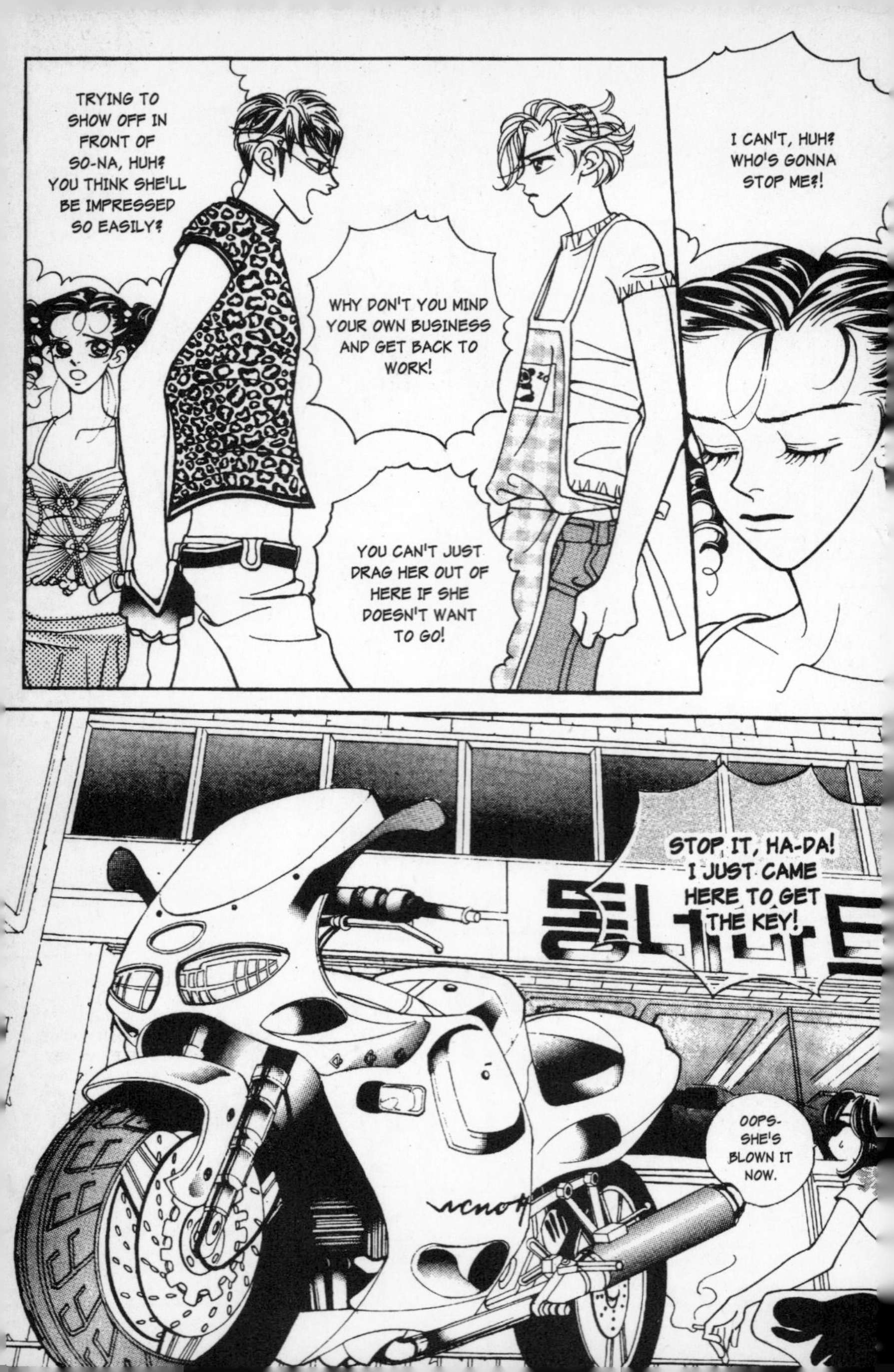
TRYING TO SHOW OFF IN FRONT OF SO-NA, HUH? YOU THINK SHE'LL BE IMPRESSED SO EASILY?
WHY DON'T YOU MIND YOUR OWN BUSINESS AND GET BACK TO WORK!
YOU CAN'T JUST DRAG HER OUT OF HERE IF SHE DOESN'T WANT TO GO!
I CAN'T, HUH? WHO'S GONNA STOP ME?!
STOP IT, HA-DA! I JUST CAME HERE TO GET THE KEY!
OOPS- SHE'S BLOWN IT NOW.

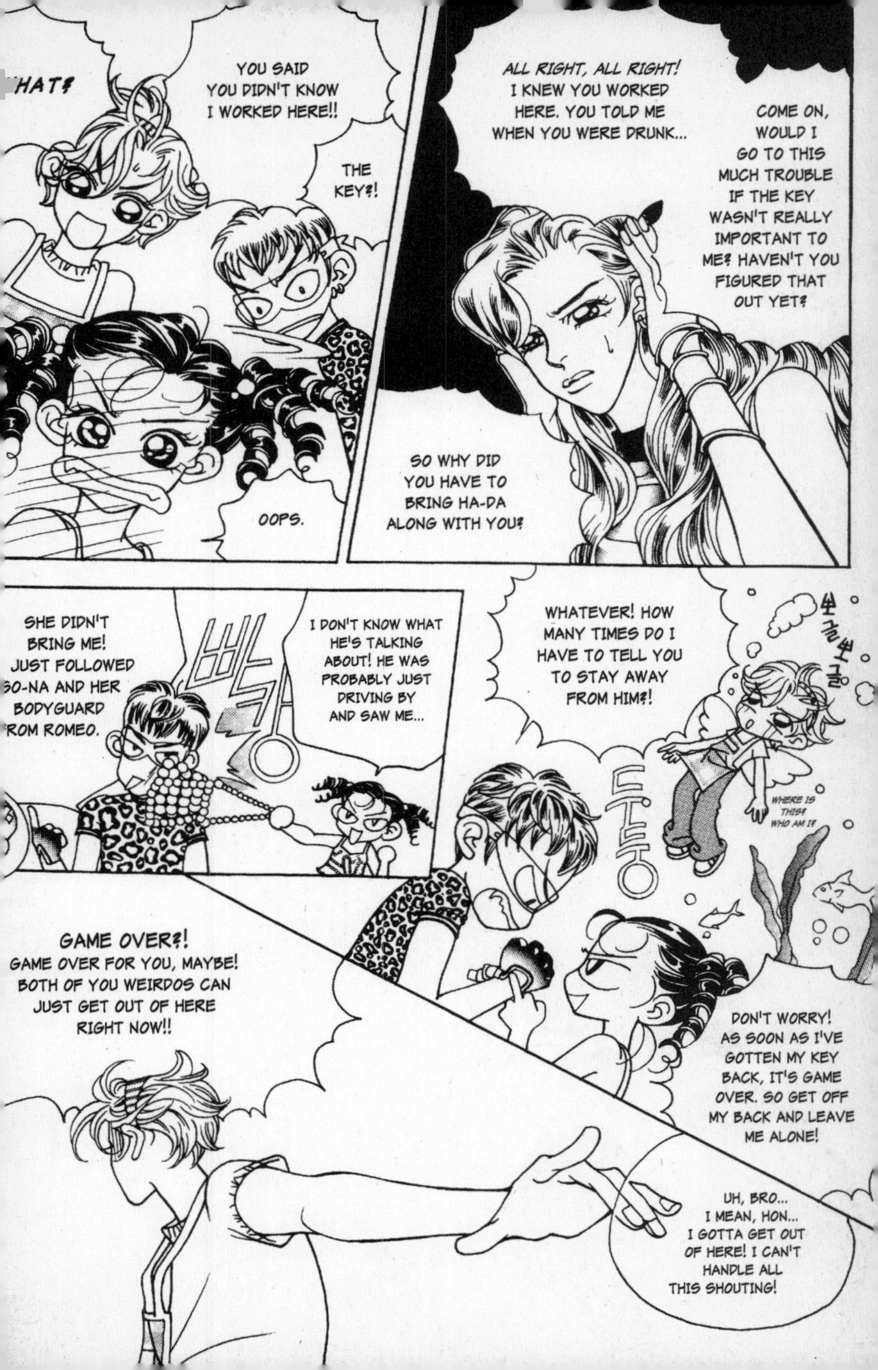
HAT?
YOU SAID YOU DIDN'T KNOW I WORKED HERE!!
THE KEY?!
OOPS.
ALL RIGHT, ALL RIGHT! I KNEW YOU WORKED HERE. YOU TOLD ME WHEN YOU WERE DRUNK...
COME ON, WOULD I GO TO THIS MUCH TROUBLE IF THE KEY WASN'T REALLY IMPORTANT TO ME? HAVEN'T YOU FIGURED THAT OUT YET?
SO WHY DID YOU HAVE TO BRING HA-DA ALONG WITH YOU?
SHE DIDN'T BRING ME! JUST FOLLOWED SO-NA AND HER BODYGUARD FROM ROMEO.
I DON'T KNOW WHAT HE'S TALKING ABOUT! HE WAS PROBABLY JUST DRIVING BY AND SAW ME...
WHATEVER! HOW MANY TIMES DO I HAVE TO TELL YOU TO STAY AWAY FROM HIM?!
WHERE IS THIS? WHO AM I?
GAME OVER?! GAME OVER FOR YOU, MAYBE! BOTH OF YOU WEIRDOS CAN JUST GET OUT OF HERE RIGHT NOW!!
DON'T WORRY! AS SOON AS I'VE GOTTEN MY KEY BACK, IT'S GAME OVER. SO GET OFF MY BACK AND LEAVE ME ALONE!
UH, BRO... I MEAN, HON... I GOTTA GET OUT OF HERE! I CAN'T HANDLE ALL THIS SHOUTING!

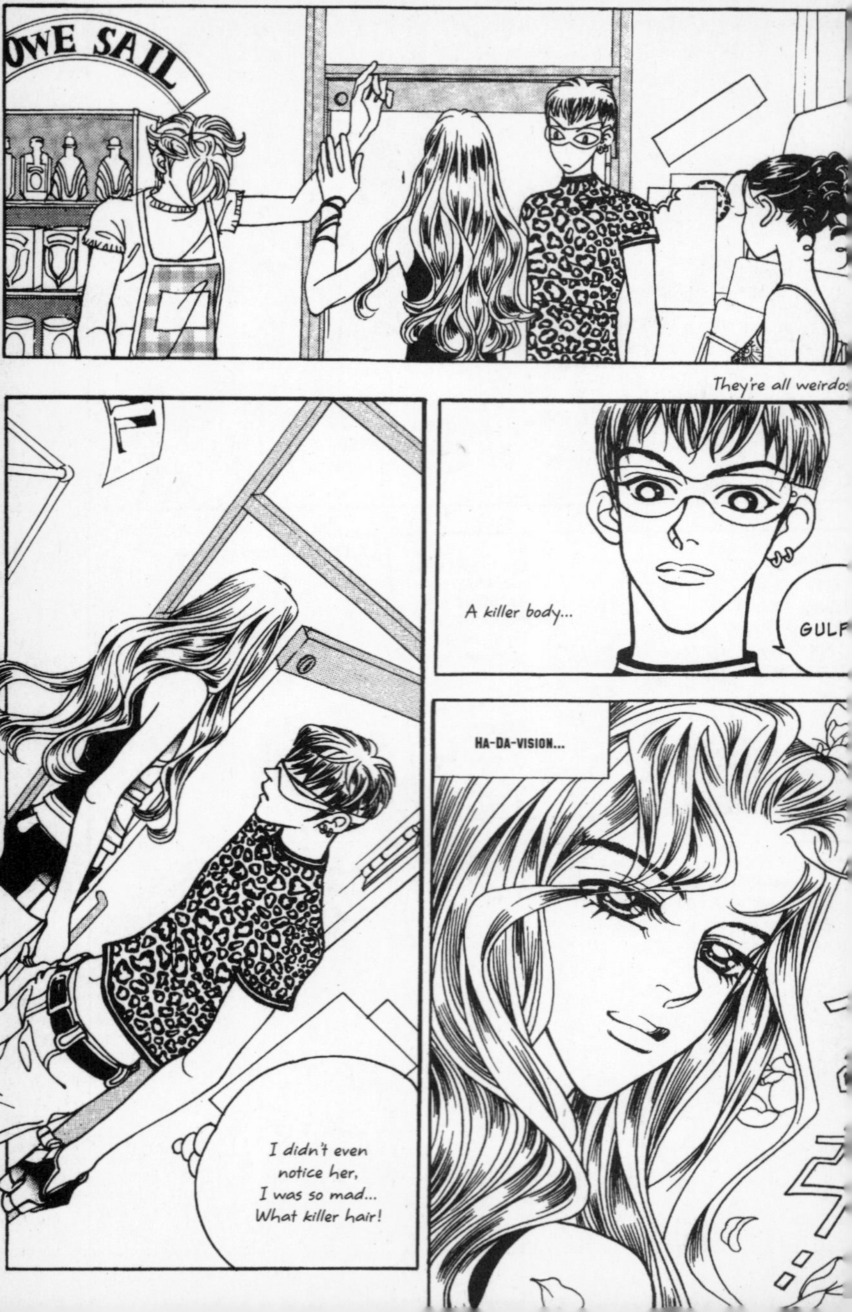
OWE SAIL
They're all weirdos
I didn't even notice her, I was so mad... What killer hair!
A killer body...
GUL
HA-DA-VISION...

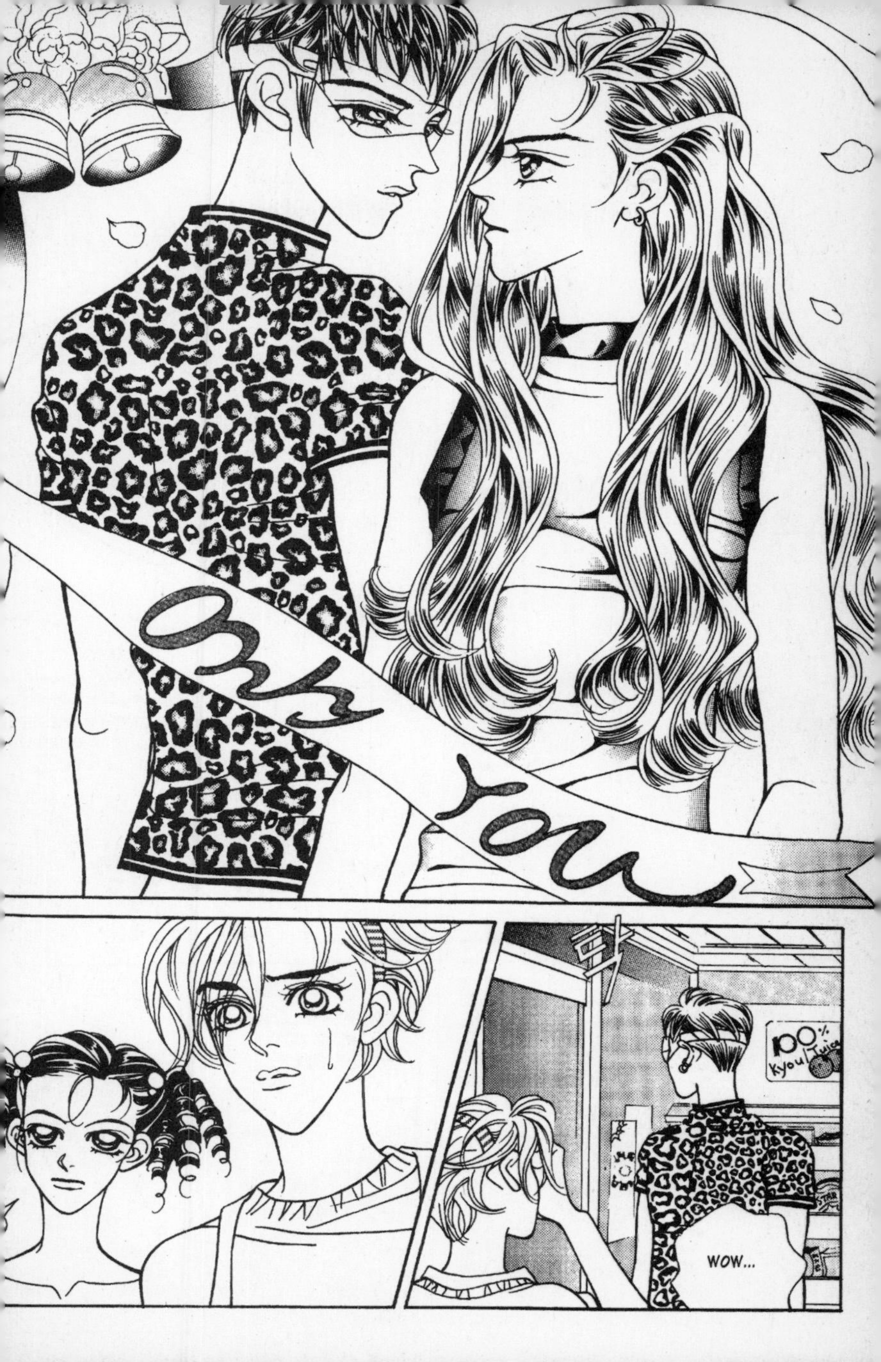
Only You
100%
Kyou
WOW...

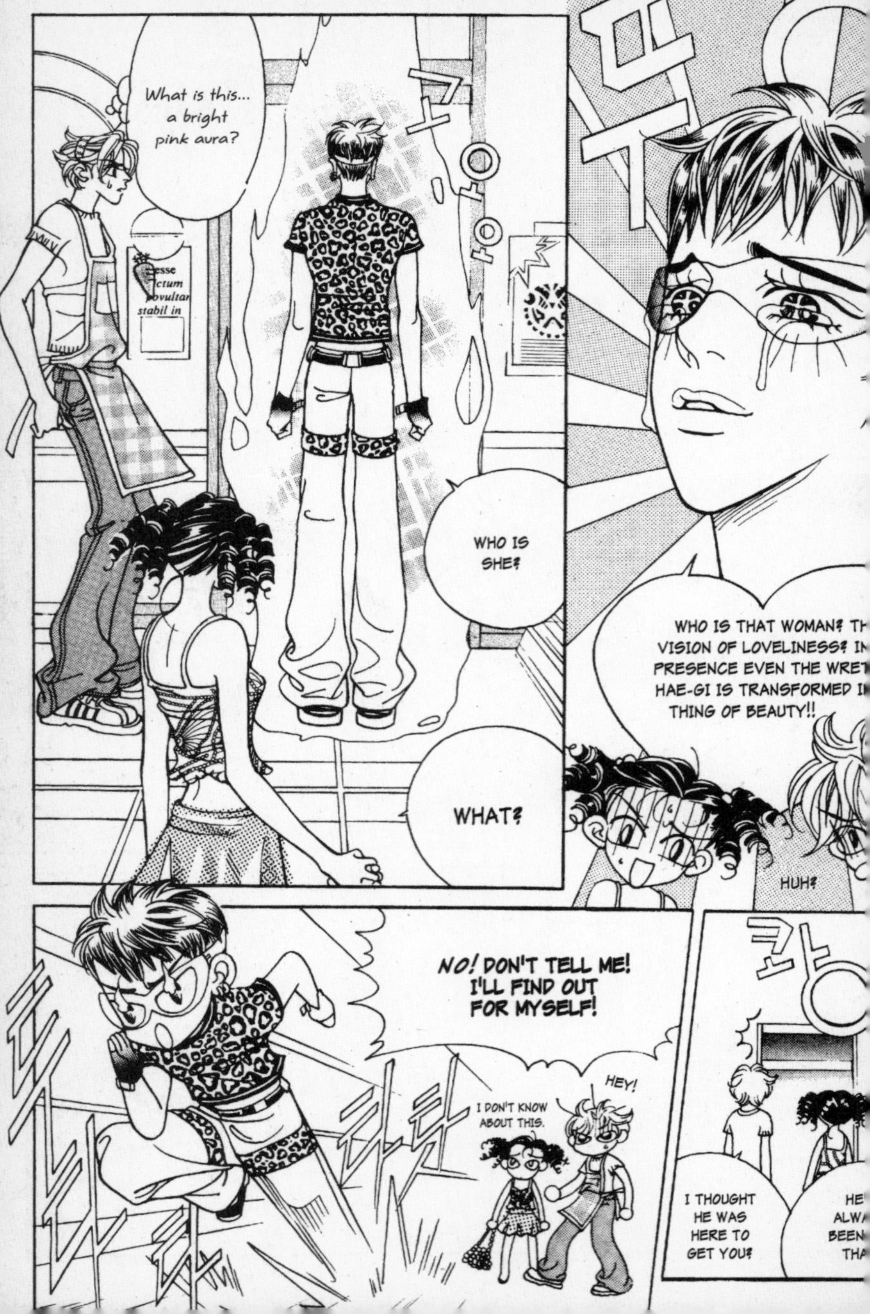
What is this... a bright pink aura?
WHO IS SHE?
WHAT?
WHO IS THAT WOMAN? TH VISION OF LOVELINESS? IN PRESENCE EVEN THE WRET HAE-GI IS TRANSFORMED I THING OF BEAUTY!!
HUH?
NO! DON'T TELL ME! I'LL FIND OUT FOR MYSELF!
HEY!
I DON'T KNOW ABOUT THIS.
I THOUGHT HE WAS HERE TO GET YOU?
HE ALWA BEEN THA

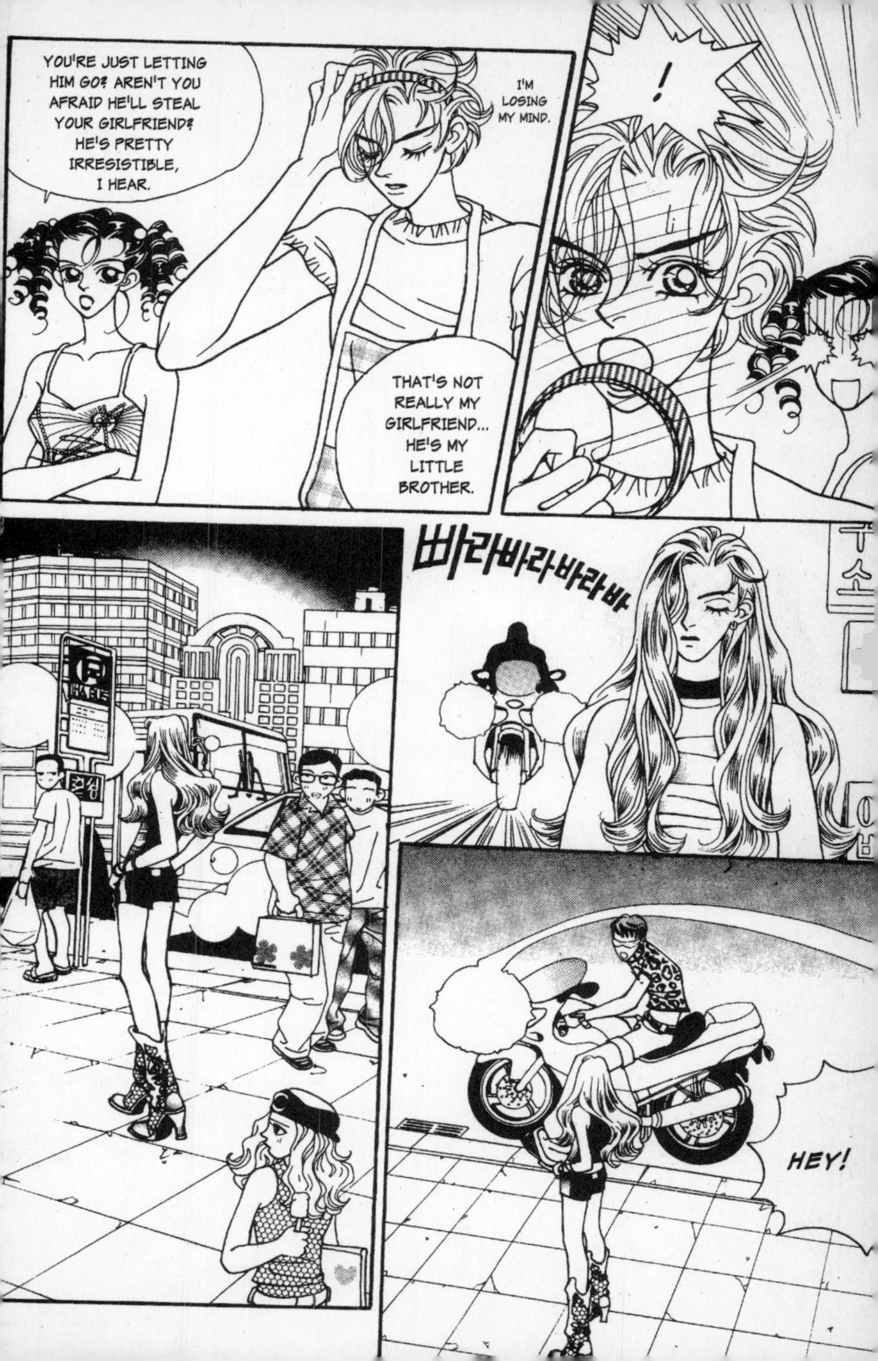
YOU'RE JUST LETTING HIM GO? AREN'T YOU AFRAID HE'LL STEAL YOUR GIRLFRIEND? HE'S PRETTY IRRESISTIBLE, I HEAR.
I'M LOSING MY MIND.
THAT'S NOT REALLY MY GIRLFRIEND... HE'S MY LITTLE BROTHER.
!
빠라빠라바라바
HEY!

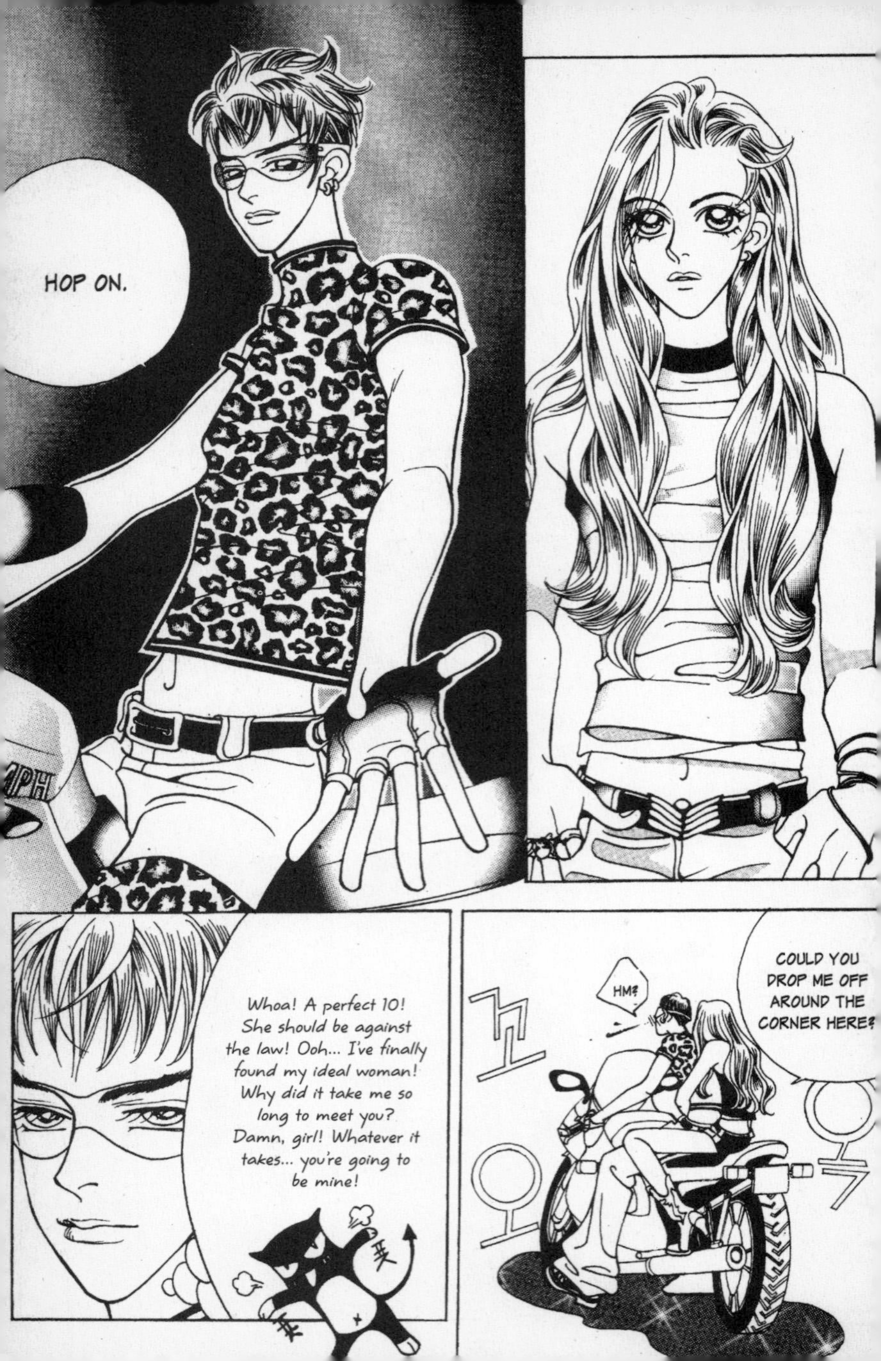
HOP ON.
Whoa! A perfect 10! She should be against the law! Ooh... I've finally found my ideal woman! Why did it take me so long to meet you? Damn, girl! Whatever it takes... you're going to be mine!
HM?
COULD YOU DROP ME OFF AROUND THE CORNER HERE?

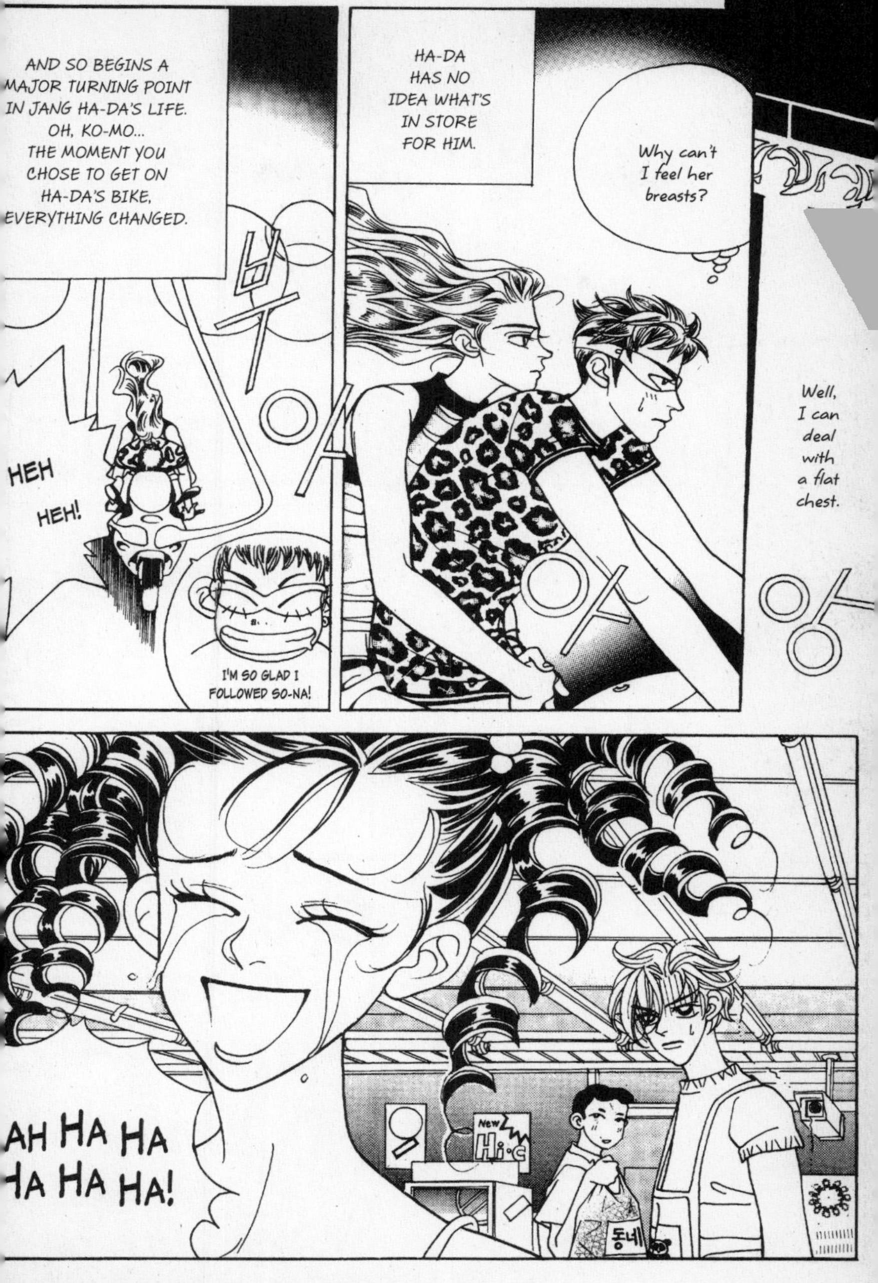

AND SO BEGINS A MAJOR TURNING POINT IN JANG HA-DA'S LIFE. OH, KO-MO... THE MOMENT YOU CHOSE TO GET ON HA-DA'S BIKE, EVERYTHING CHANGED.
HEH
HEH!
I'M SO GLAD I FOLLOWED SO-NA!
HA-DA HAS NO IDEA WHAT'S IN STORE FOR HIM.
Why can't I feel her breasts?
Well, I can deal with a flat chest.
AH HA HA HA HA HA HA!
New Hi-C
동네

HAE-GI TRIES TO LOOK CALM.

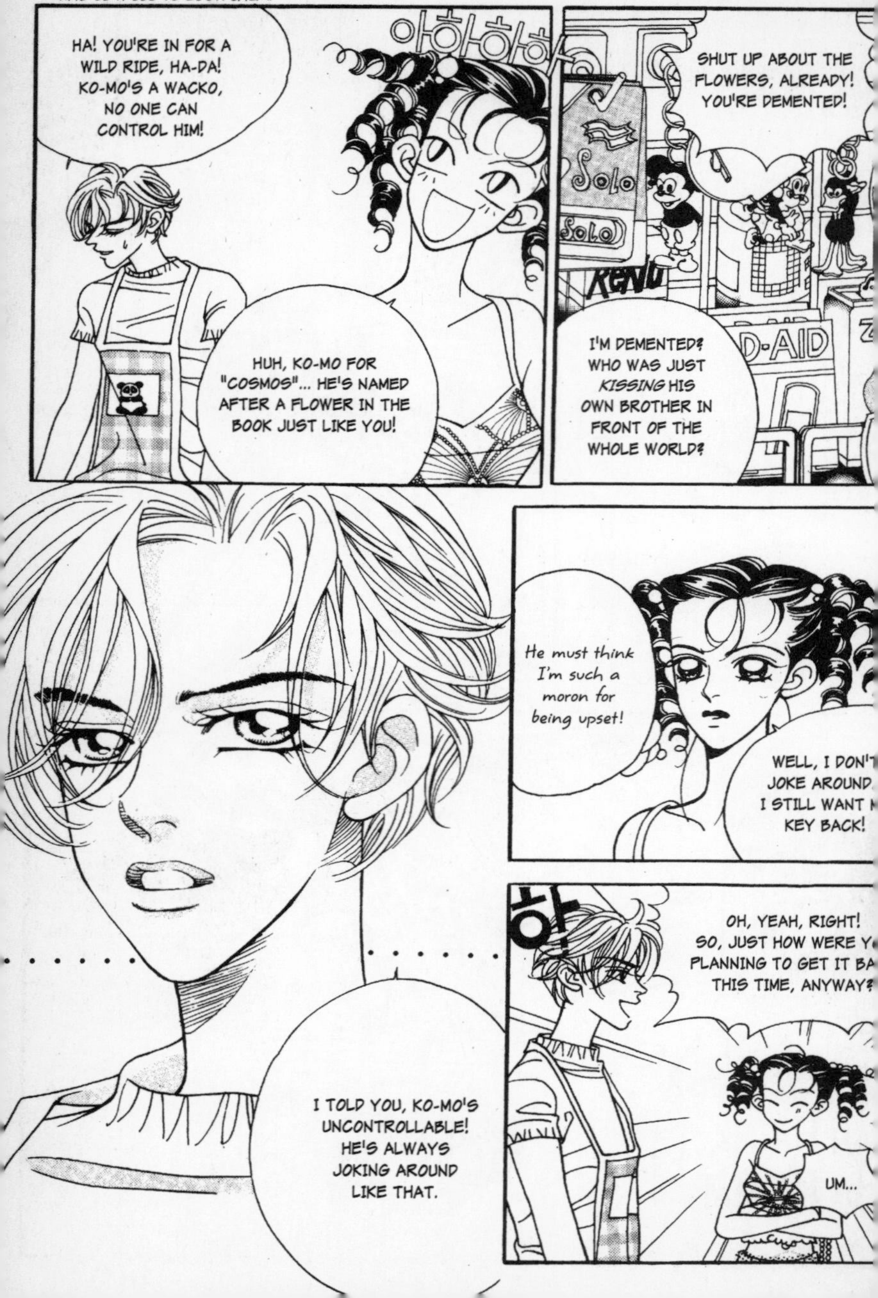
HA! YOU'RE IN FOR A WILD RIDE, HA-DA! KO-MO'S A WACKO, NO ONE CAN CONTROL HIM!
아하하하
HUH, KO-MO FOR "COSMOS"... HE'S NAMED AFTER A FLOWER IN THE BOOK JUST LIKE YOU!
SHUT UP ABOUT THE FLOWERS, ALREADY! YOU'RE DEMENTED!
Solo
Solo
D-AID
I'M DEMENTED? WHO WAS JUST *KISSING* HIS OWN BROTHER IN FRONT OF THE WHOLE WORLD?
I TOLD YOU, KO-MO'S UNCONTROLLABLE! HE'S ALWAYS JOKING AROUND LIKE THAT.
He must think I'm such a moron for being upset!
WELL, I DON'T JOKE AROUND. I STILL WANT KEY BACK!
하
OH, YEAH, RIGHT! SO, JUST HOW WERE PLANNING TO GET IT BA THIS TIME, ANYWAY?
UM...

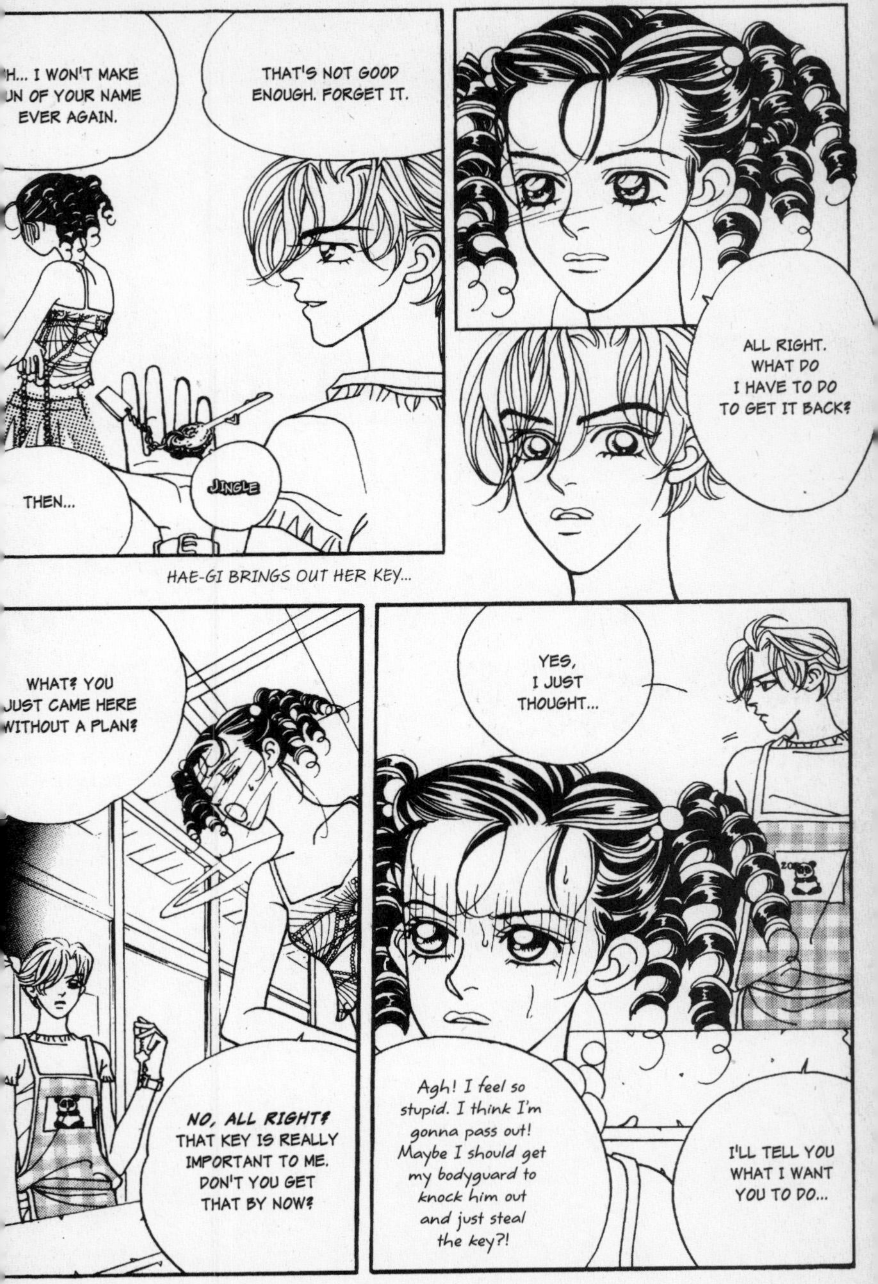
H... I WON'T MAKE
UN OF YOUR NAME
EVER AGAIN.
THAT'S NOT GOOD ENOUGH. FORGET IT.
THEN...
JINGLE
ALL RIGHT. WHAT DO I HAVE TO DO TO GET IT BACK?
HAE-GI BRINGS OUT HER KEY...
WHAT? YOU
JUST CAME HERE
WITHOUT A PLAN?
NO, ALL RIGHT? THAT KEY IS REALLY IMPORTANT TO ME. DON'T YOU GET THAT BY NOW?
YES, I JUST THOUGHT...
Agh! I feel so stupid. I think I'm gonna pass out! Maybe I should get my bodyguard to knock him out and just steal the key?!
I'LL TELL YOU WHAT I WANT YOU TO DO...

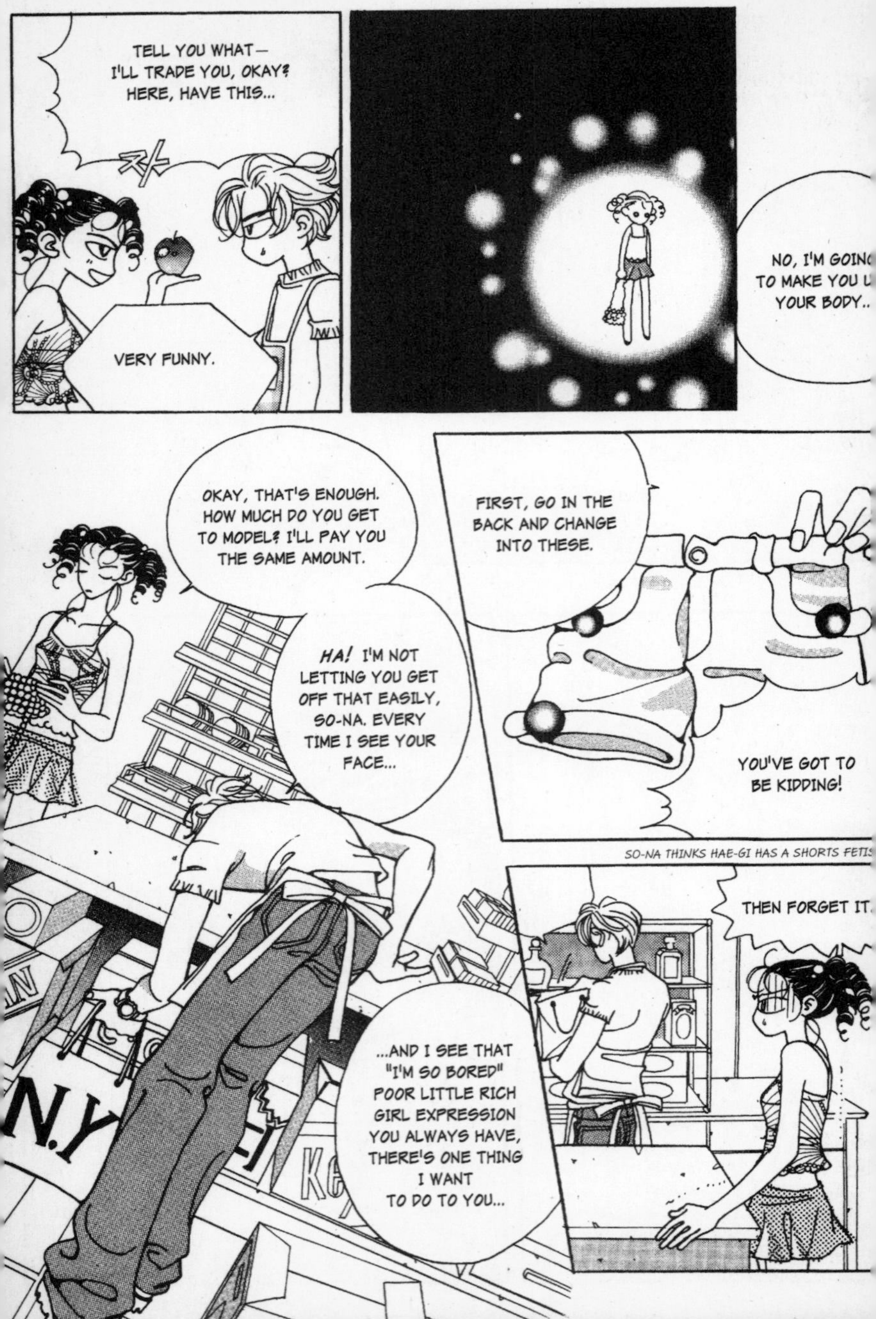
TELL YOU WHAT— I'LL TRADE YOU, OKAY? HERE, HAVE THIS...
VERY FUNNY.
NO, I'M GOIN
TO MAKE YOU L
YOUR BODY..
OKAY, THAT'S ENOUGH. HOW MUCH DO YOU GET TO MODEL? I'LL PAY YOU THE SAME AMOUNT.
HA! I'M NOT LETTING YOU GET OFF THAT EASILY, SO-NA. EVERY TIME I SEE YOUR FACE...
...AND I SEE THAT "I'M SO BORED" POOR LITTLE RICH GIRL EXPRESSION YOU ALWAYS HAVE, THERE'S ONE THING I WANT TO DO TO YOU...
FIRST, GO IN THE BACK AND CHANGE INTO THESE.
YOU'VE GOT TO BE KIDDING!
SO-NA THINKS HAE-GI HAS A SHORTS FETIS
THEN FORGET IT.

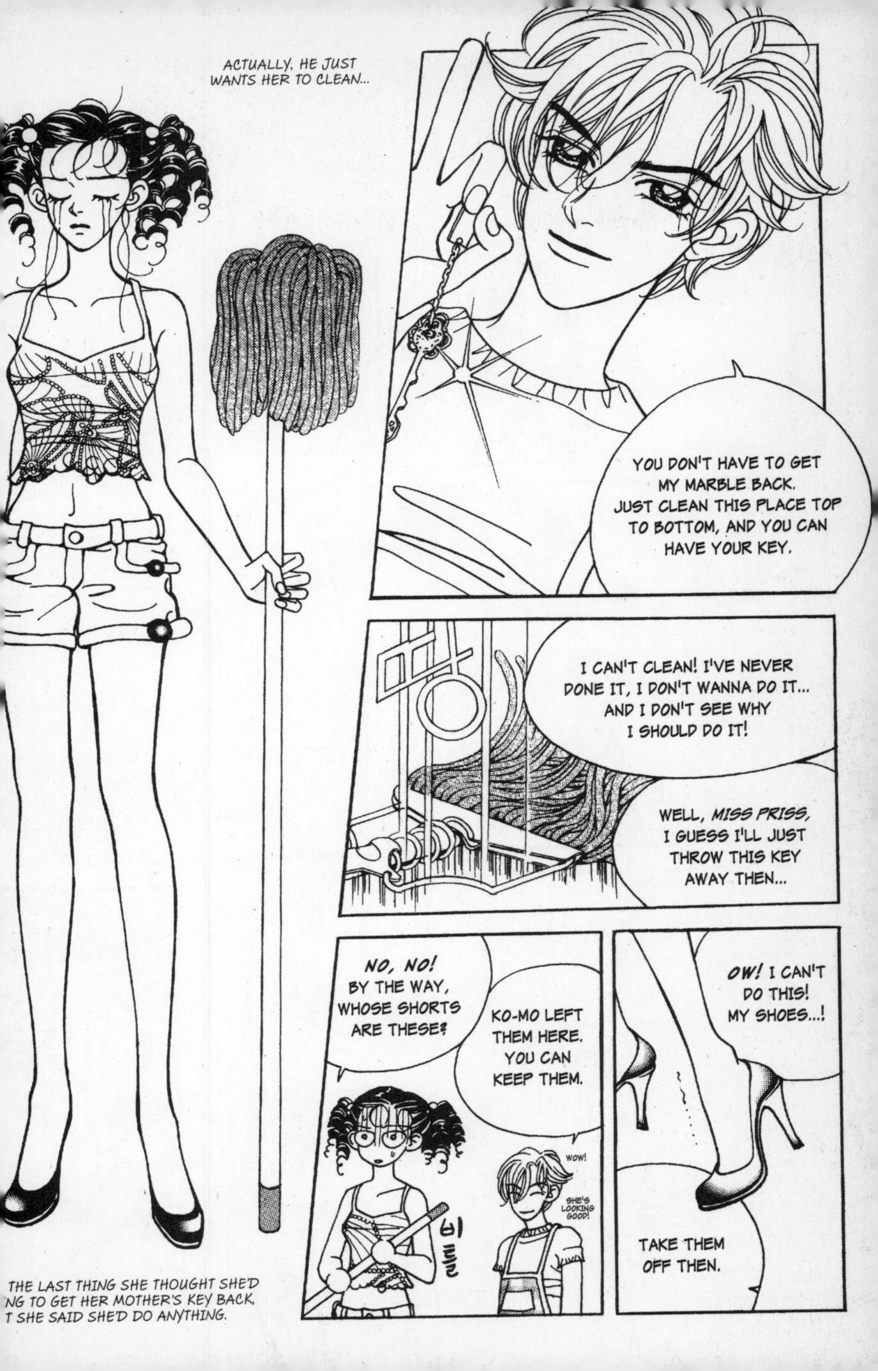
ACTUALLY, HE JUST WANTS HER TO CLEAN...
THE LAST THING SHE THOUGHT SHE'D
NG TO GET HER MOTHER'S KEY BACK,
T SHE SAID SHE'D DO ANYTHING.
YOU DON'T HAVE TO GET MY MARBLE BACK. JUST CLEAN THIS PLACE TOP TO BOTTOM, AND YOU CAN HAVE YOUR KEY.
I CAN'T CLEAN! I'VE NEVER DONE IT, I DON'T WANNA DO IT... AND I DON'T SEE WHY I SHOULD DO IT!
WELL, *MISS PRISS,* I GUESS I'LL JUST THROW THIS KEY AWAY THEN...
NO, NO! BY THE WAY, WHOSE SHORTS ARE THESE?
KO-MO LEFT THEM HERE. YOU CAN KEEP THEM.
WOW!
SHE'S LOOKING GOOD!
OW! I CAN'T DO THIS! MY SHOES...!
TAKE THEM OFF THEN.

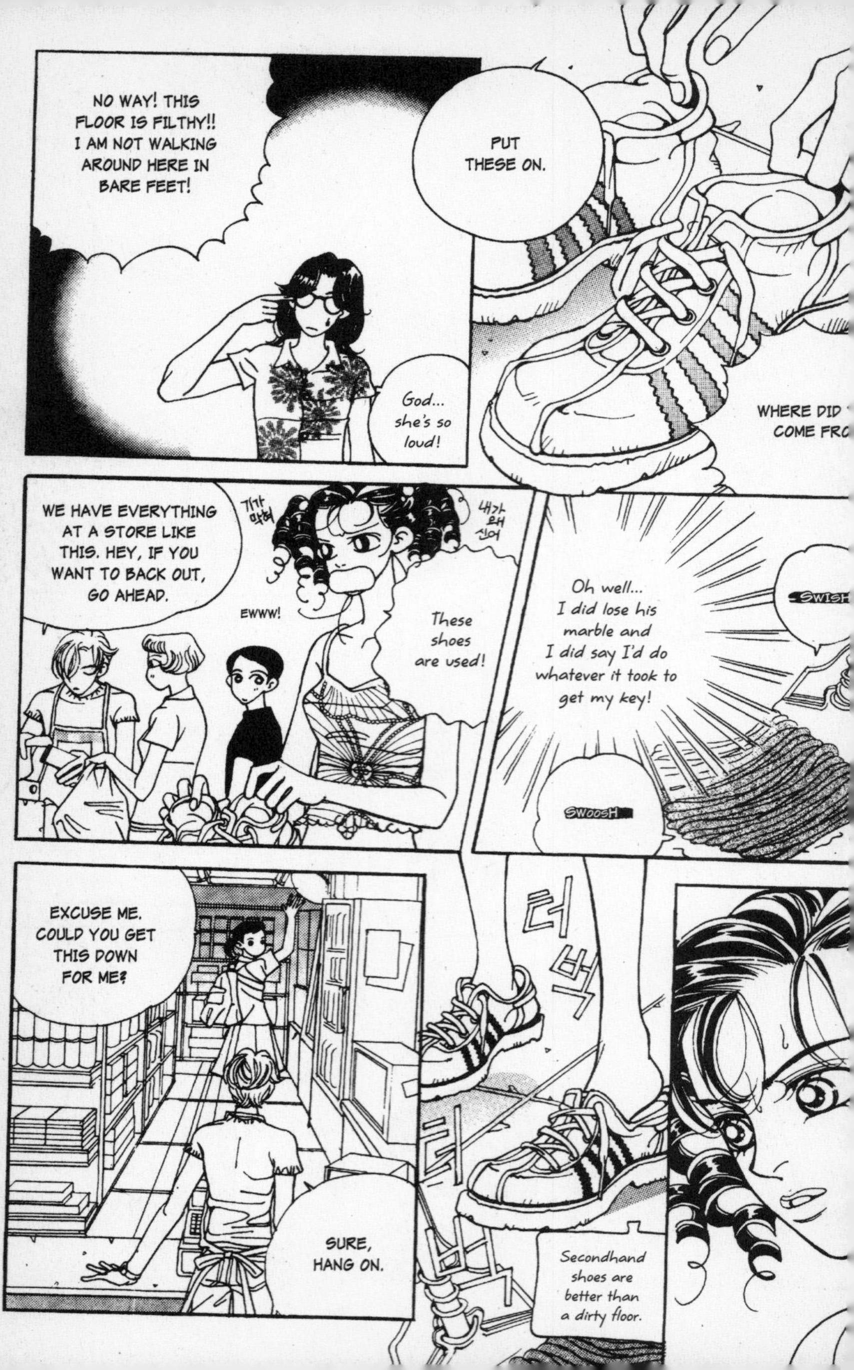
NO WAY! THIS FLOOR IS FILTHY!! I AM NOT WALKING AROUND HERE IN BARE FEET!
God... she's so loud!
PUT THESE ON.
WHERE DID
COME FRO
WE HAVE EVERYTHING AT A STORE LIKE THIS. HEY, IF YOU WANT TO BACK OUT, GO AHEAD.
기가 막혀
내가 왜 신어
EWWW!
These shoes are used!
Oh well... I did lose his marble and I did say I'd do whatever it took to get my key!
SWISH
SWOOSH
EXCUSE ME. COULD YOU GET THIS DOWN FOR ME?
SURE, HANG ON.
Secondhand shoes are better than a dirty floor.

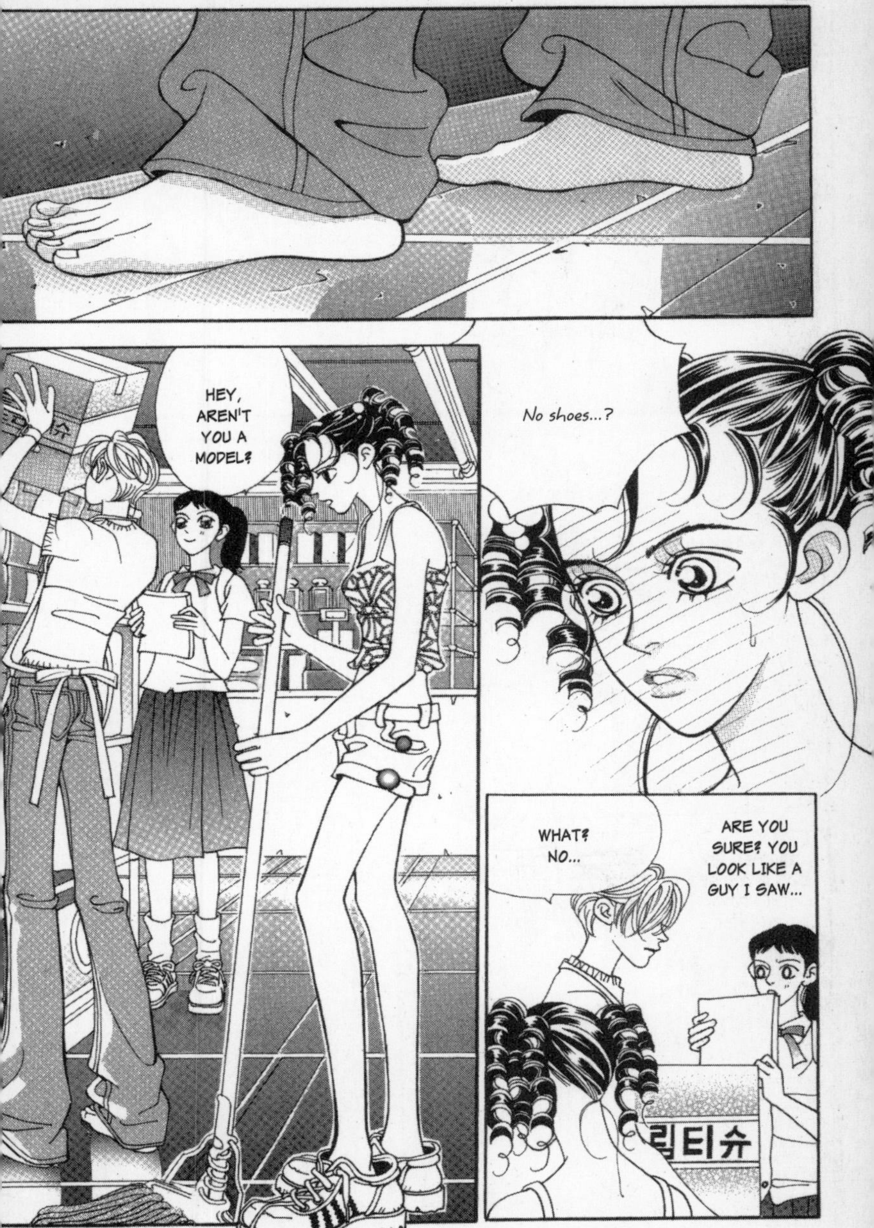
HEY, AREN'T YOU A MODEL?
No shoes...?
WHAT? NO...
ARE YOU SURE? YOU LOOK LIKE A GUY I SAW...
릭티슈

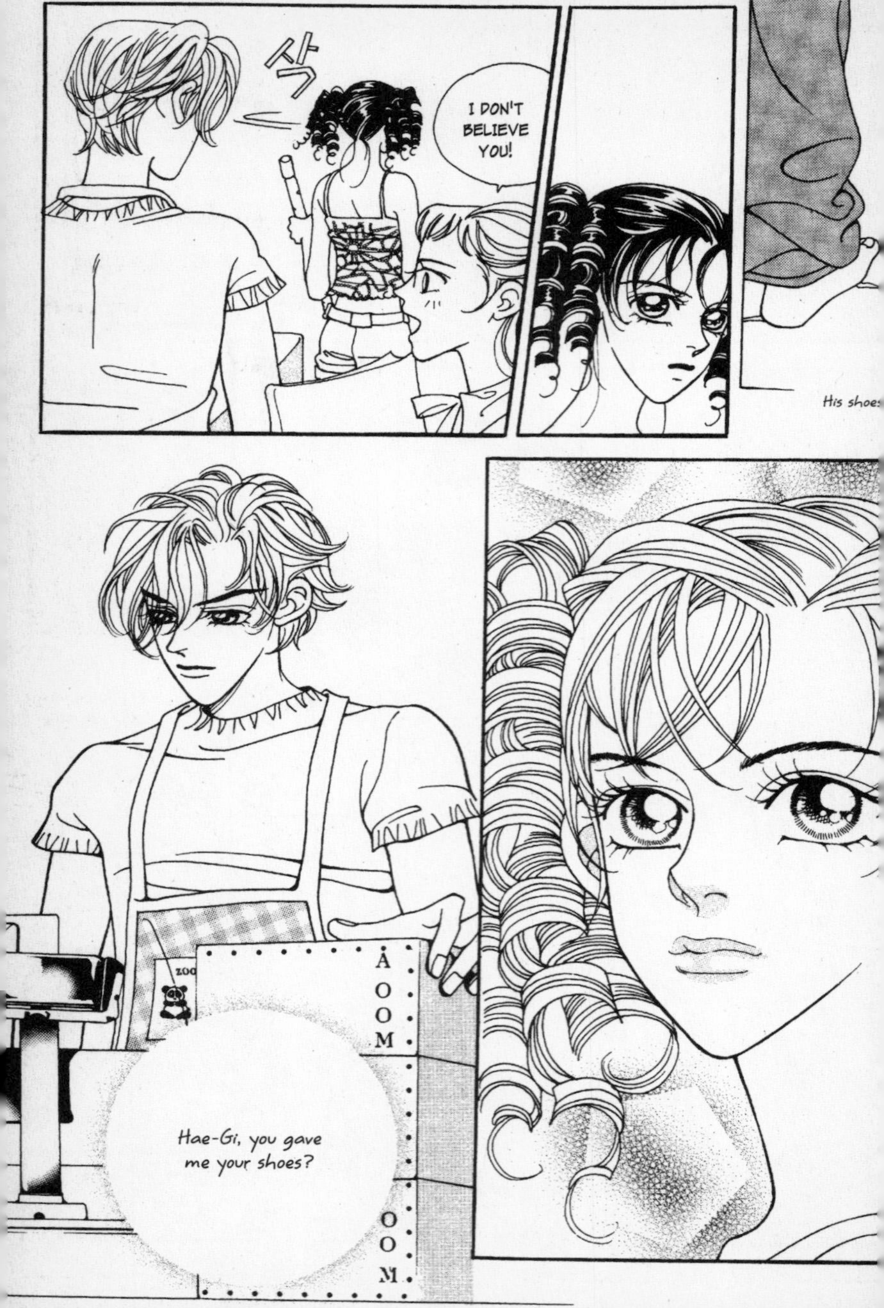
삭
I DON'T BELIEVE YOU!
His shoes
ZOO
AOOM
Hae-Gi, you gave me your shoes?
OOM

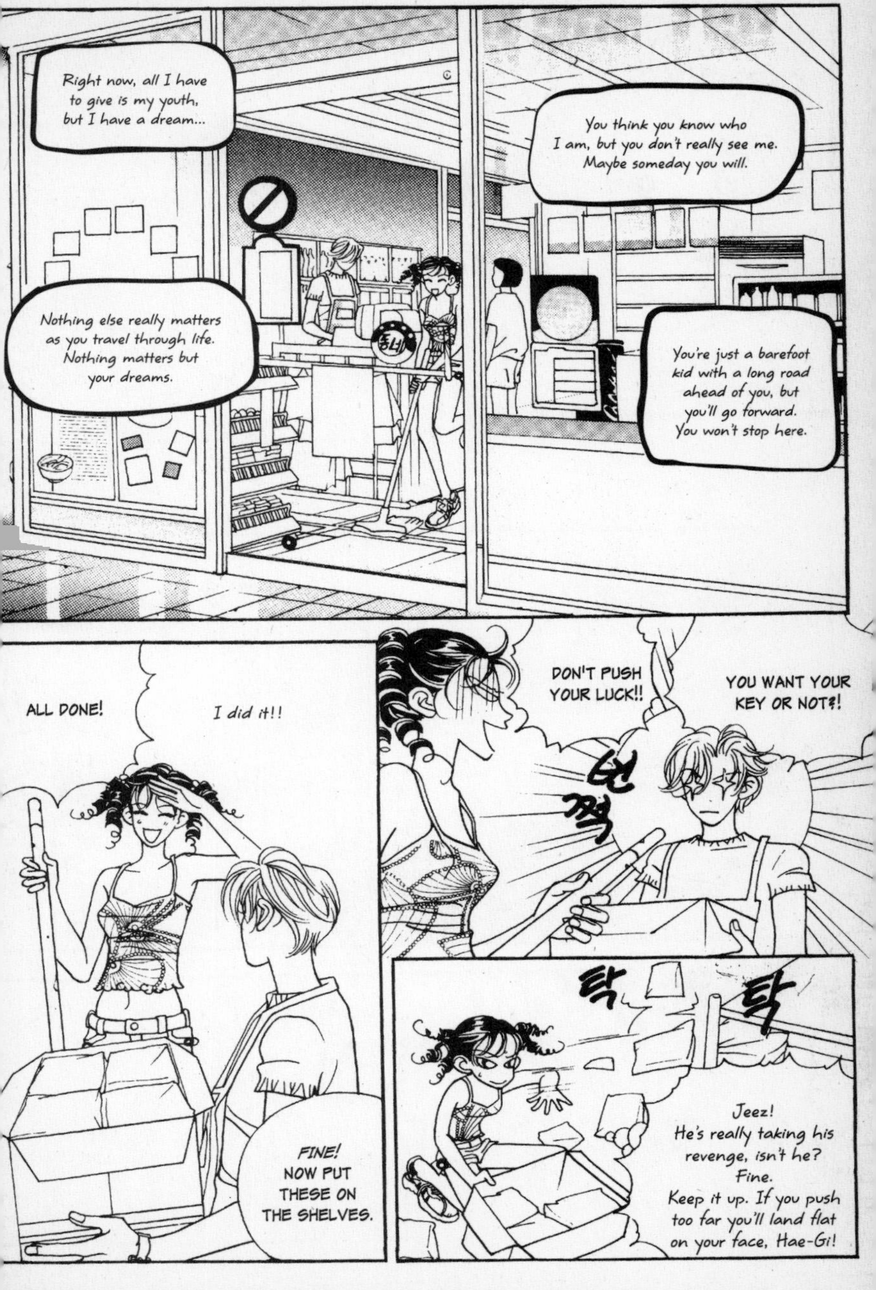
Right now, all I have to give is my youth, but I have a dream...
Nothing else really matters as you travel through life. Nothing matters but your dreams.
You think you know who I am, but you don't really see me. Maybe someday you will.
You're just a barefoot kid with a long road ahead of you, but you'll go forward. You won't stop here.
ALL DONE!
I did it!!
FINE! NOW PUT THESE ON THE SHELVES.
DON'T PUSH YOUR LUCK!!
YOU WANT YOUR KEY OR NOT?!
번쩍
탁
탁
Jeez! He's really taking his revenge, isn't he? Fine. Keep it up. If you push too far you'll land flat on your face, Hae-Gi!

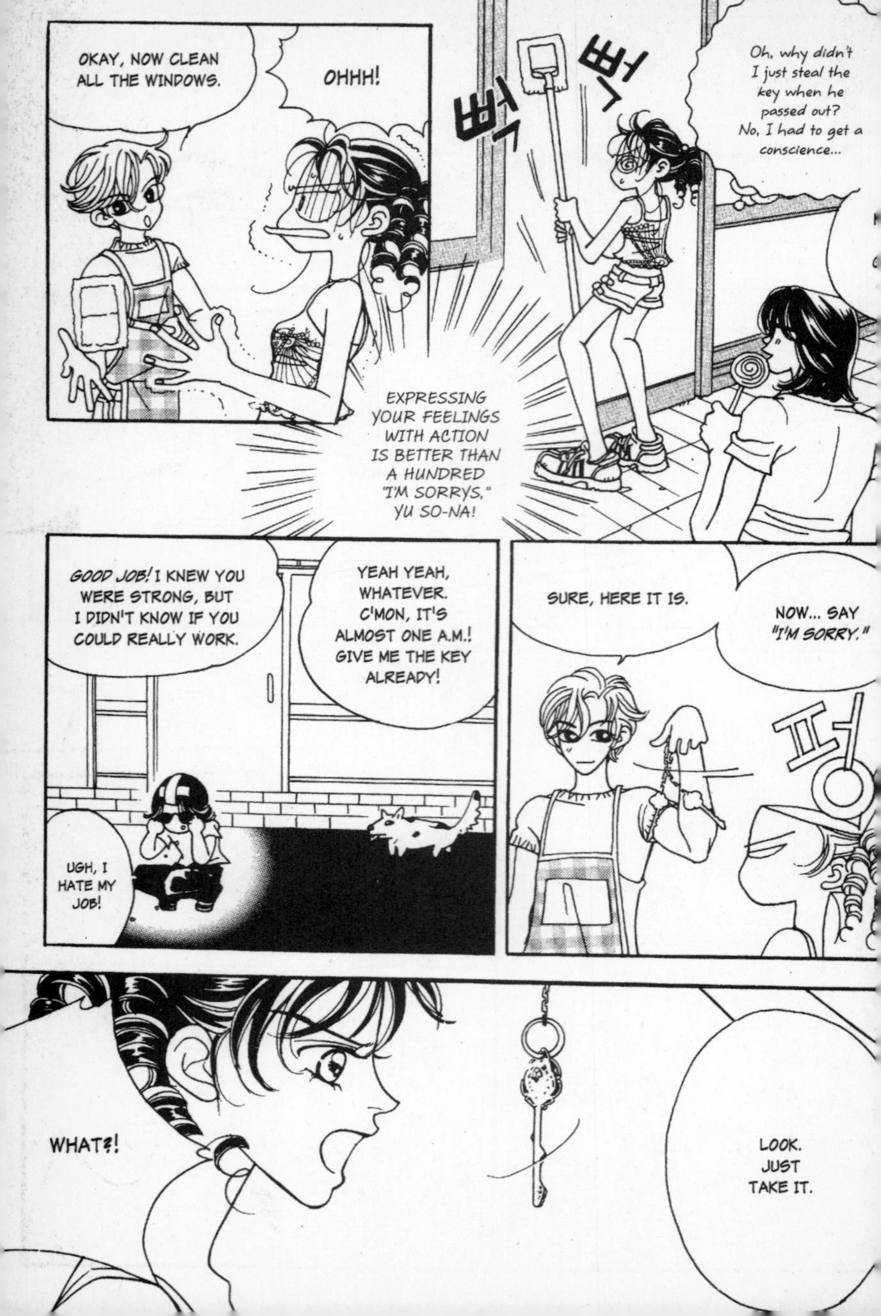

OKAY, NOW CLEAN ALL THE WINDOWS.
OHHH!
빡
빡
Oh, why didn't I just steal the key when he passed out? No, I had to get a conscience...
EXPRESSING YOUR FEELINGS WITH ACTION IS BETTER THAN A HUNDRED "I'M SORRYS," YU SO-NA!
GOOD JOB! I KNEW YOU WERE STRONG, BUT I DIDN'T KNOW IF YOU COULD REALLY WORK.
YEAH YEAH, WHATEVER. C'MON, IT'S ALMOST ONE A.M.! GIVE ME THE KEY ALREADY!
UGH, I HATE MY JOB!
SURE, HERE IT IS.
NOW... SAY "I'M SORRY."
펑
WHAT?!
LOOK. JUST TAKE IT.

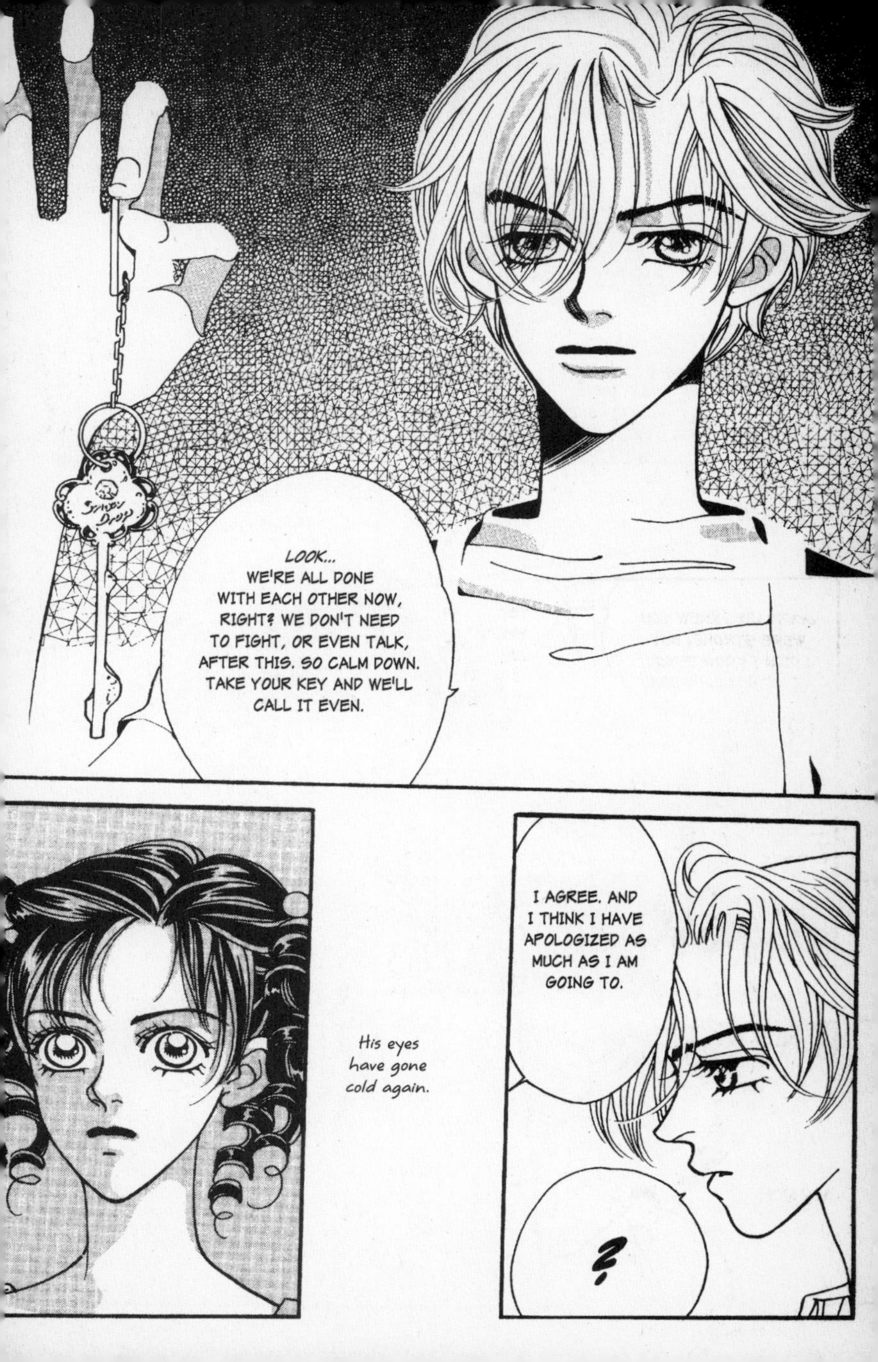
LOOK... WE'RE ALL DONE WITH EACH OTHER NOW, RIGHT? WE DON'T NEED TO FIGHT, OR EVEN TALK, AFTER THIS. SO CALM DOWN. TAKE YOUR KEY AND WE'LL CALL IT EVEN.
His eyes have gone cold again.
I AGREE. AND I THINK I HAVE APOLOGIZED AS MUCH AS I AM GOING TO.
?

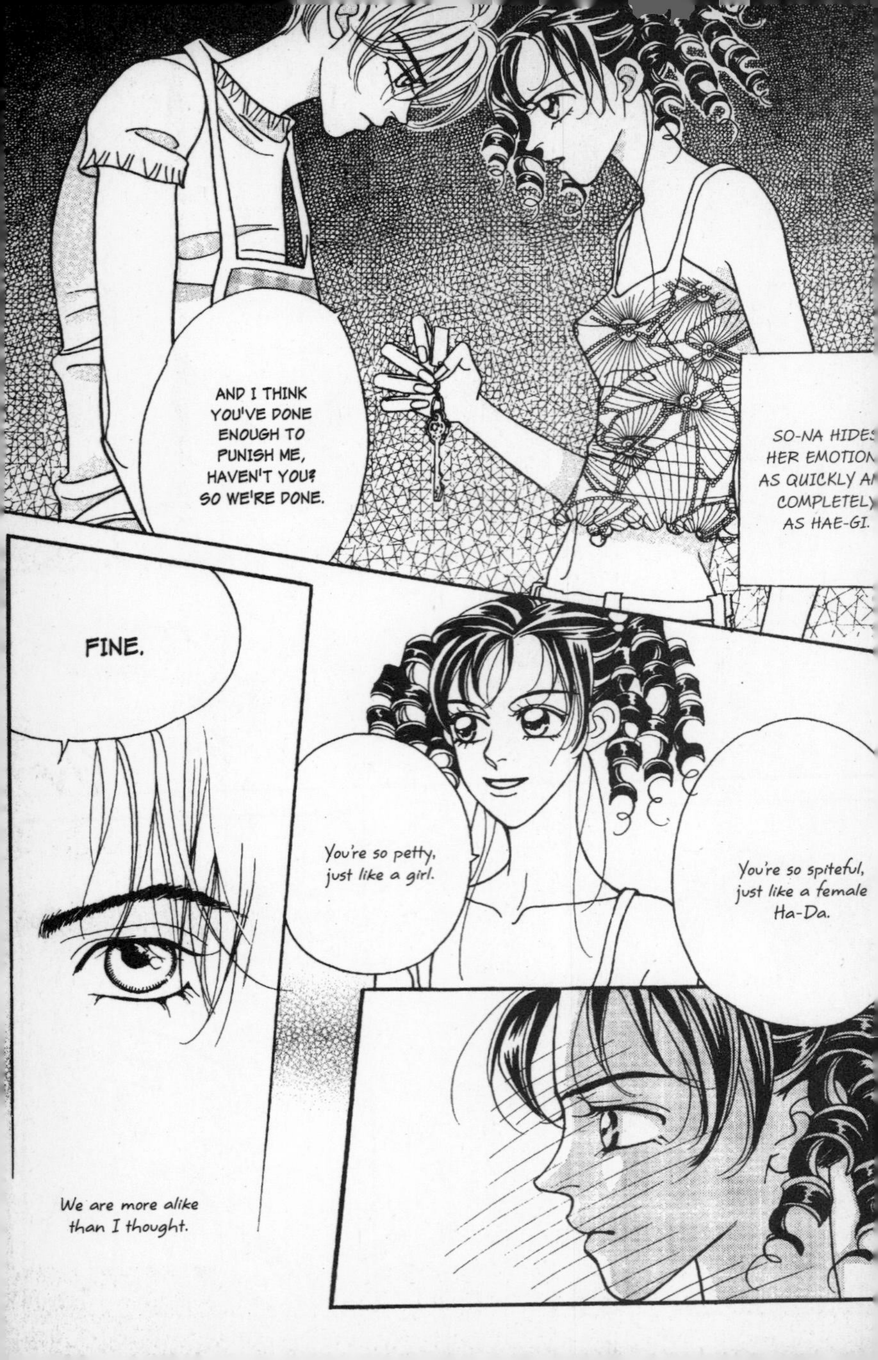
AND I THINK YOU'VE DONE ENOUGH TO PUNISH ME, HAVEN'T YOU? SO WE'RE DONE.
SO-NA HIDES HER EMOTION AS QUICKLY A COMPLETELY AS HAE-GI.
FINE.
You're so petty, just like a girl.
You're so spiteful, just like a female Ha-Da.
We are more alike than I thought.

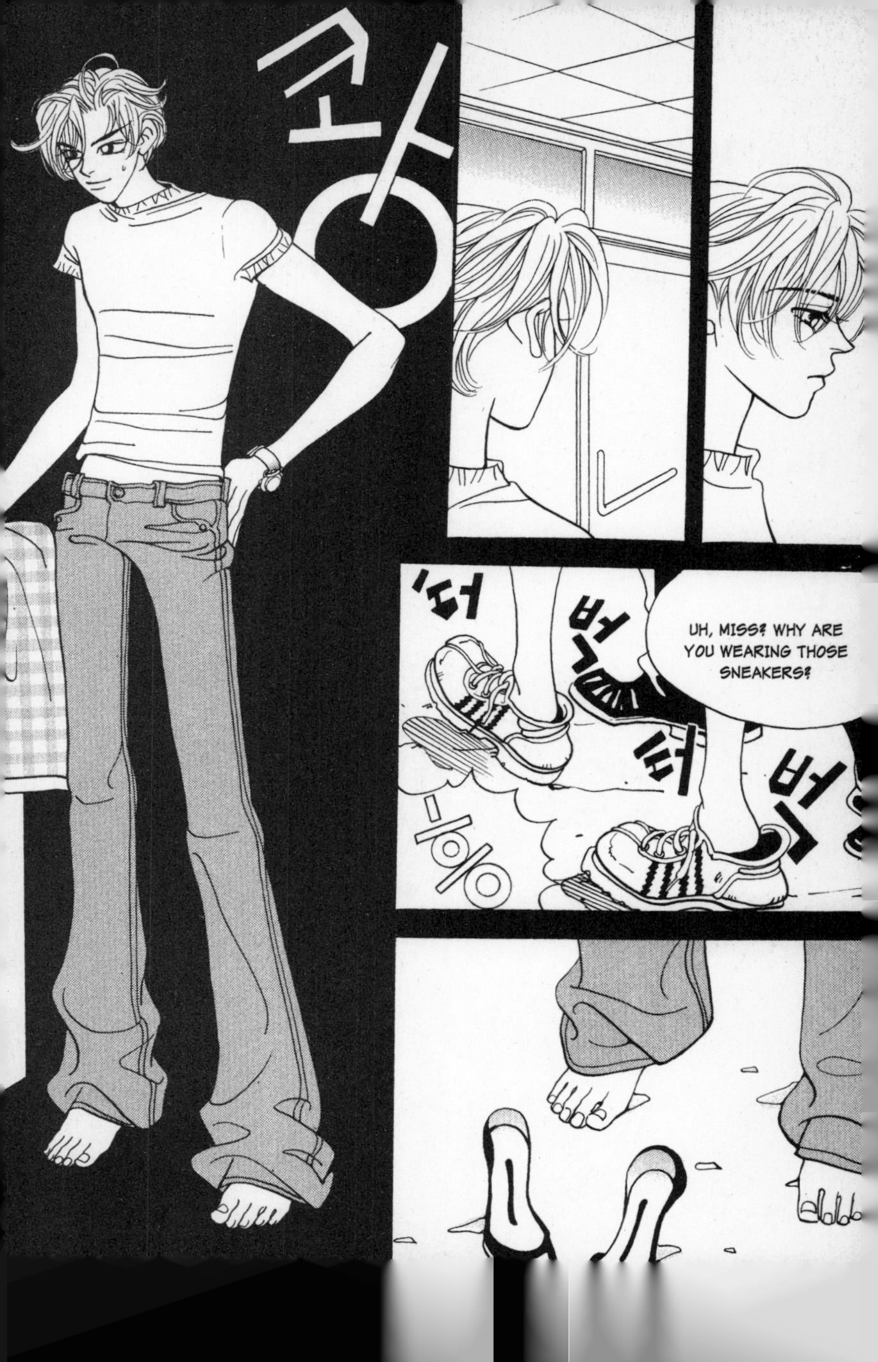
UH, MISS? WHY ARE YOU WEARING THOSE SNEAKERS?

Snow Drop

Jang • Ha • Da

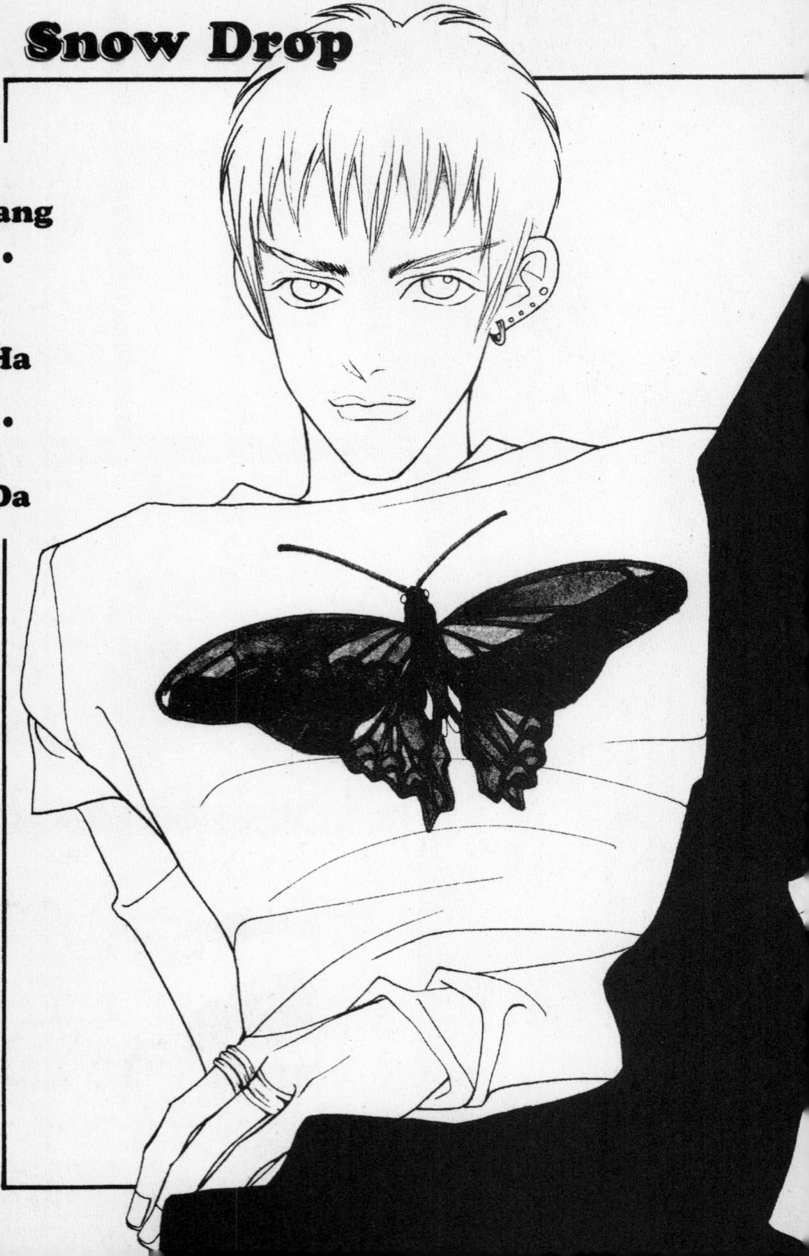

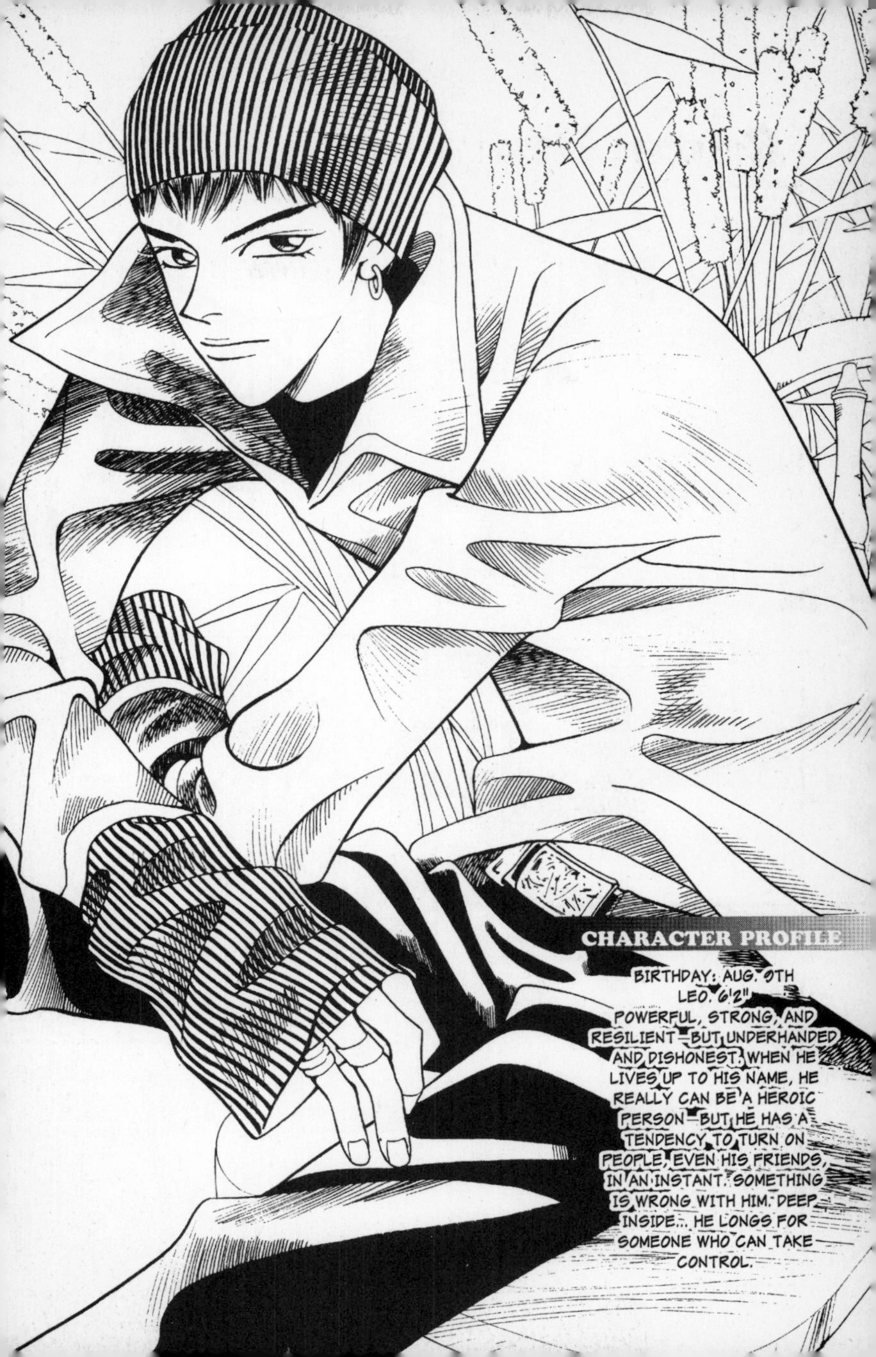
CHARACTER PROFILE
BIRTHDAY: AUG. 9TH
LEO. 6'2"
POWERFUL, STRONG, AND RESILIENT—BUT UNDERHANDED AND DISHONEST. WHEN HE LIVES UP TO HIS NAME, HE REALLY CAN BE A HEROIC PERSON—BUT HE HAS A TENDENCY TO TURN ON PEOPLE, EVEN HIS FRIENDS, IN AN INSTANT. SOMETHING IS WRONG WITH HIM. DEEP INSIDE... HE LONGS FOR SOMEONE WHO CAN TAKE CONTROL.

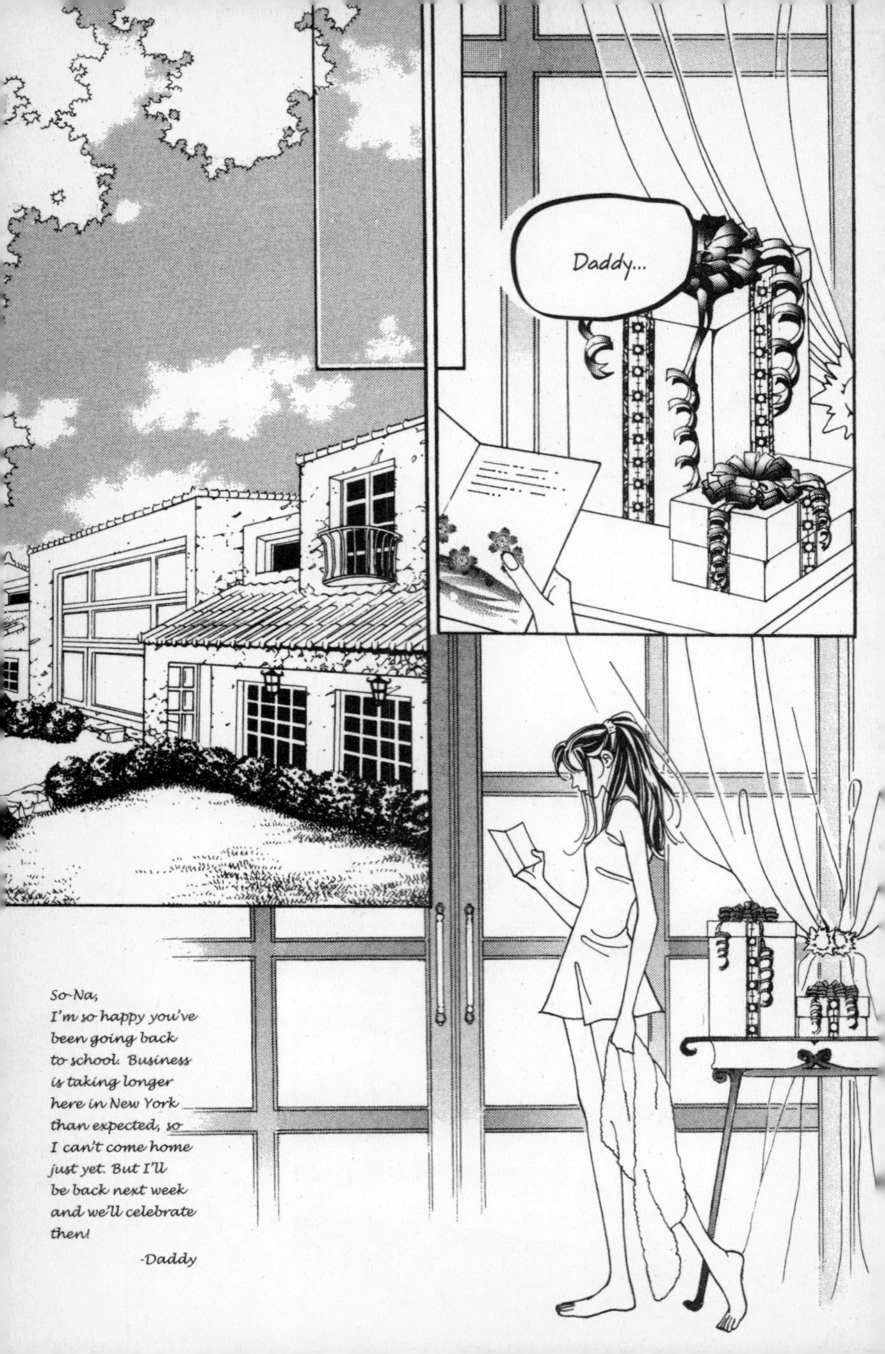
Daddy...
So-Na,
I'm so happy you've been going back to school. Business is taking longer here in New York than expected, so I can't come home just yet. But I'll be back next week and we'll celebrate then!
-Daddy

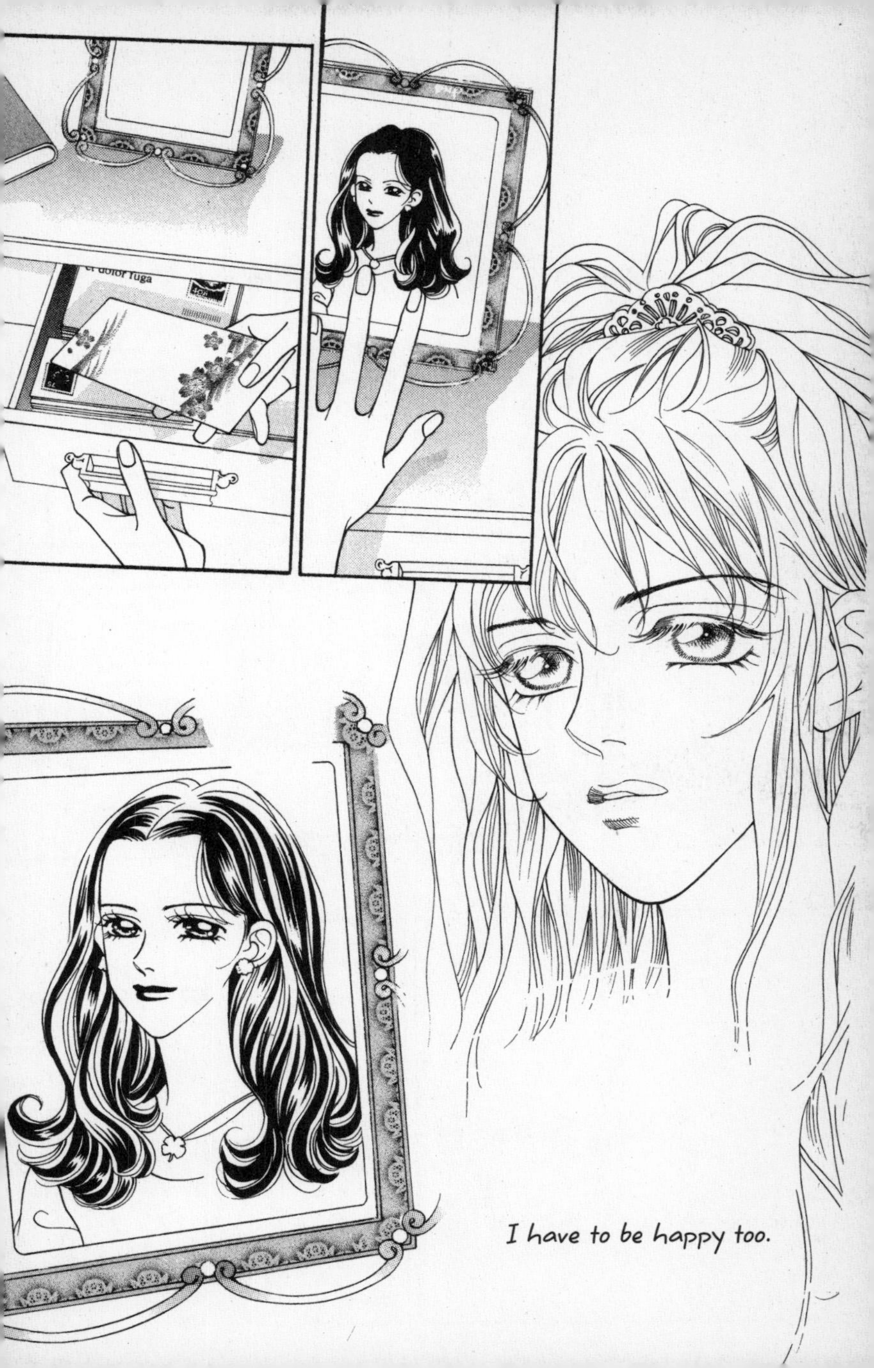
I have to be happy too.

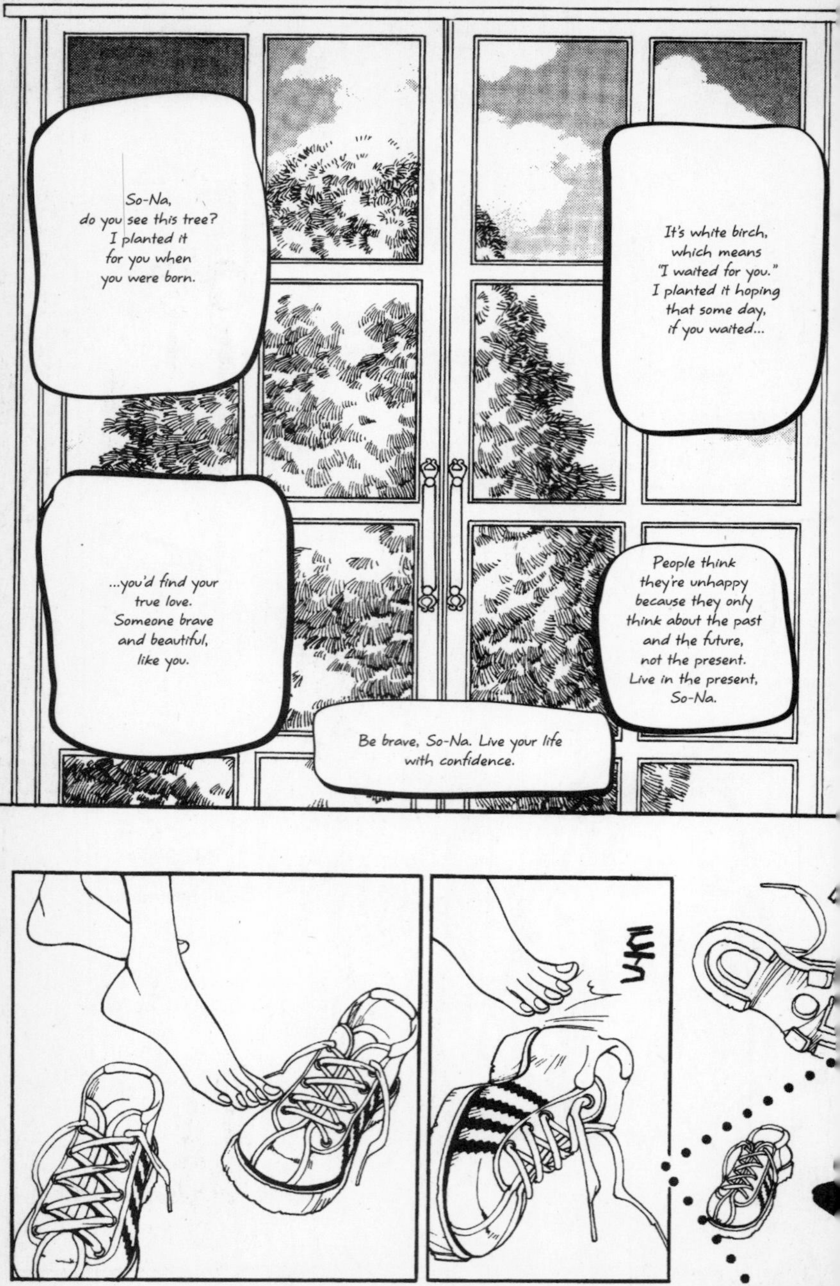
So-Na, do you see this tree? I planted it for you when you were born.
It's white birch, which means "I waited for you." I planted it hoping that some day, if you waited...
...you'd find your true love. Someone brave and beautiful, like you.
People think they're unhappy because they only think about the past and the future, not the present. Live in the present, So-Na.
Be brave, So-Na. Live your life with confidence.

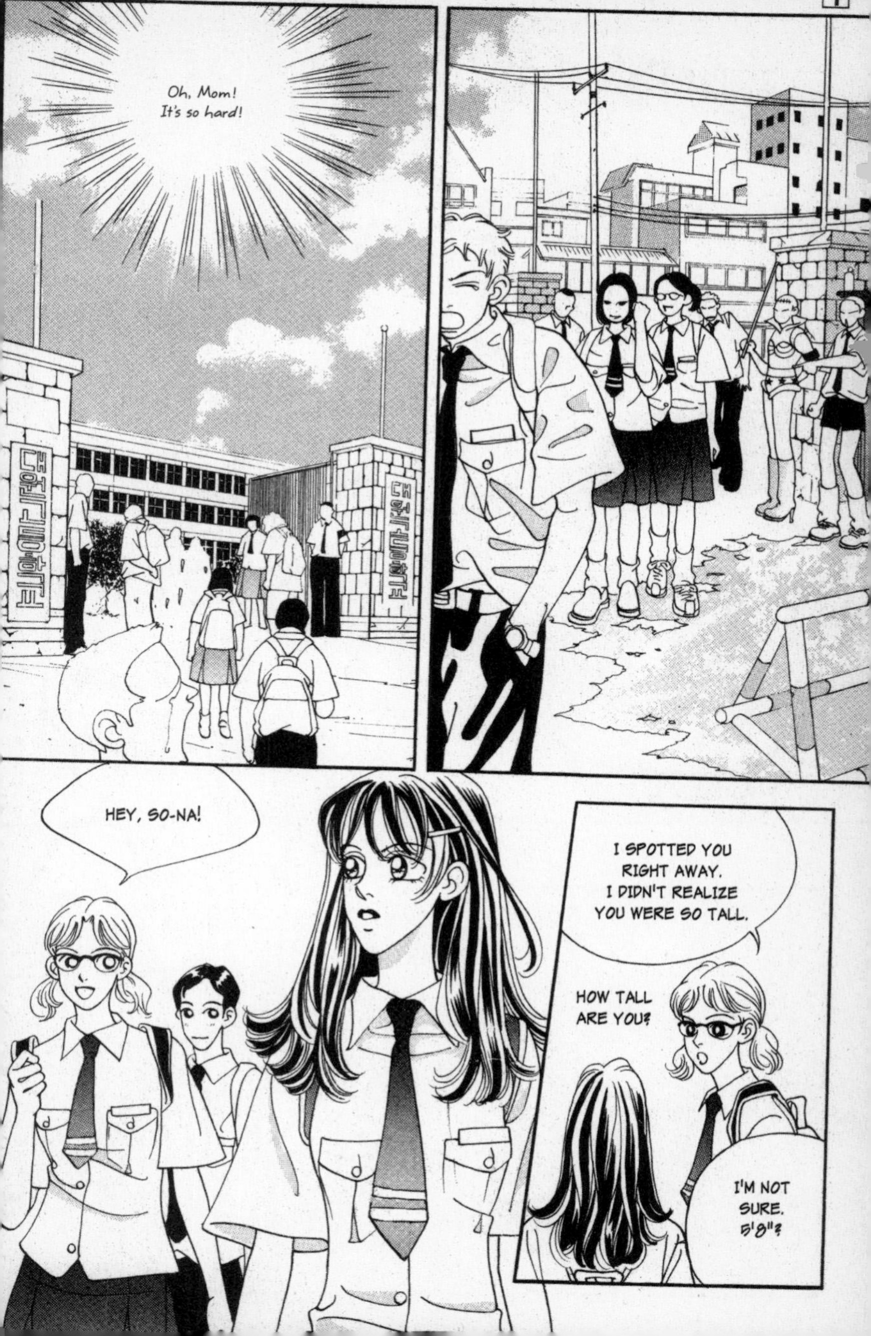
Oh, Mom!
It's so hard!
HEY, SO-NA!
I SPOTTED YOU RIGHT AWAY. I DIDN'T REALIZE YOU WERE SO TALL.
HOW TALL ARE YOU?
I'M NOT SURE. 5'8"?

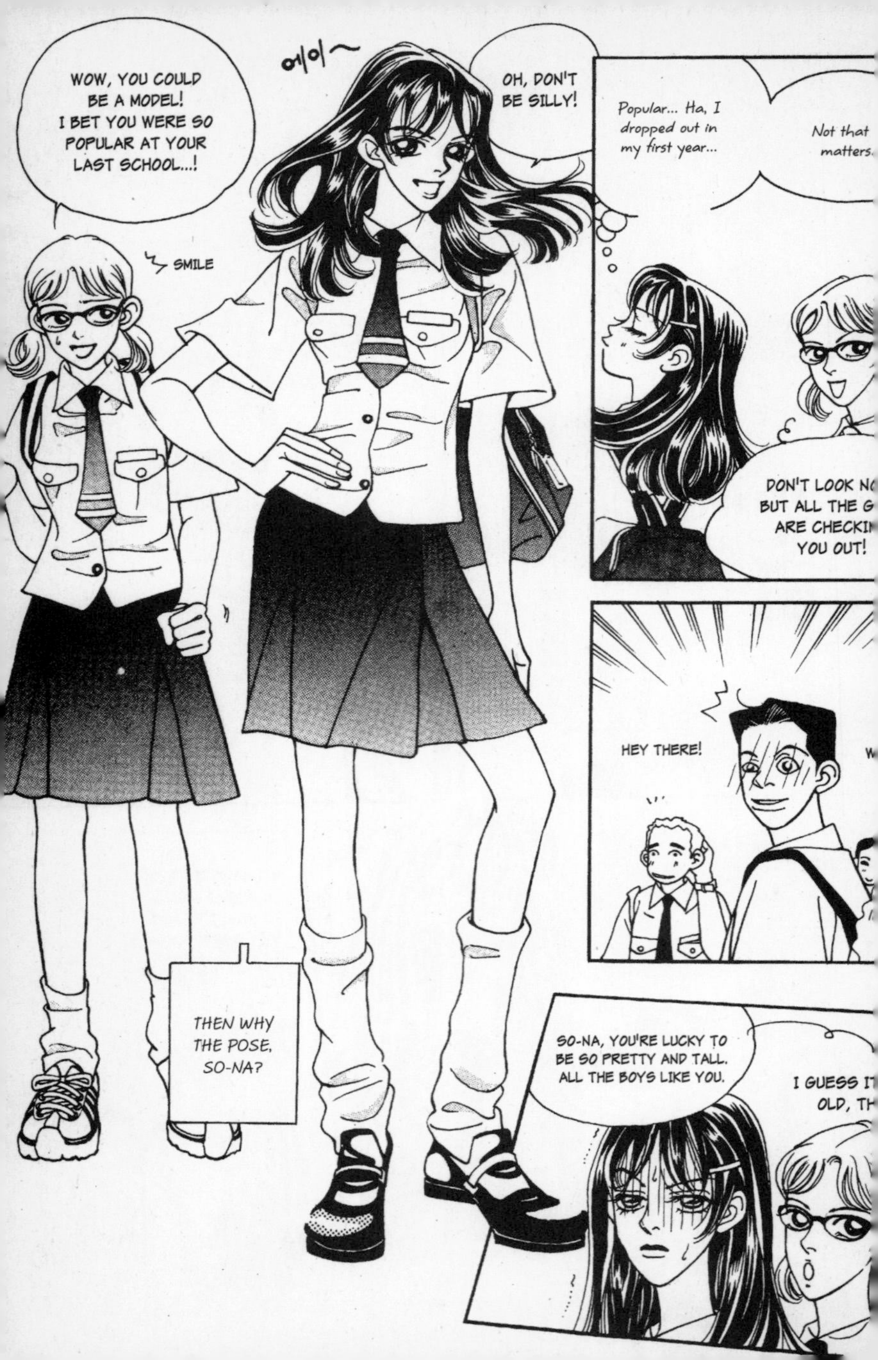
WOW, YOU COULD BE A MODEL! I BET YOU WERE SO POPULAR AT YOUR LAST SCHOOL...!
에이~
OH, DON'T BE SILLY!
SMILE
THEN WHY THE POSE, SO-NA?
Popular... Ha, I dropped out in my first year...
Not that matters.
DON'T LOOK N BUT ALL THE G ARE CHECKI YOU OUT!
HEY THERE!
SO-NA, YOU'RE LUCKY TO BE SO PRETTY AND TALL. ALL THE BOYS LIKE YOU.
I GUESS IT OLD, TH

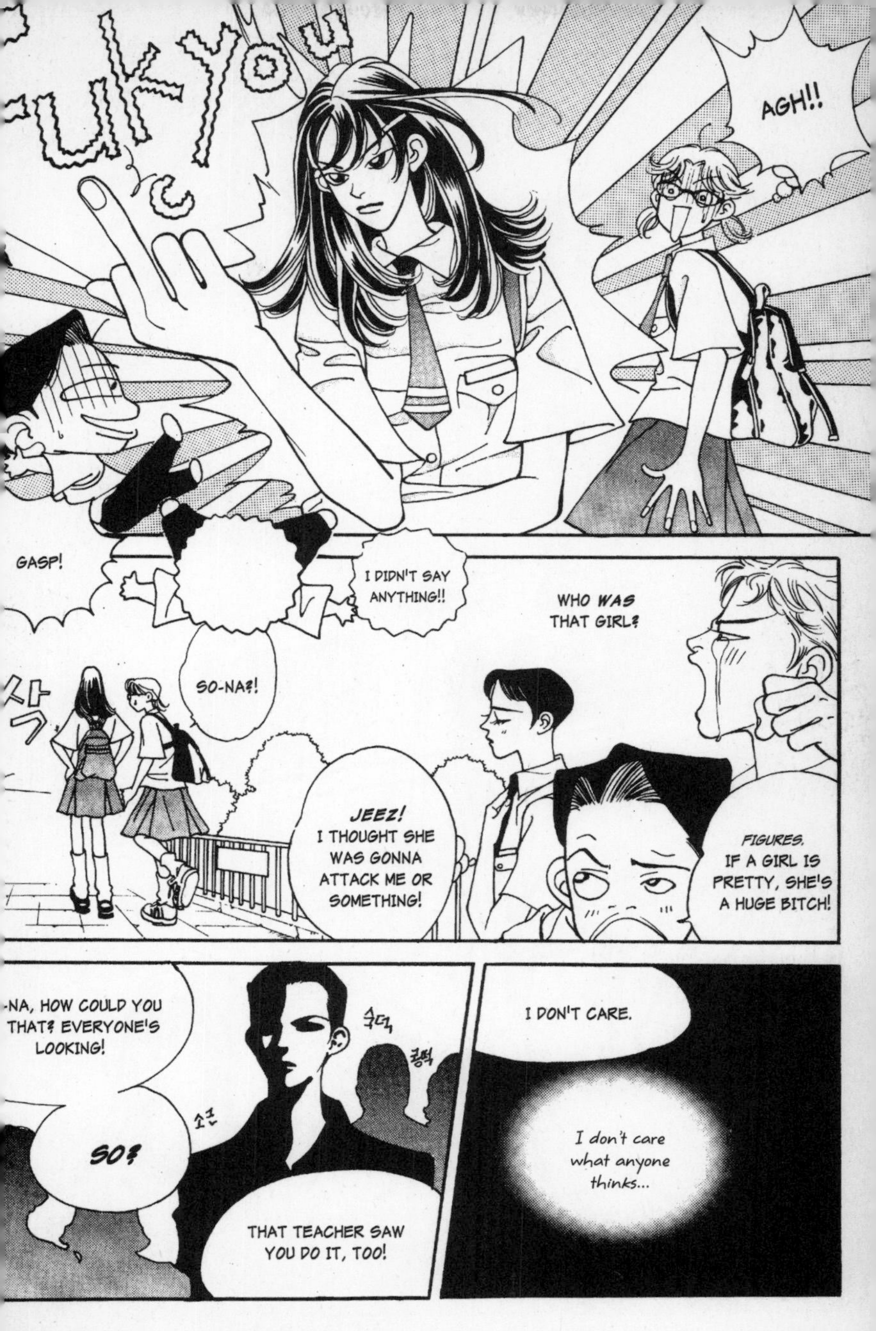

UK YOU
AGH!!
GASP!
I DIDN'T SAY ANYTHING!!
SO-NA?!
JEEZ! I THOUGHT SHE WAS GONNA ATTACK ME OR SOMETHING!
WHO WAS THAT GIRL?
FIGURES. IF A GIRL IS PRETTY, SHE'S A HUGE BITCH!
-NA, HOW COULD YOU THAT? EVERYONE'S LOOKING!
SO?
THAT TEACHER SAW YOU DO IT, TOO!
I DON'T CARE.
I don't care what anyone thinks...

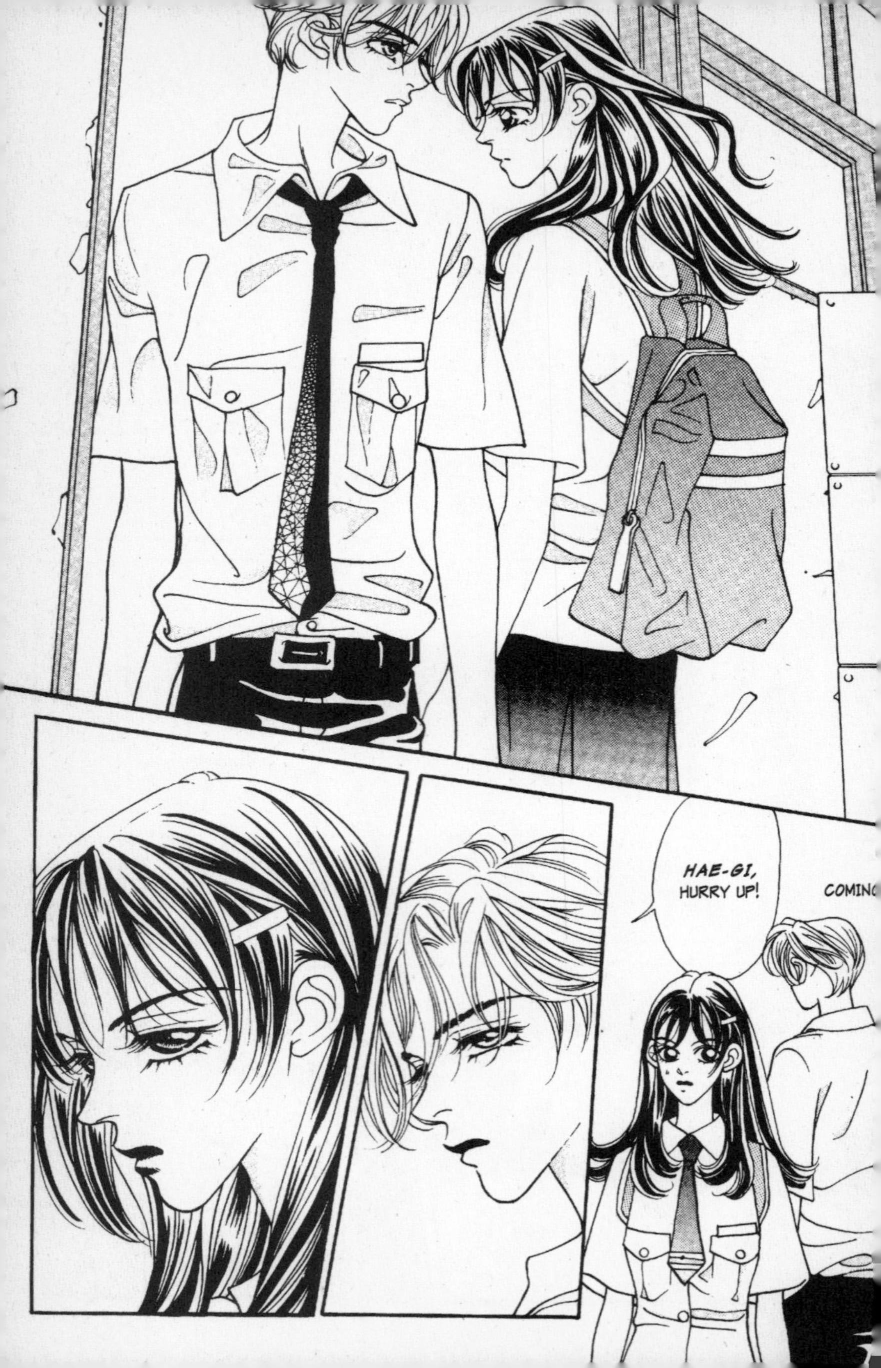
HAE-GI, HURRY UP!
COMING

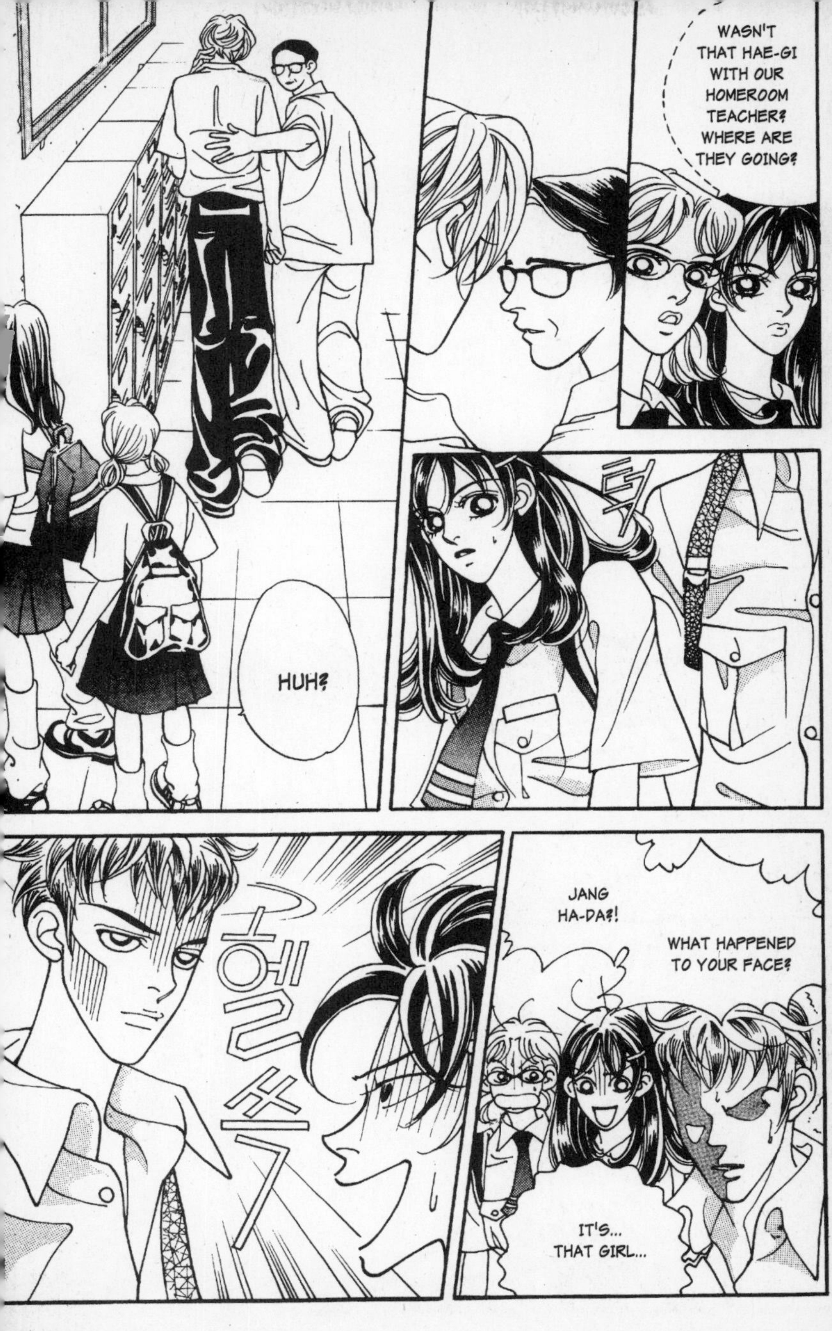
HUH?
WASN'T THAT HAE-GI WITH OUR HOMEROOM TEACHER? WHERE ARE THEY GOING?
JANG HA-DA?!
WHAT HAPPENED TO YOUR FACE?
IT'S... THAT GIRL...

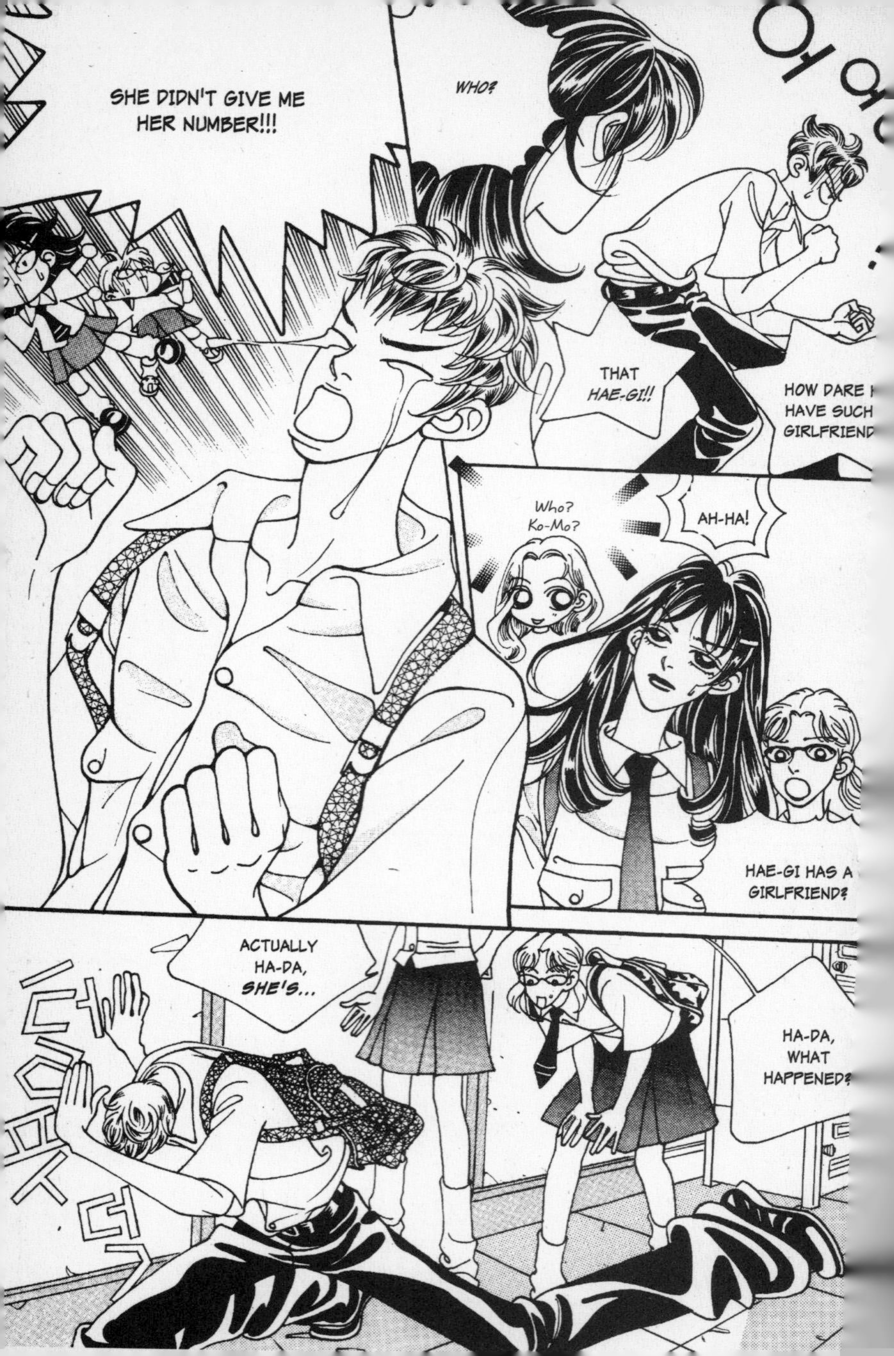
SHE DIDN'T GIVE ME HER NUMBER!!!
WHO?
THAT HAE-GI!!
HOW DARE H
HAVE SUCH
GIRLFRIEND
Who? Ko-Mo?
AH-HA!
HAE-GI HAS A
GIRLFRIEND?
ACTUALLY HA-DA, SHE'S...
HA-DA, WHAT HAPPENED?

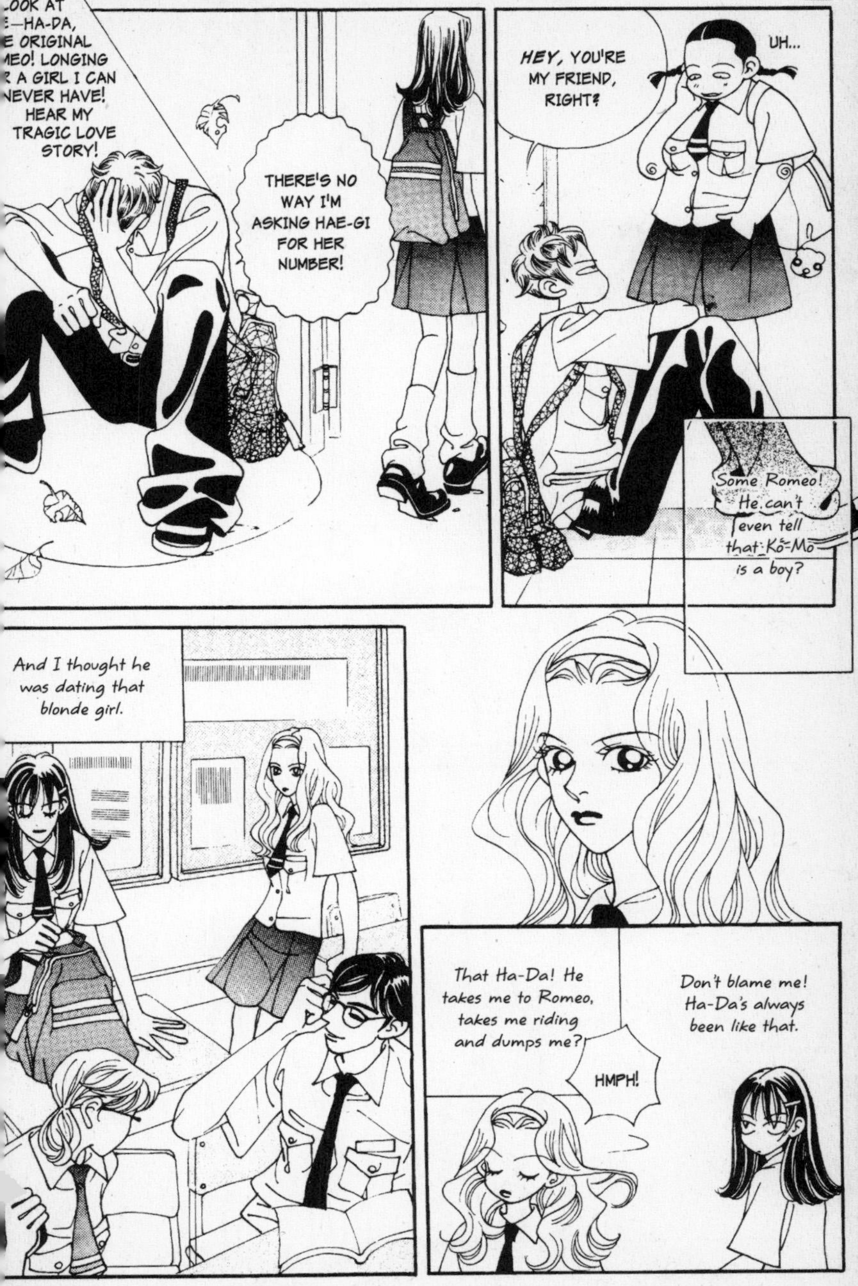

OOK AT E—HA-DA, E ORIGINAL MEO! LONGING R A GIRL I CAN NEVER HAVE! HEAR MY TRAGIC LOVE STORY!
THERE'S NO WAY I'M ASKING HAE-GI FOR HER NUMBER!
HEY, YOU'RE MY FRIEND, RIGHT?
UH...
Some Romeo! He can't even tell that Ko-Mo is a boy?
And I thought he was dating that blonde girl.
That Ha-Da! He takes me to Romeo, takes me riding and dumps me?
HMPH!
Don't blame me! Ha-Da's always been like that.

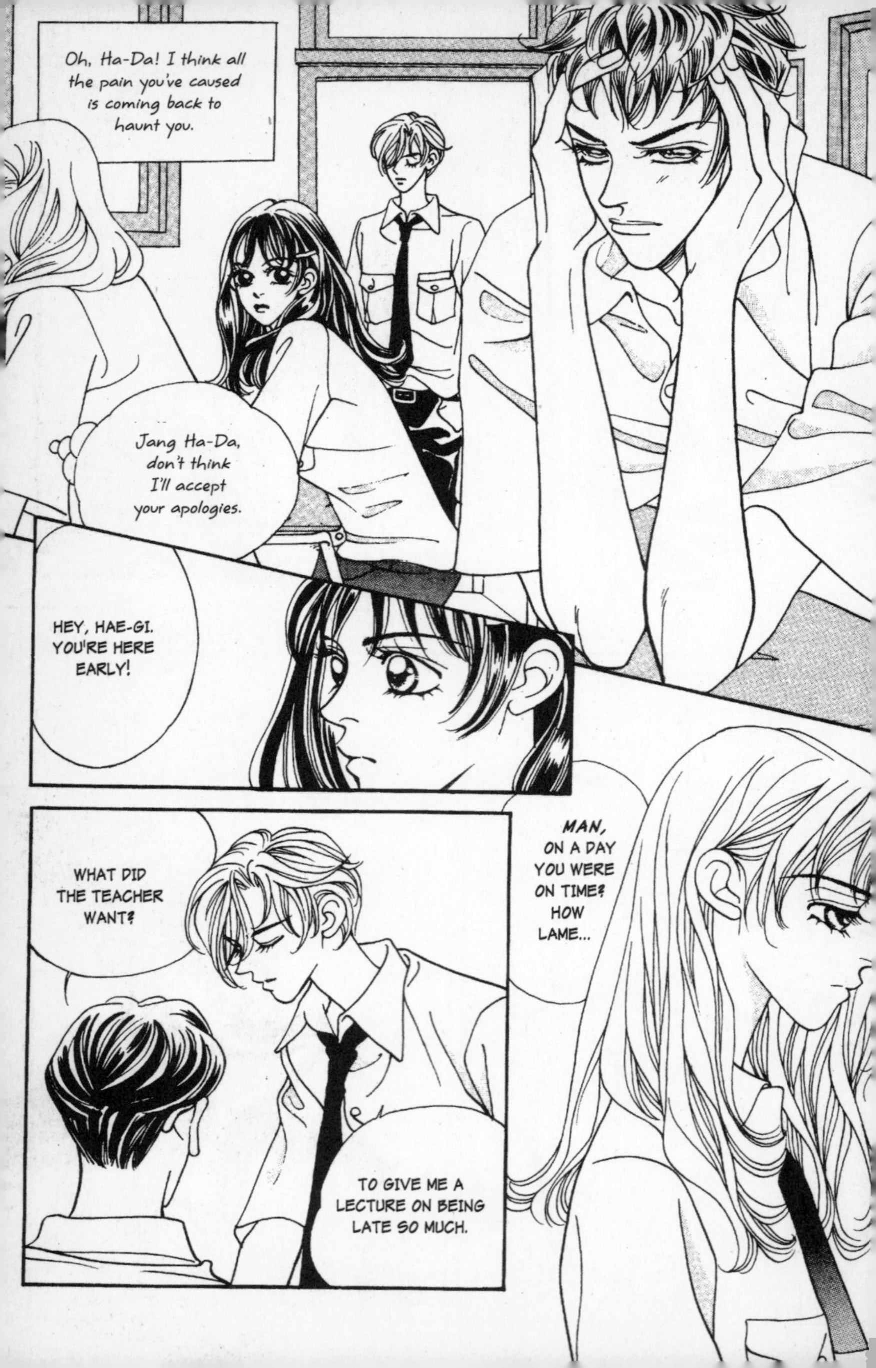
Oh, Ha-Da! I think all the pain you've caused is coming back to haunt you.
Jang Ha-Da, don't think I'll accept your apologies.
HEY, HAE-GI. YOU'RE HERE EARLY!
MAN, ON A DAY YOU WERE ON TIME? HOW LAME...
WHAT DID THE TEACHER WANT?
TO GIVE ME A LECTURE ON BEING LATE SO MUCH.

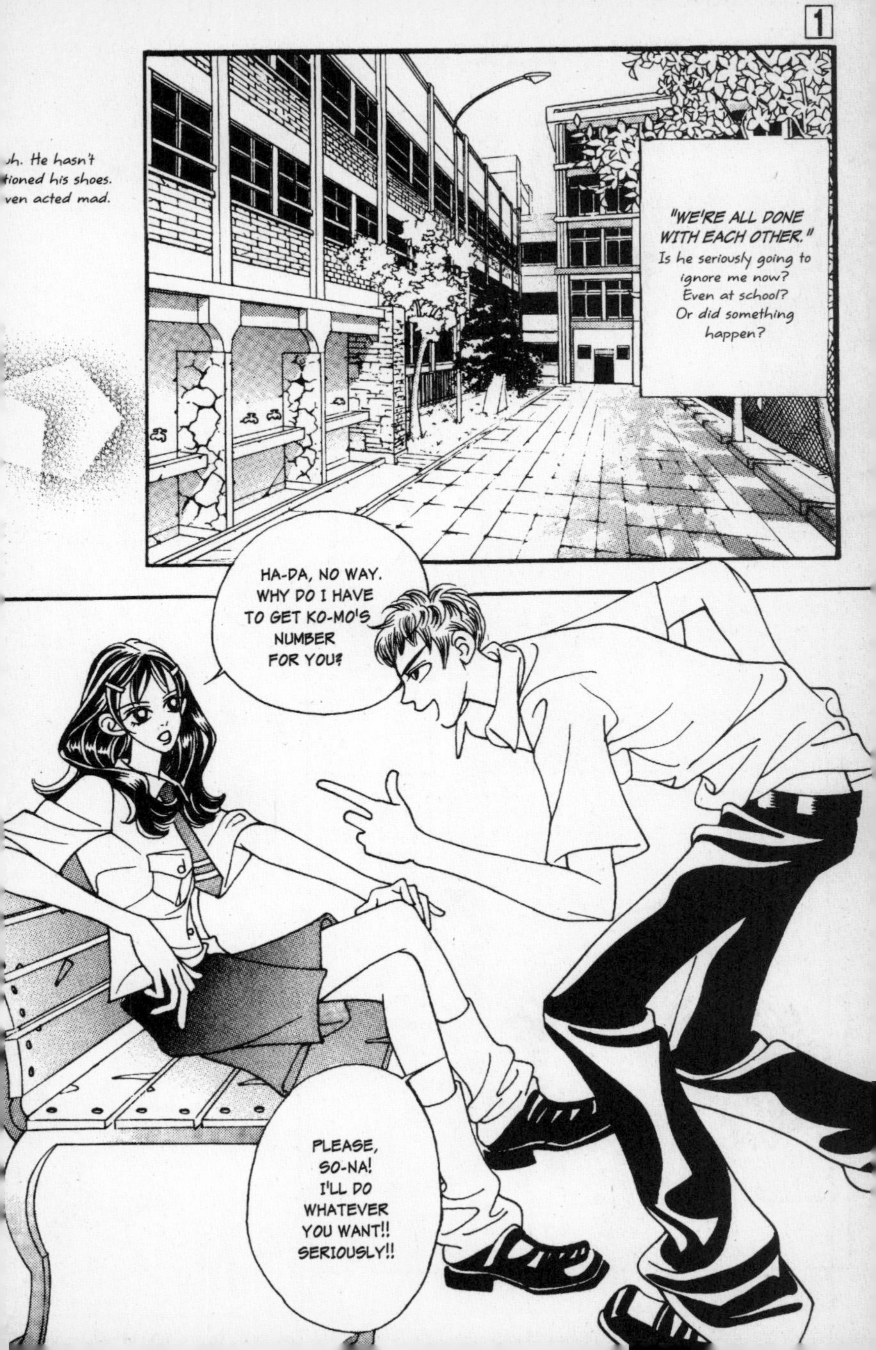
1
h. He hasn't tioned his shoes. ven acted mad.
"WE'RE ALL DONE WITH EACH OTHER." Is he seriously going to ignore me now? Even at school? Or did something happen?
HA-DA, NO WAY. WHY DO I HAVE TO GET KO-MO'S NUMBER FOR YOU?
PLEASE, SO-NA! I'LL DO WHATEVER YOU WANT!! SERIOUSLY!!

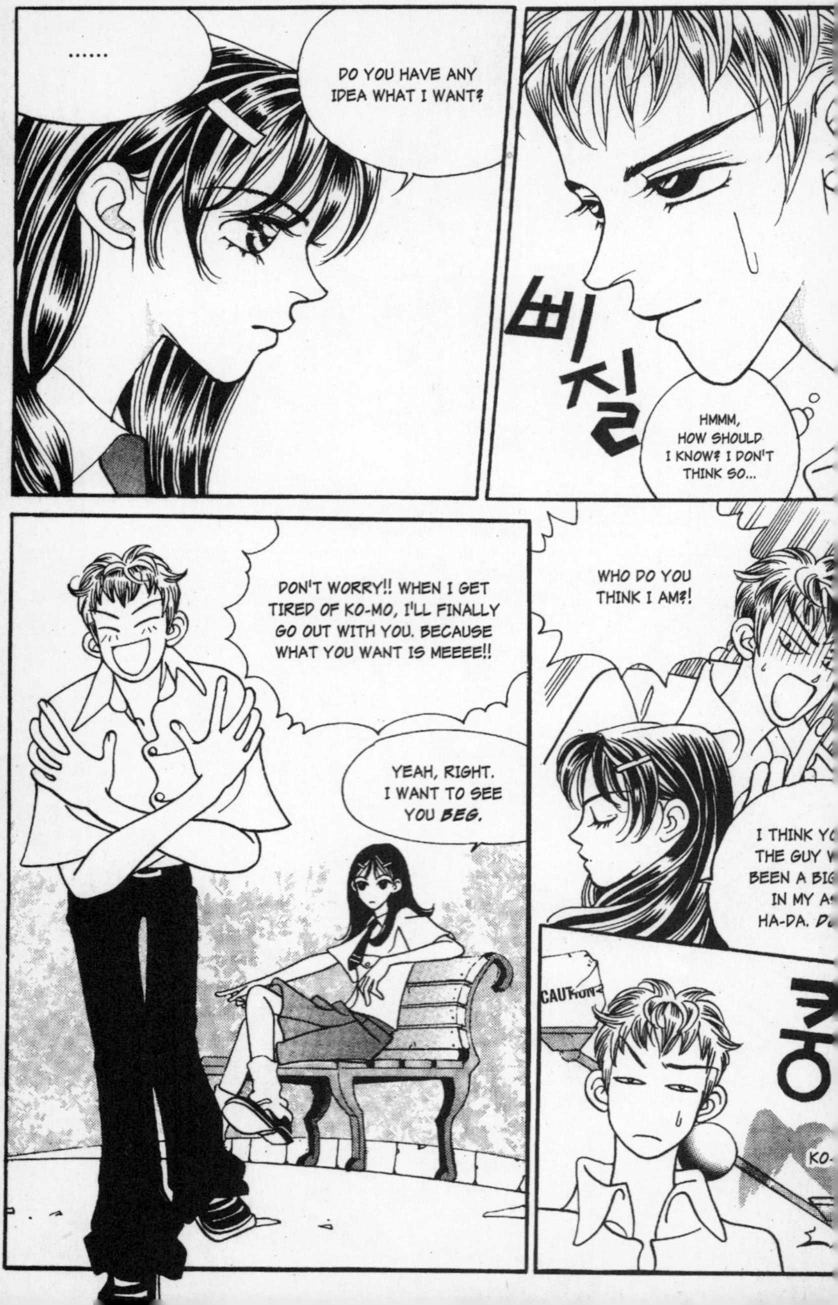
......
DO YOU HAVE ANY IDEA WHAT I WANT?
삐실
HMMM, HOW SHOULD I KNOW? I DON'T THINK SO...
DON'T WORRY!! WHEN I GET TIRED OF KO-MO, I'LL FINALLY GO OUT WITH YOU. BECAUSE WHAT YOU WANT IS MEEEE!!
YEAH, RIGHT. I WANT TO SEE YOU *BEG.*
WHO DO YOU THINK I AM?!
CAUTION

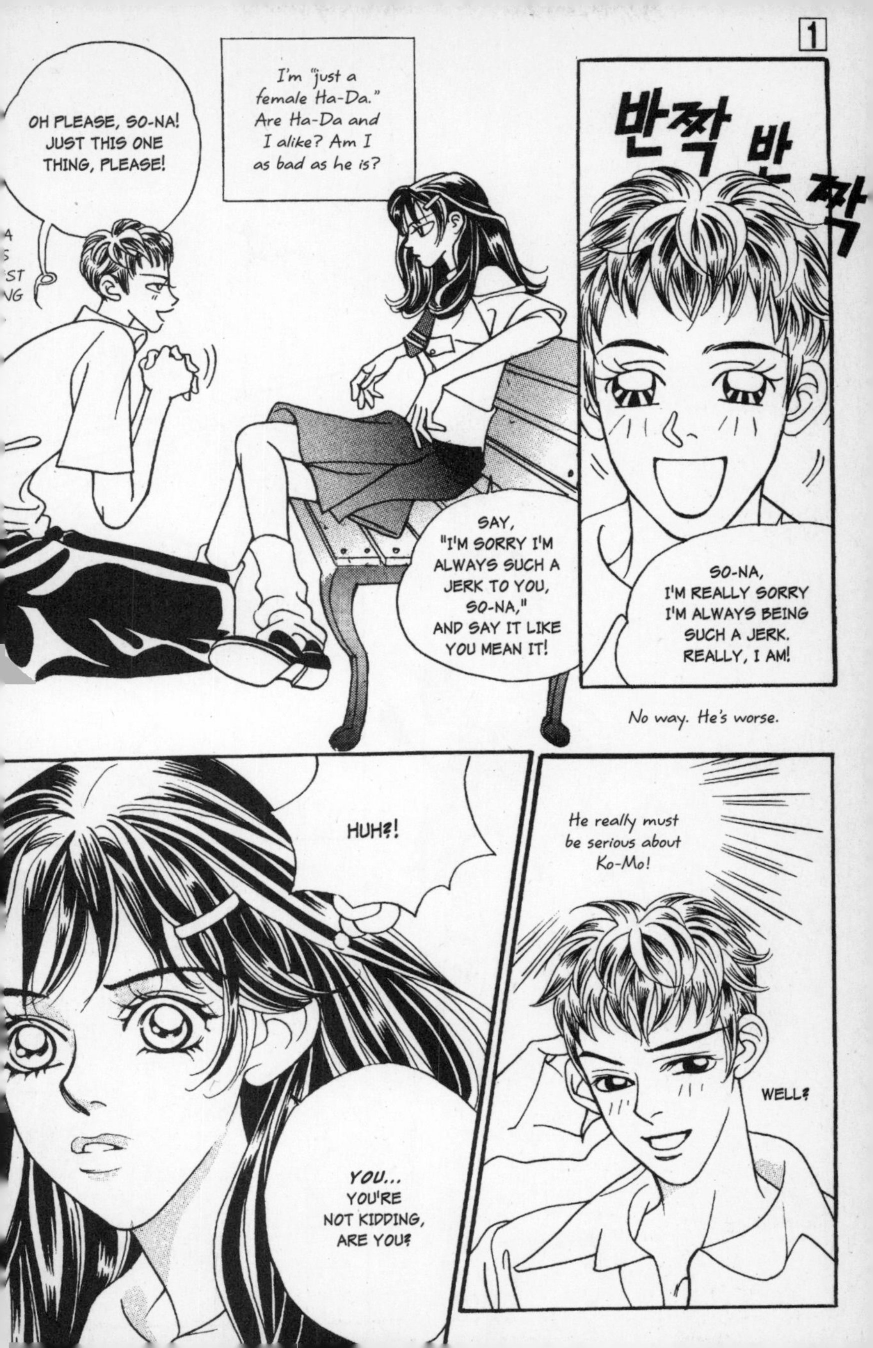
1
OH PLEASE, SO-NA! JUST THIS ONE THING, PLEASE!
I'm "just a female Ha-Da." Are Ha-Da and I alike? Am I as bad as he is?
SAY, "I'M SORRY I'M ALWAYS SUCH A JERK TO YOU, SO-NA," AND SAY IT LIKE YOU MEAN IT!
반짝 반짝
SO-NA, I'M REALLY SORRY I'M ALWAYS BEING SUCH A JERK. REALLY, I AM!
No way. He's worse.
HUH?!
YOU... YOU'RE NOT KIDDING, ARE YOU?
He really must be serious about Ko-Mo!
WELL?

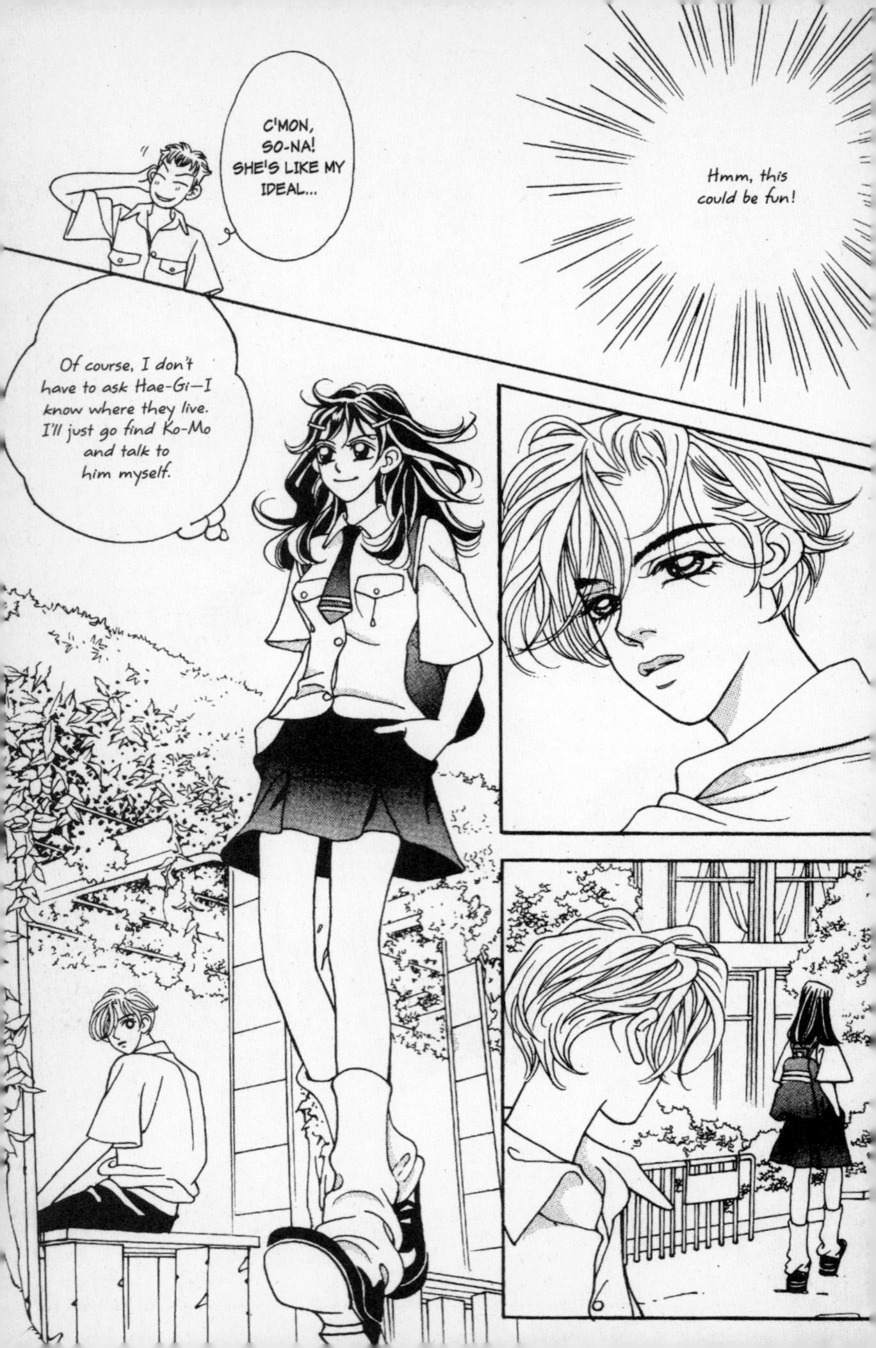
C'MON, SO-NA! SHE'S LIKE MY IDEAL...
Hmm, this could be fun!
Of course, I don't have to ask Hae-Gi—I know where they live. I'll just go find Ko-Mo and talk to him myself.

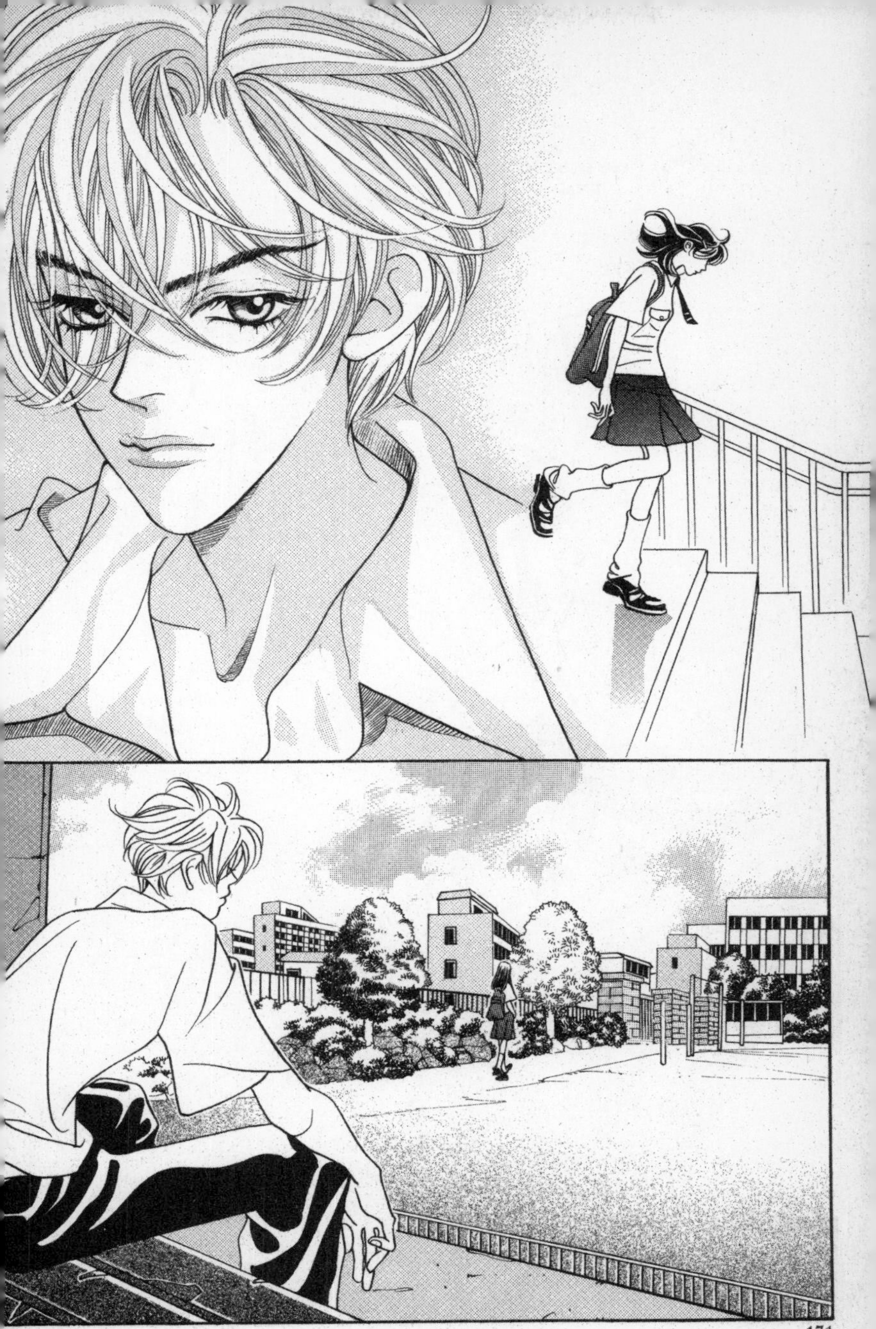

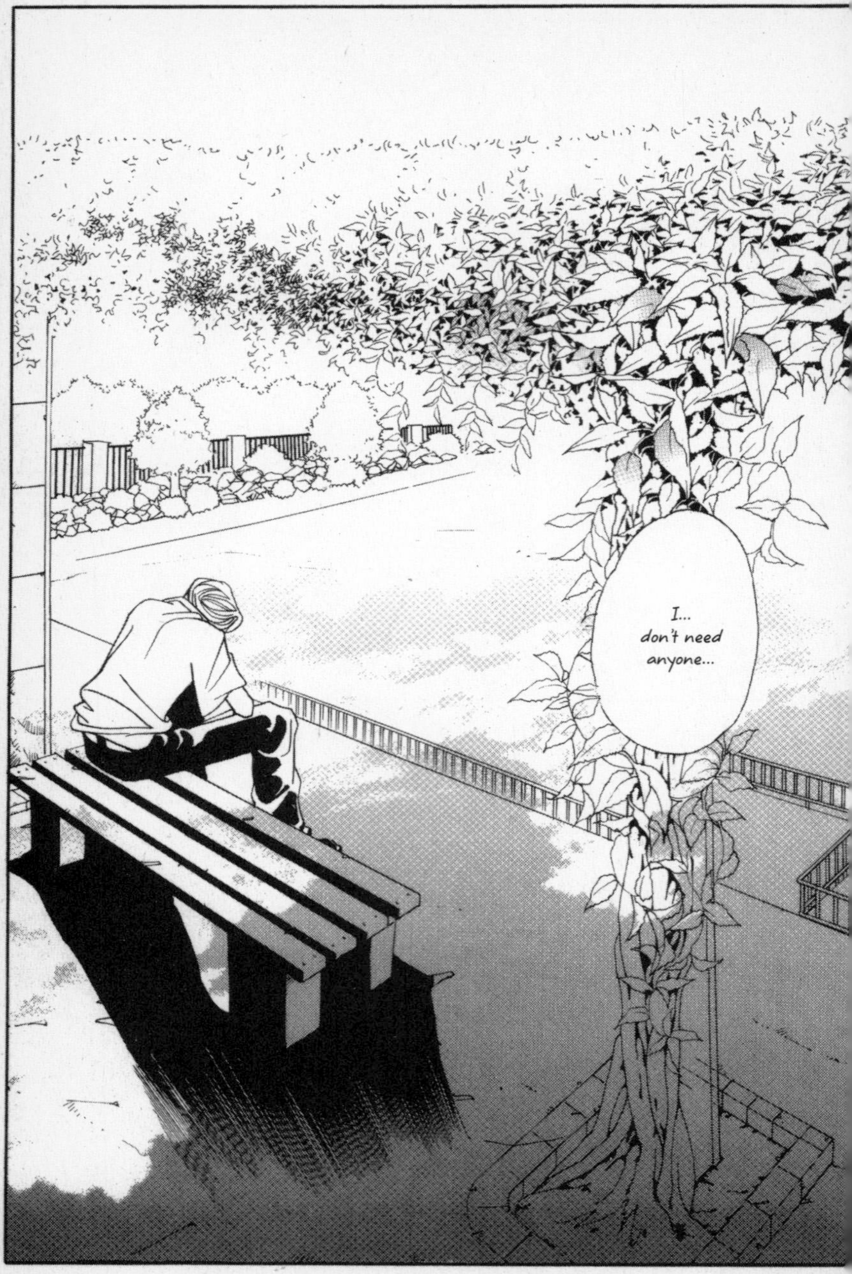
I... don't need anyone...

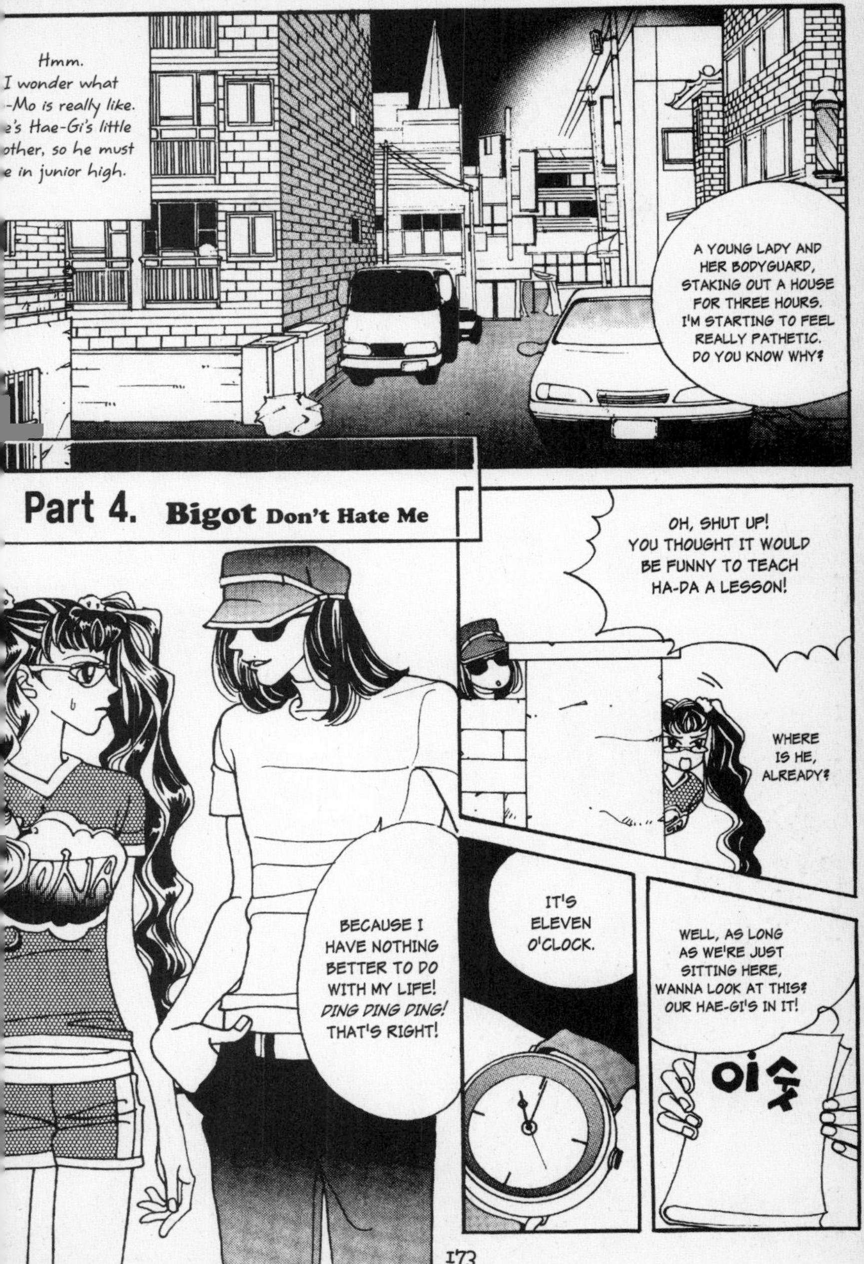
Hmm.
I wonder what
-Mo is really like.
e's Hae-Gi's little
other, so he must
e in junior high.
A YOUNG LADY AND HER BODYGUARD, STAKING OUT A HOUSE FOR THREE HOURS. I'M STARTING TO FEEL REALLY PATHETIC. DO YOU KNOW WHY?
Part 4. Bigot Don't Hate Me
BECAUSE I HAVE NOTHING BETTER TO DO WITH MY LIFE! *DING DING DING!* THAT'S RIGHT!
OH, SHUT UP! YOU THOUGHT IT WOULD BE FUNNY TO TEACH HA-DA A LESSON!
WHERE IS HE, ALREADY?
IT'S ELEVEN O'CLOCK.
WELL, AS LONG AS WE'RE JUST SITTING HERE, WANNA LOOK AT THIS? OUR HAE-GI'S IN IT!

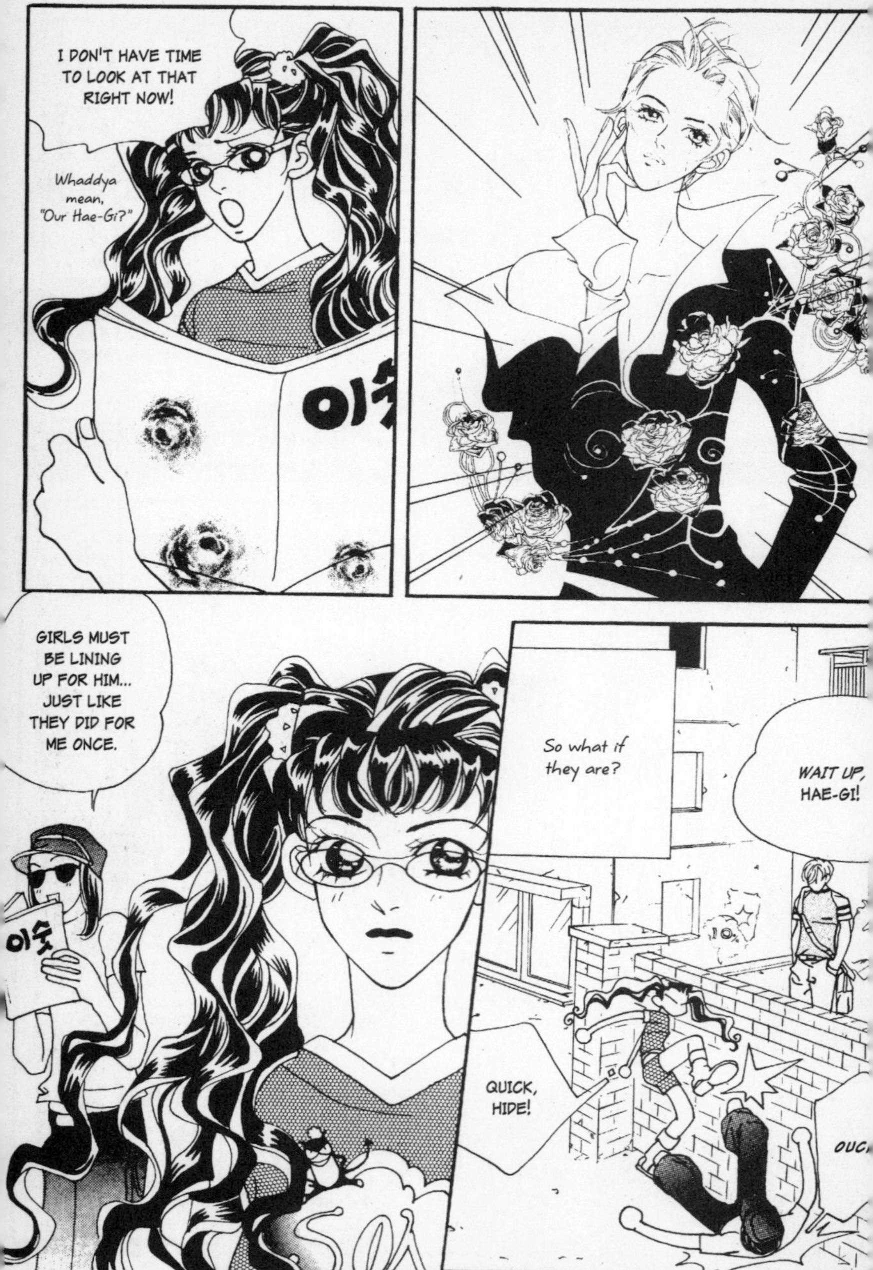
I DON'T HAVE TIME TO LOOK AT THAT RIGHT NOW!
Whaddya mean, "Our Hae-Gi?"
이숙
GIRLS MUST BE LINING UP FOR HIM... JUST LIKE THEY DID FOR ME ONCE.
이숙
So what if they are?
WAIT UP, HAE-GI!
QUICK, HIDE!
OUC

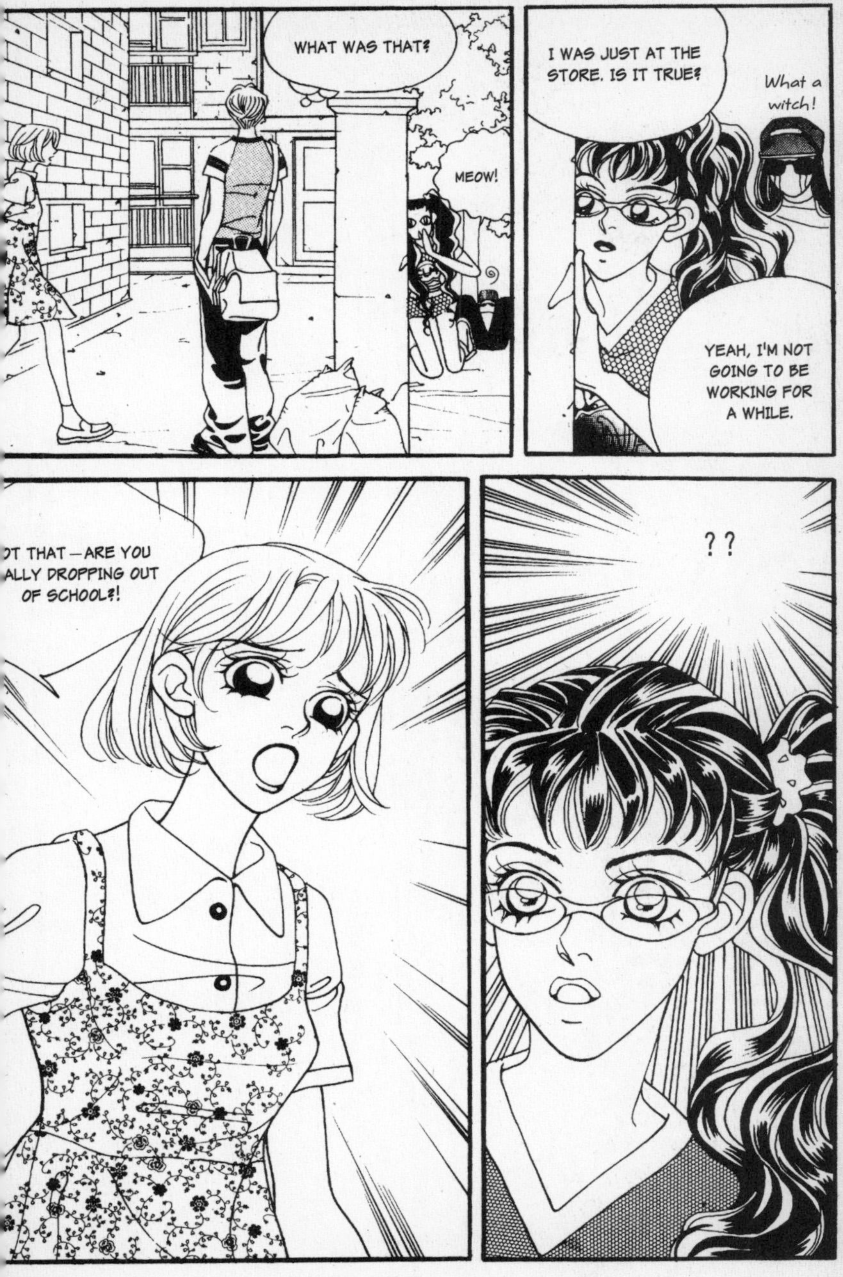
WHAT WAS THAT?
MEOW!
I WAS JUST AT THE STORE. IS IT TRUE?
What a witch!
YEAH, I'M NOT GOING TO BE WORKING FOR A WHILE.
OT THAT—ARE YOU ALLY DROPPING OUT OF SCHOOL?!
? ?

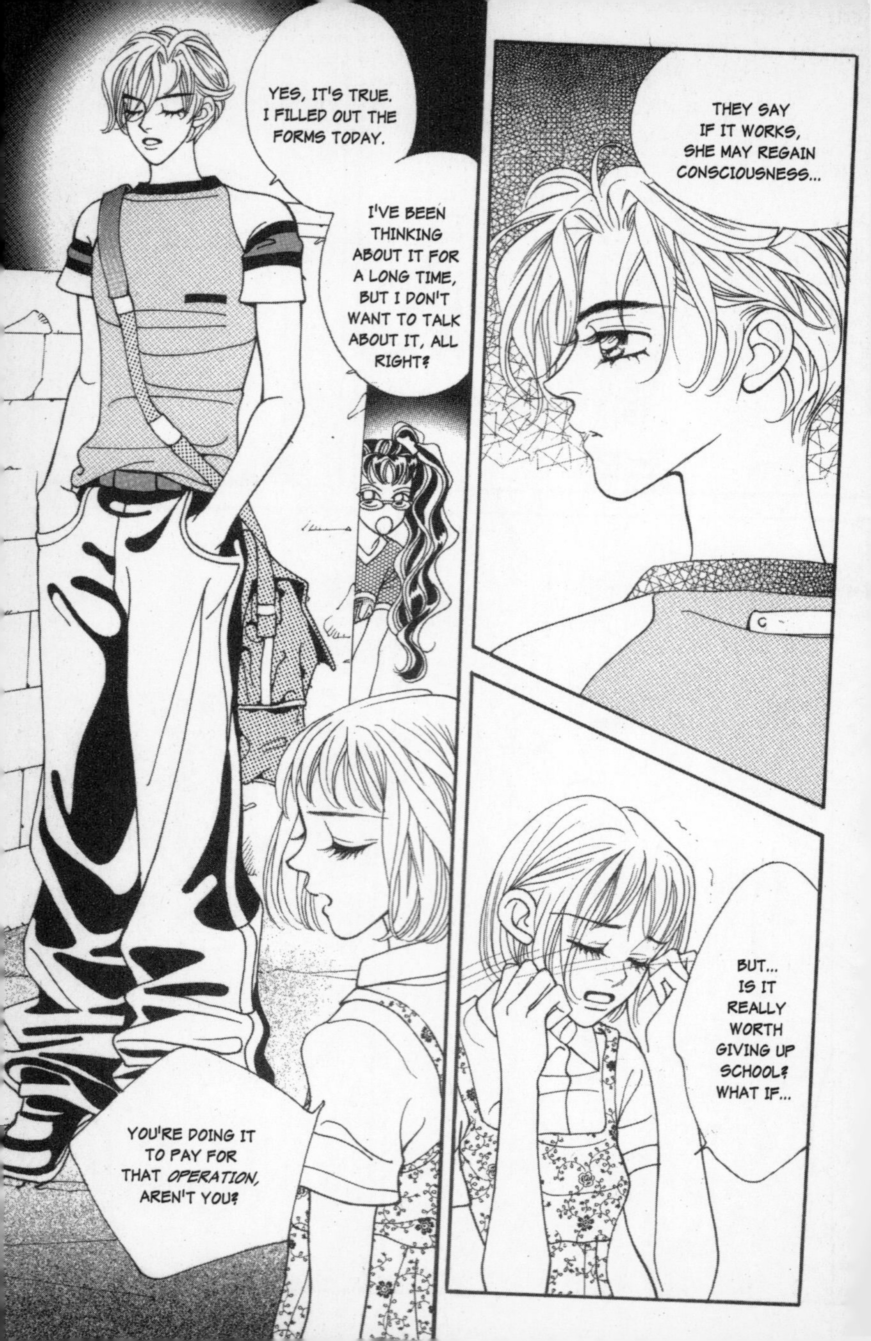
YES, IT'S TRUE. I FILLED OUT THE FORMS TODAY.
I'VE BEEN THINKING ABOUT IT FOR A LONG TIME, BUT I DON'T WANT TO TALK ABOUT IT, ALL RIGHT?
YOU'RE DOING IT TO PAY FOR THAT *OPERATION*, AREN'T YOU?
THEY SAY IF IT WORKS, SHE MAY REGAIN CONSCIOUSNESS...
BUT... IS IT REALLY WORTH GIVING UP SCHOOL? WHAT IF...

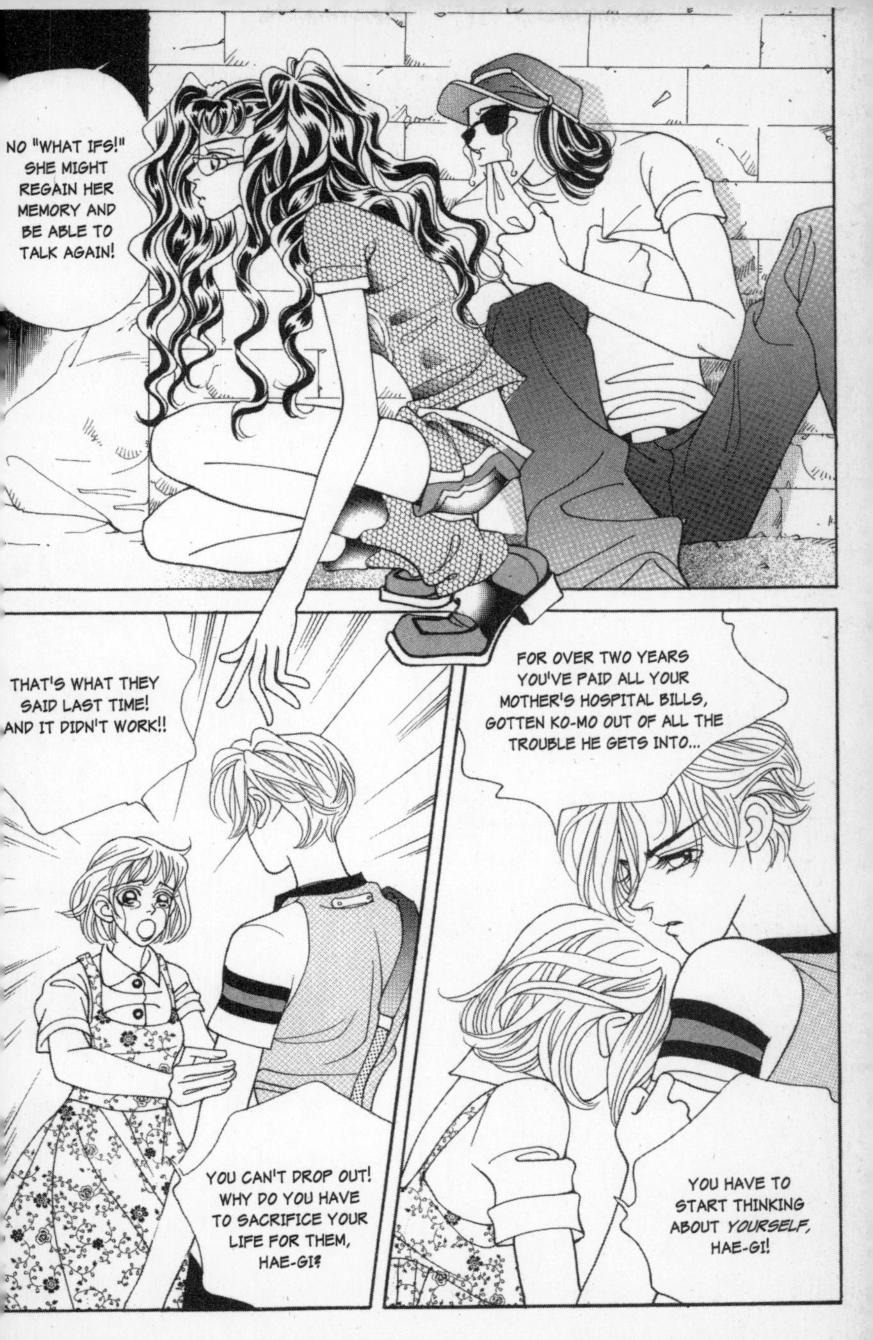
NO "WHAT IFS!" SHE MIGHT REGAIN HER MEMORY AND BE ABLE TO TALK AGAIN!
THAT'S WHAT THEY SAID LAST TIME! AND IT DIDN'T WORK!!
YOU CAN'T DROP OUT! WHY DO YOU HAVE TO SACRIFICE YOUR LIFE FOR THEM, HAE-GI?
FOR OVER TWO YEARS YOU'VE PAID ALL YOUR MOTHER'S HOSPITAL BILLS, GOTTEN KO-MO OUT OF ALL THE TROUBLE HE GETS INTO...
YOU HAVE TO START THINKING ABOUT *YOURSELF*, HAE-GI!

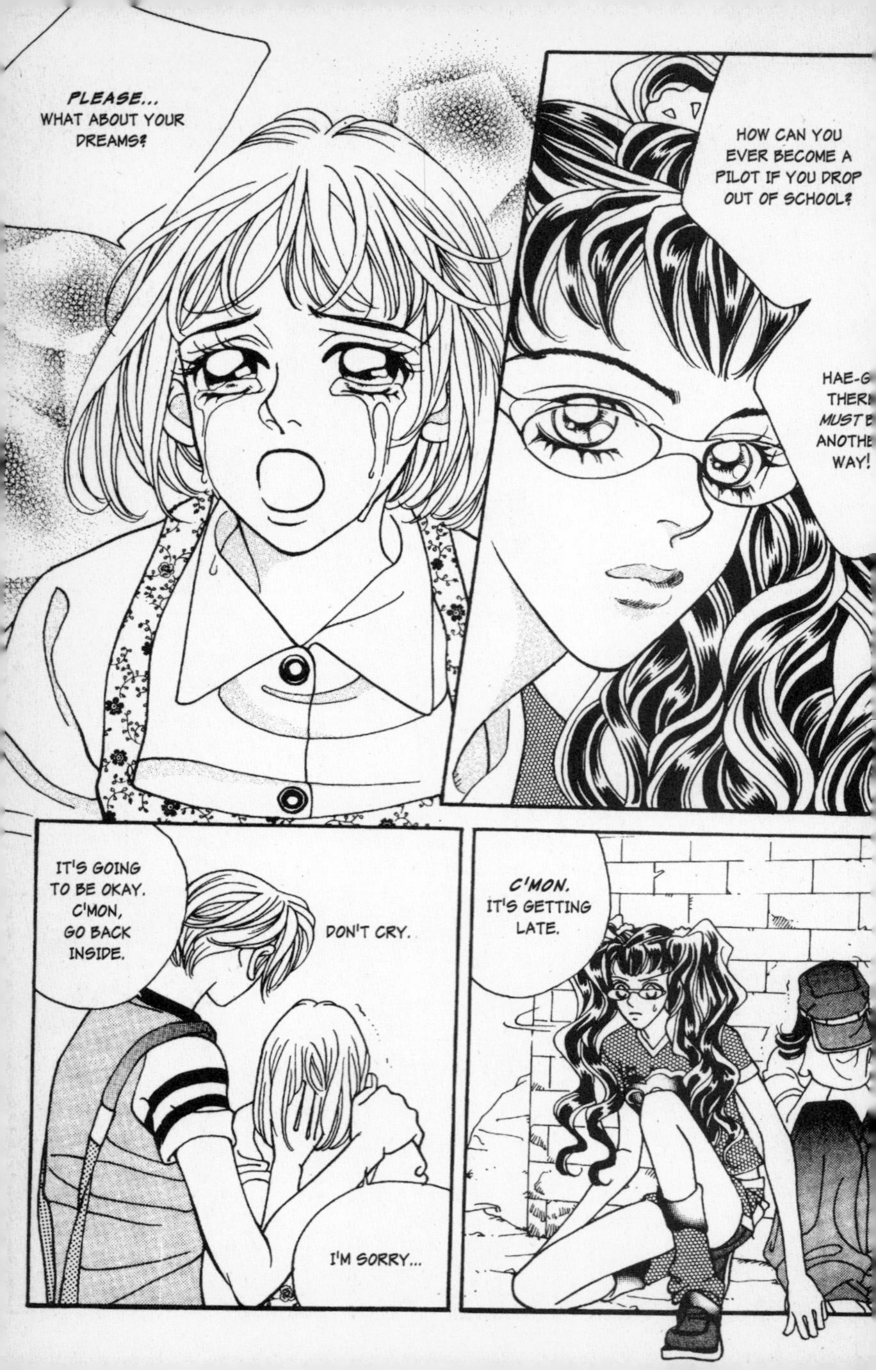
PLEASE... WHAT ABOUT YOUR DREAMS?
HOW CAN YOU EVER BECOME A PILOT IF YOU DROP OUT OF SCHOOL?
IT'S GOING TO BE OKAY. C'MON, GO BACK INSIDE.
DON'T CRY.
I'M SORRY...
C'MON. IT'S GETTING LATE.

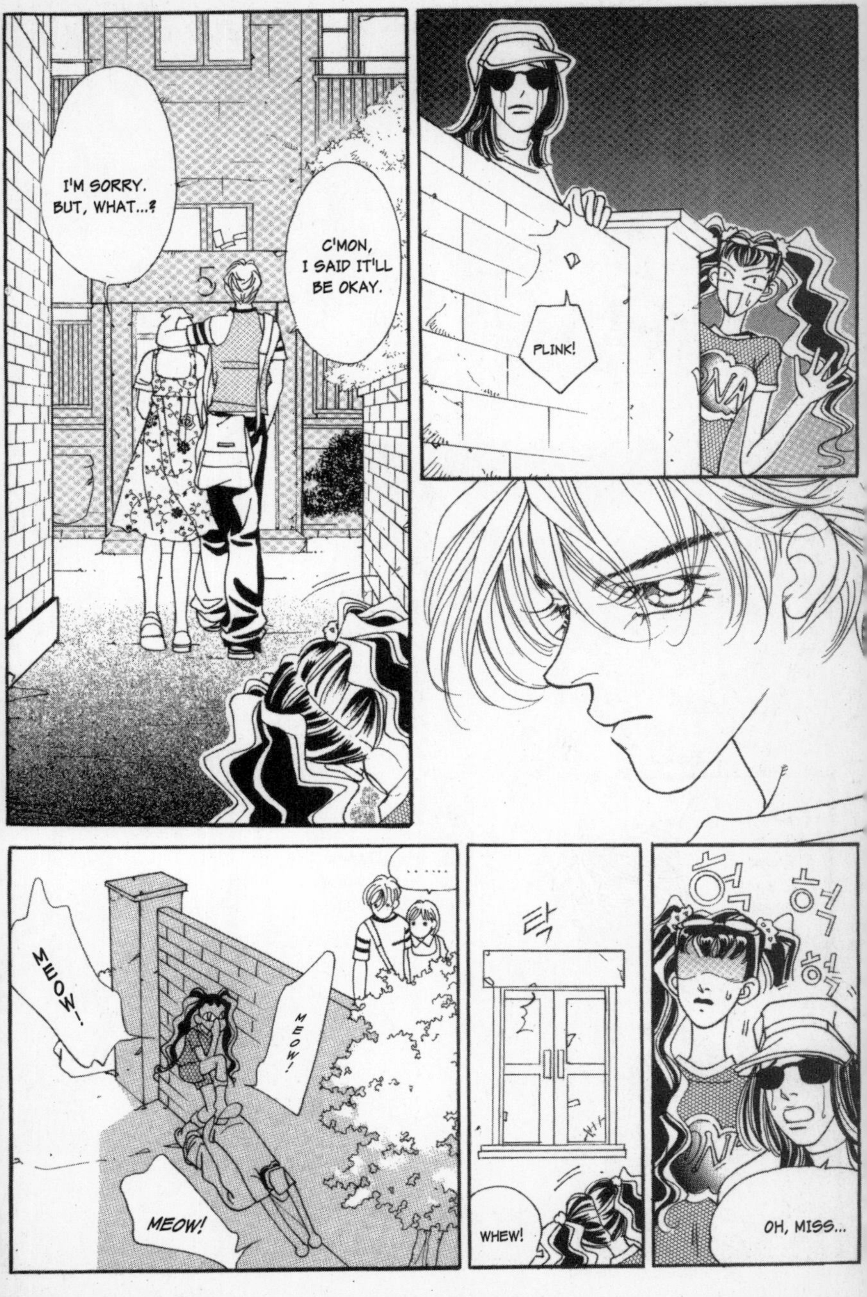
I'M SORRY.
BUT, WHAT...?
C'MON,
I SAID IT'LL
BE OKAY.
PLINK!
MEOW!
. . . . . .
MEOW!
MEOW!
탁
WHEW!
헉
헉
헉
OH, MISS...

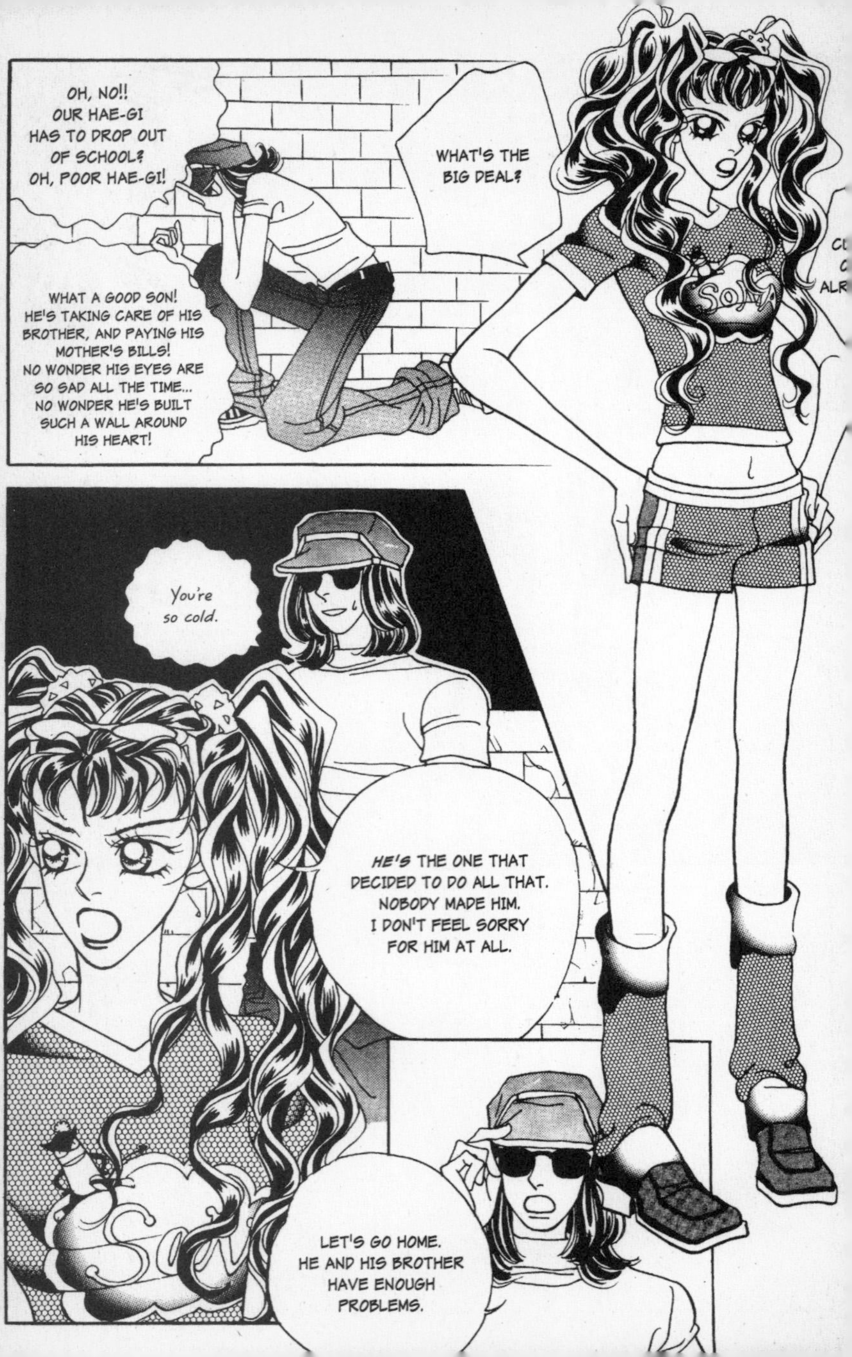
OH, NO!!
OUR HAE-GI
HAS TO DROP OUT
OF SCHOOL?
OH, POOR HAE-GI!
WHAT A GOOD SON!
HE'S TAKING CARE OF HIS
BROTHER, AND PAYING HIS
MOTHER'S BILLS!
NO WONDER HIS EYES ARE
SO SAD ALL THE TIME...
NO WONDER HE'S BUILT
SUCH A WALL AROUND
HIS HEART!
WHAT'S THE
BIG DEAL?
You're
so cold.
HE'S THE ONE THAT
DECIDED TO DO ALL THAT.
NOBODY MADE HIM.
I DON'T FEEL SORRY
FOR HIM AT ALL.
LET'S GO HOME.
HE AND HIS BROTHER
HAVE ENOUGH
PROBLEMS.

NO WAY. I NEED TO HAVE A LITTLE TALK WITH KO-MO.

KO-MO, YOU JACKASS. YOUR BROTHER IS GIVING UP HIS DREAMS FOR YOU AND YOUR MOM, AND WHAT ARE YOU DOING—JUST PLAYING AROUND!

No big deal, huh?

Is he really leaving school?

Everyone told me that he doesn't have any close friends. He never lets anything bother him, never gets involved.

Is this why? Hae-Gi, you didn't want to make friends because you knew...

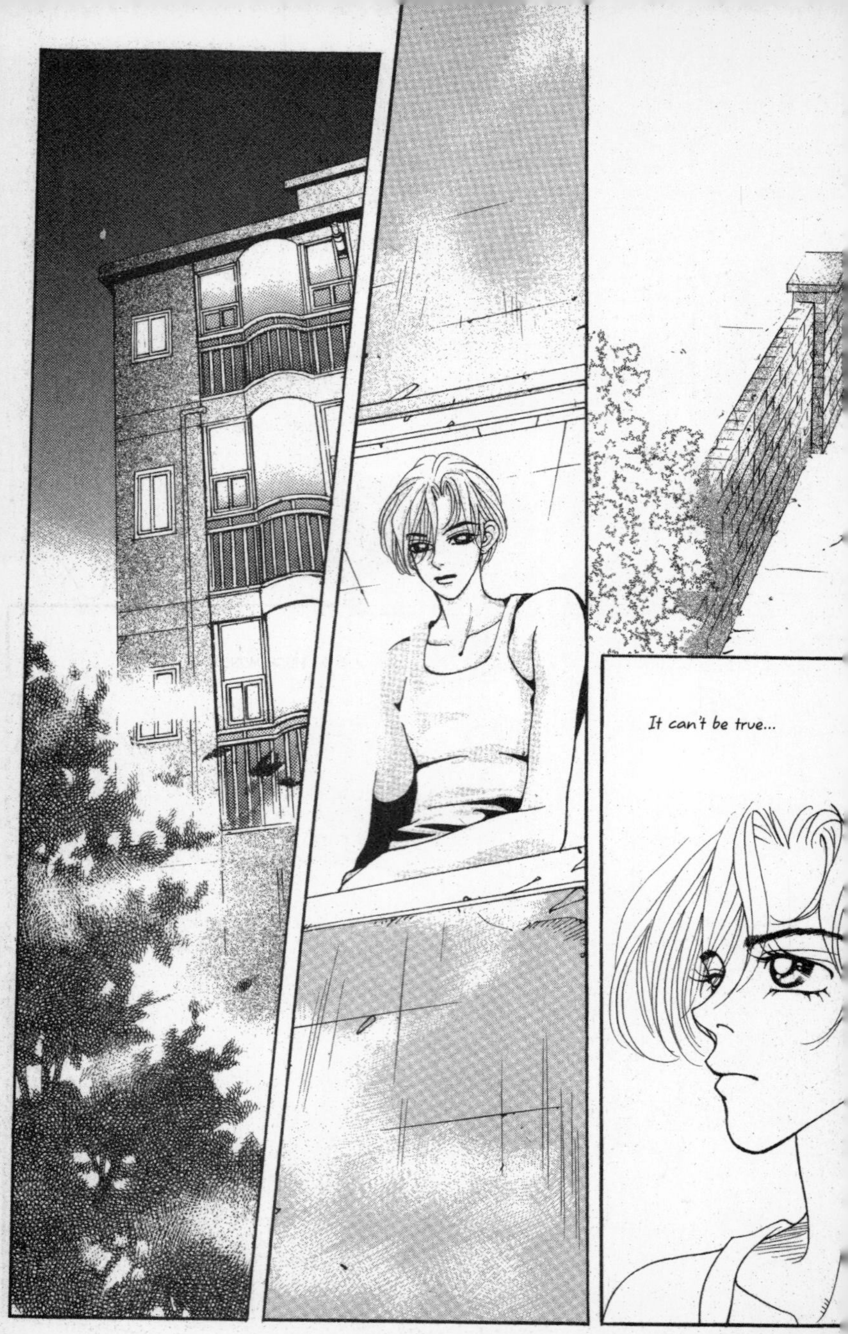
It can't be true...

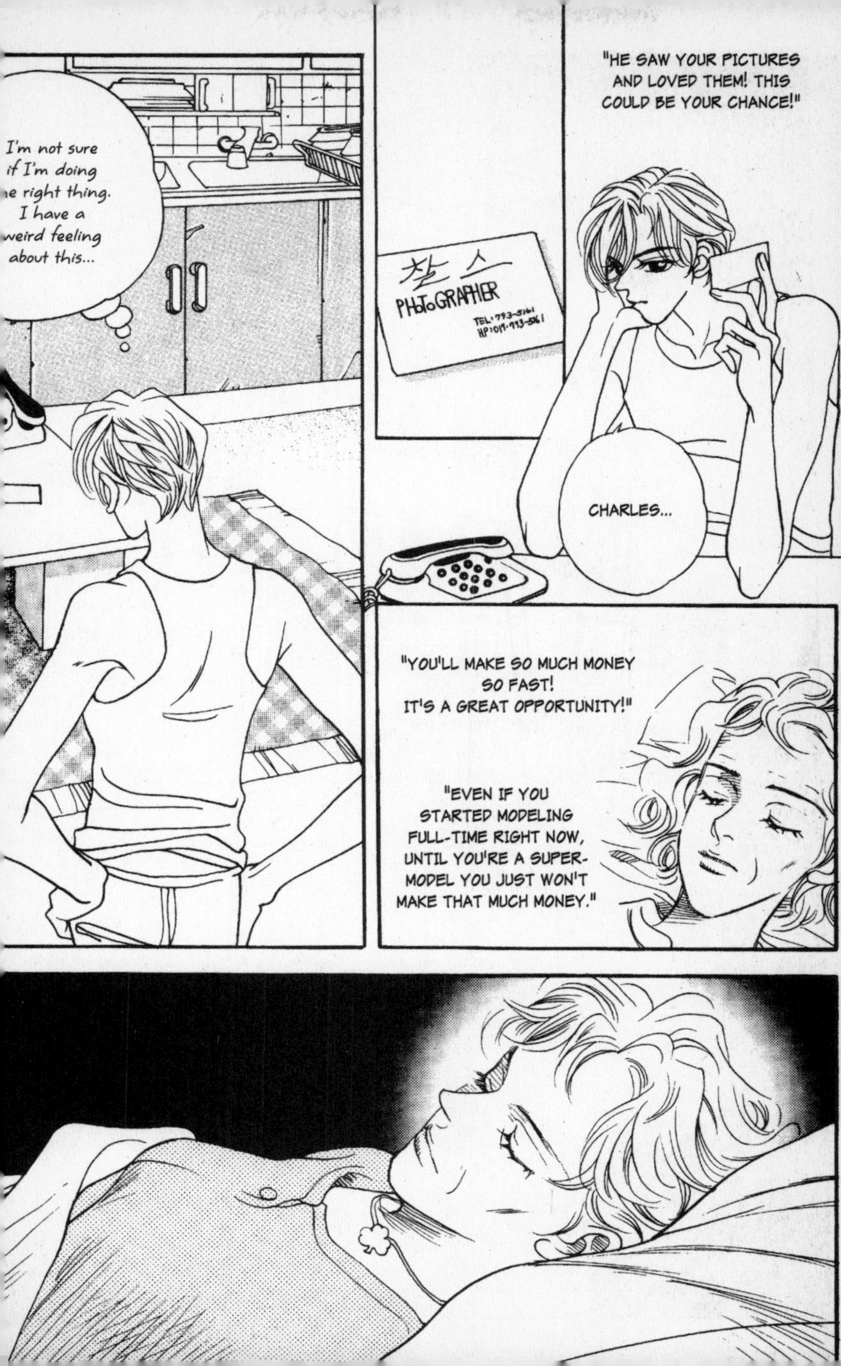
I'm not sure if I'm doing e right thing. I have a weird feeling about this...
"HE SAW YOUR PICTURES AND LOVED THEM! THIS COULD BE YOUR CHANCE!"
찰스
PHoToGRAPHER
TEL:793-5161
HP:017-793-5161
CHARLES...
"YOU'LL MAKE SO MUCH MONEY SO FAST! IT'S A GREAT OPPORTUNITY!"
"EVEN IF YOU STARTED MODELING FULL-TIME RIGHT NOW, UNTIL YOU'RE A SUPER-MODEL YOU JUST WON'T MAKE THAT MUCH MONEY."

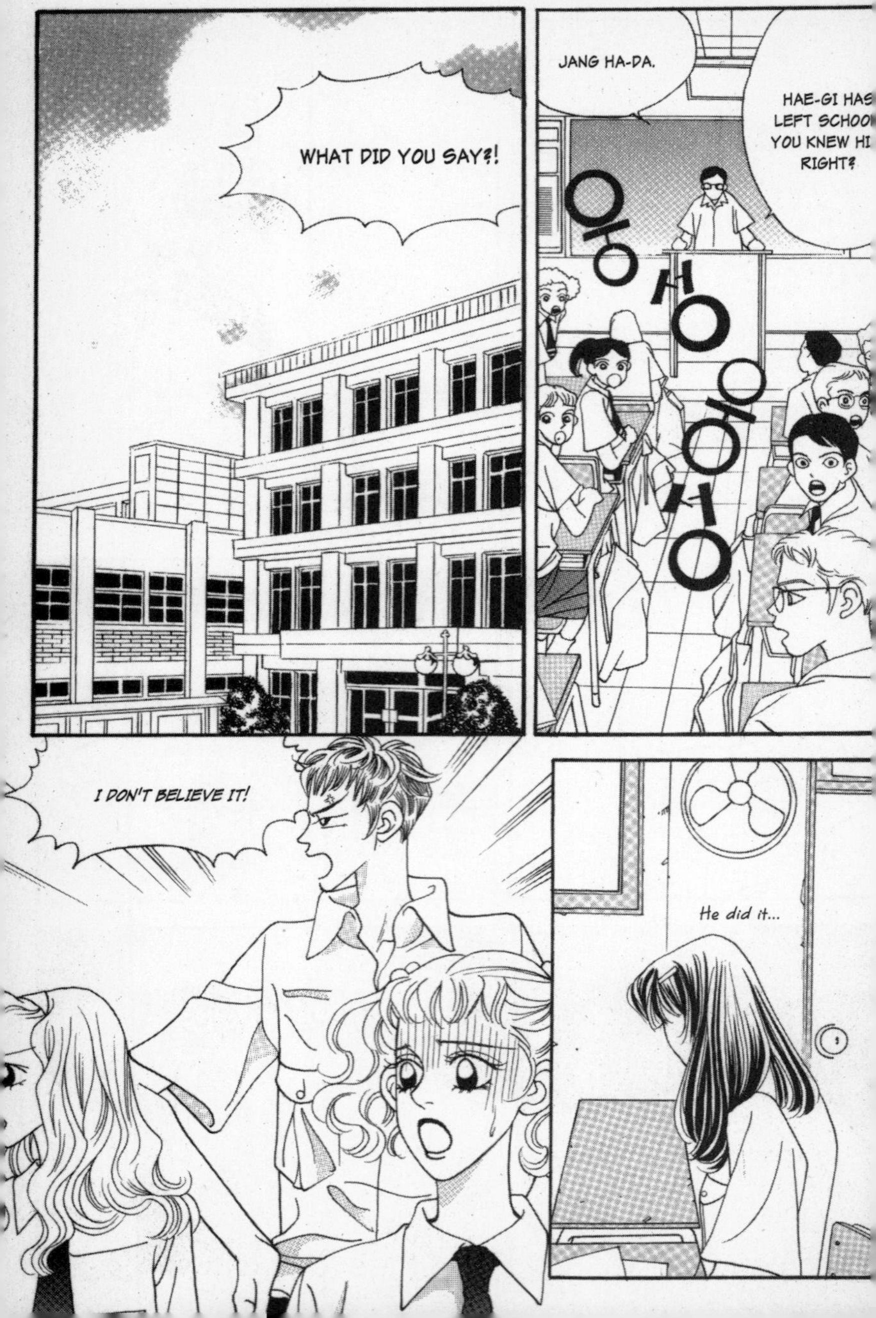
WHAT DID YOU SAY?!
JANG HA-DA.
HAE-GI HAS LEFT SCHOO YOU KNEW HI RIGHT?
I DON'T BELIEVE IT!
He did it...

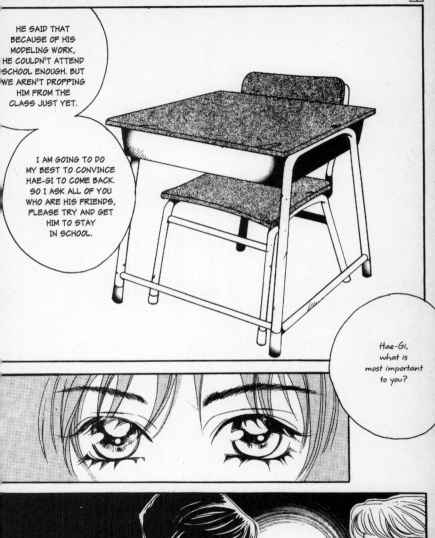

HE SAID THAT BECAUSE OF HIS MODELING WORK, HE COULDN'T ATTEND SCHOOL ENOUGH. BUT WE AREN'T DROPPING HIM FROM THE CLASS JUST YET.

I AM GOING TO DO MY BEST TO CONVINCE HAE-GI TO COME BACK. SO I ASK ALL OF YOU WHO ARE HIS FRIENDS, PLEASE TRY AND GET HIM TO STAY IN SCHOOL.

Hae-Gi, what is most important to you?

HE'S REALLY DROPPING OUT?

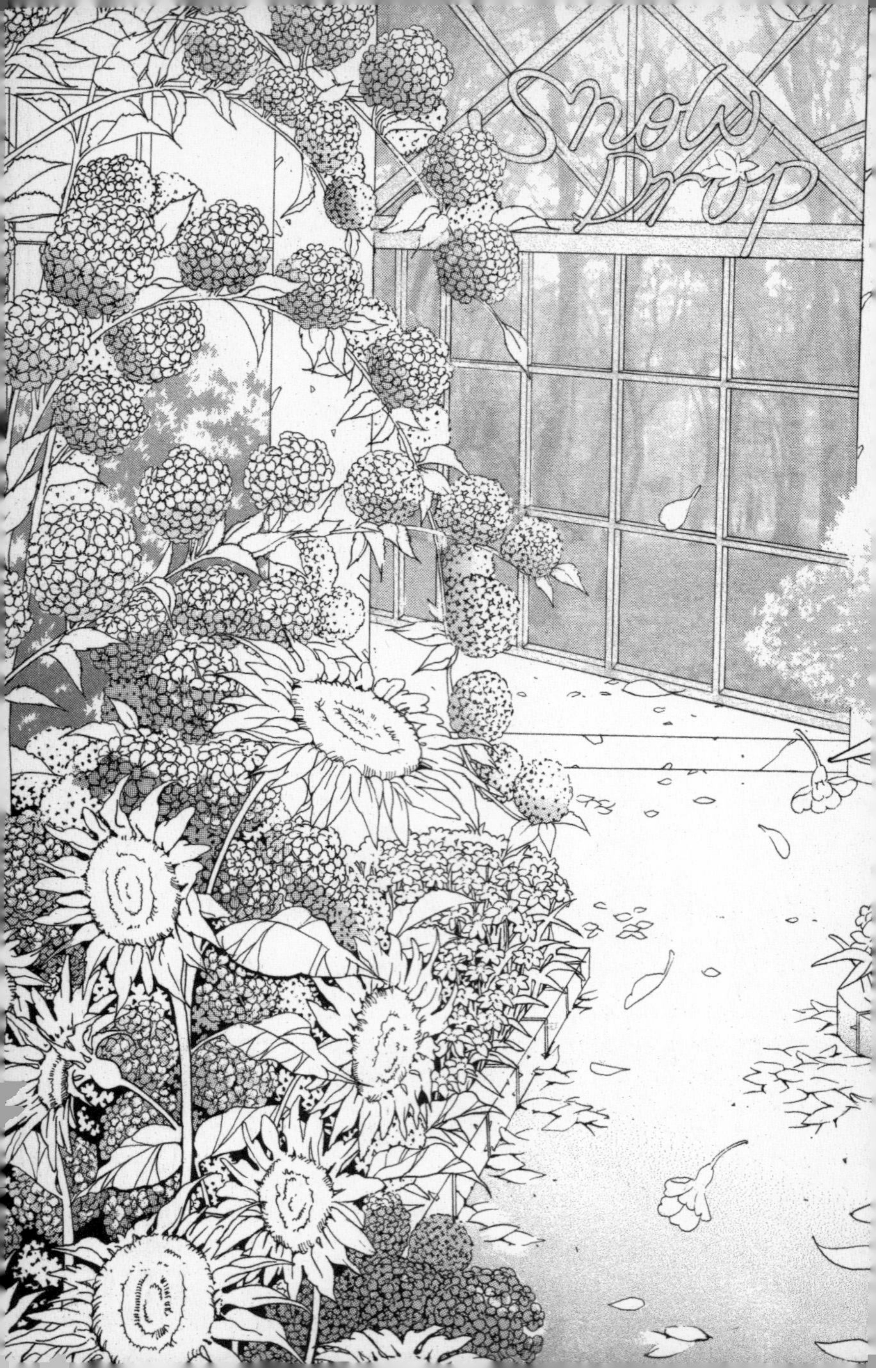
Snow Drop

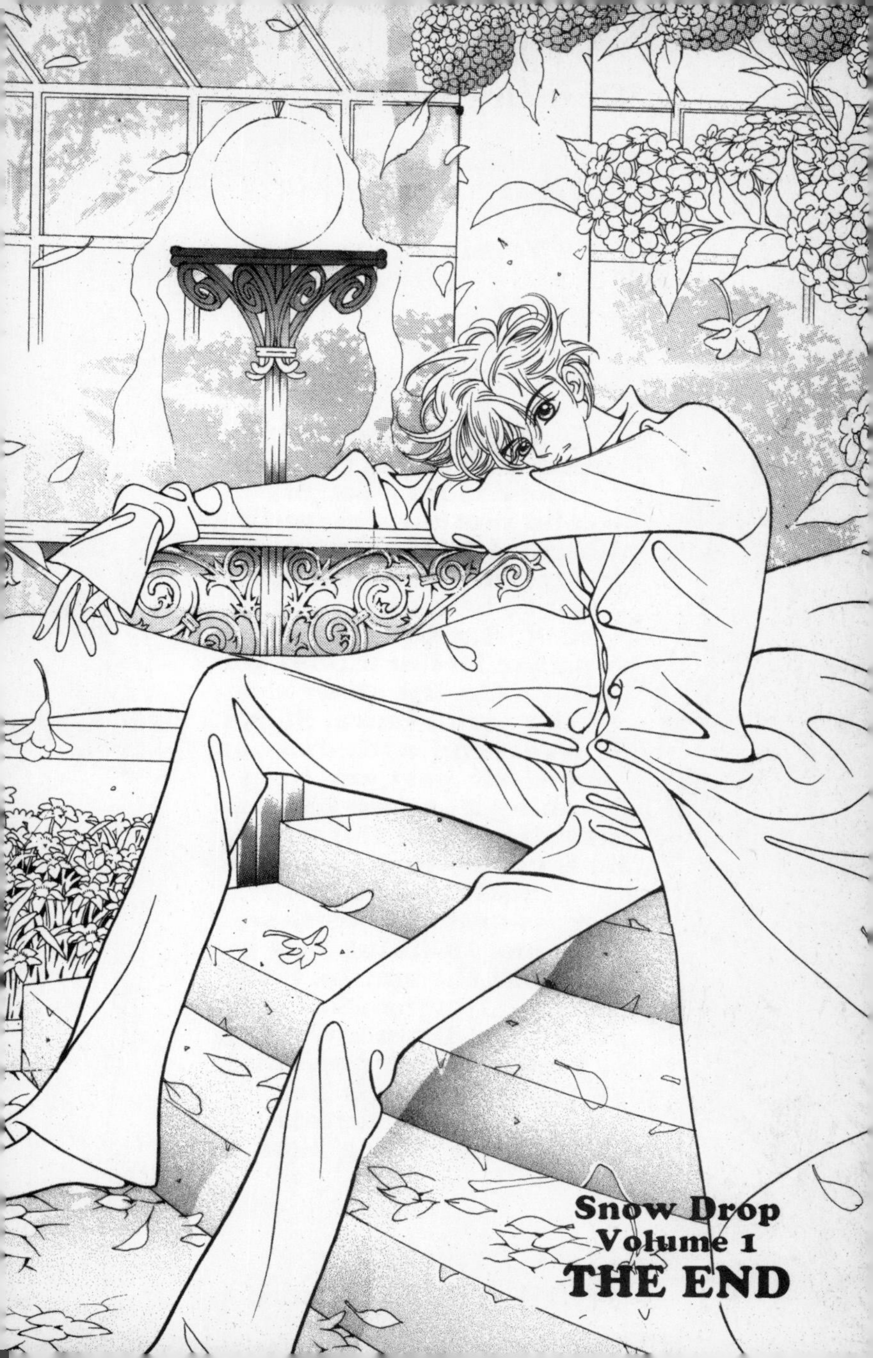
Snow Drop
Volume 1
THE END

Coming in March...

Snow Drop

Volume Two

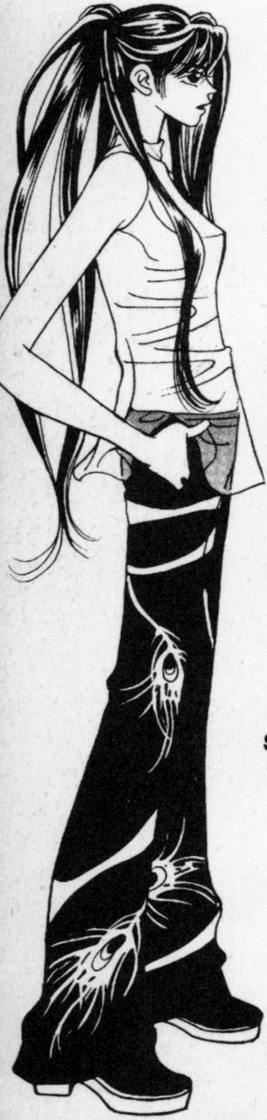

Hae-Gi has quit school in order to earn more money for his invalid mother's mounting hospital bills. But when his regular modeling gigs fail to bring in enough cash, Hae-Gi begins to consider less orthodox job offers. On the other side of the social fence, So-Na is wrestling with demons from her past and questioning her own future at school. All the while, Ha-Da continues to pursue Hae-Gi's beautiful, cross-dressing brother, Ko-mo, thinking he's a she. But the sparks really start to fly when Sun-Mi, a young girl from a wealthy family, arrives on the scene and sets her sights on a certain handsome young man...

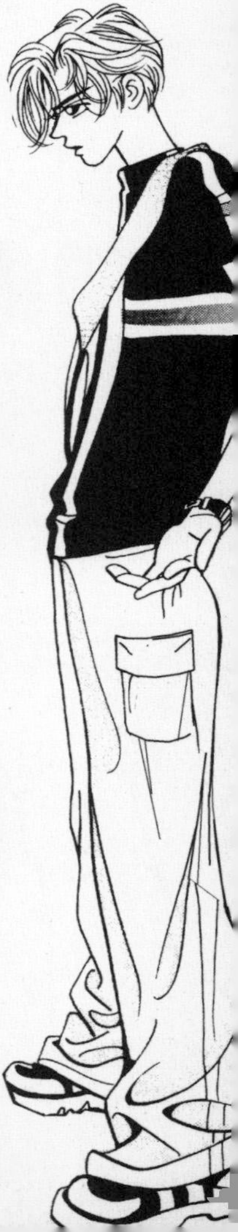

Drop in for SNOW DROP, Volume 2!

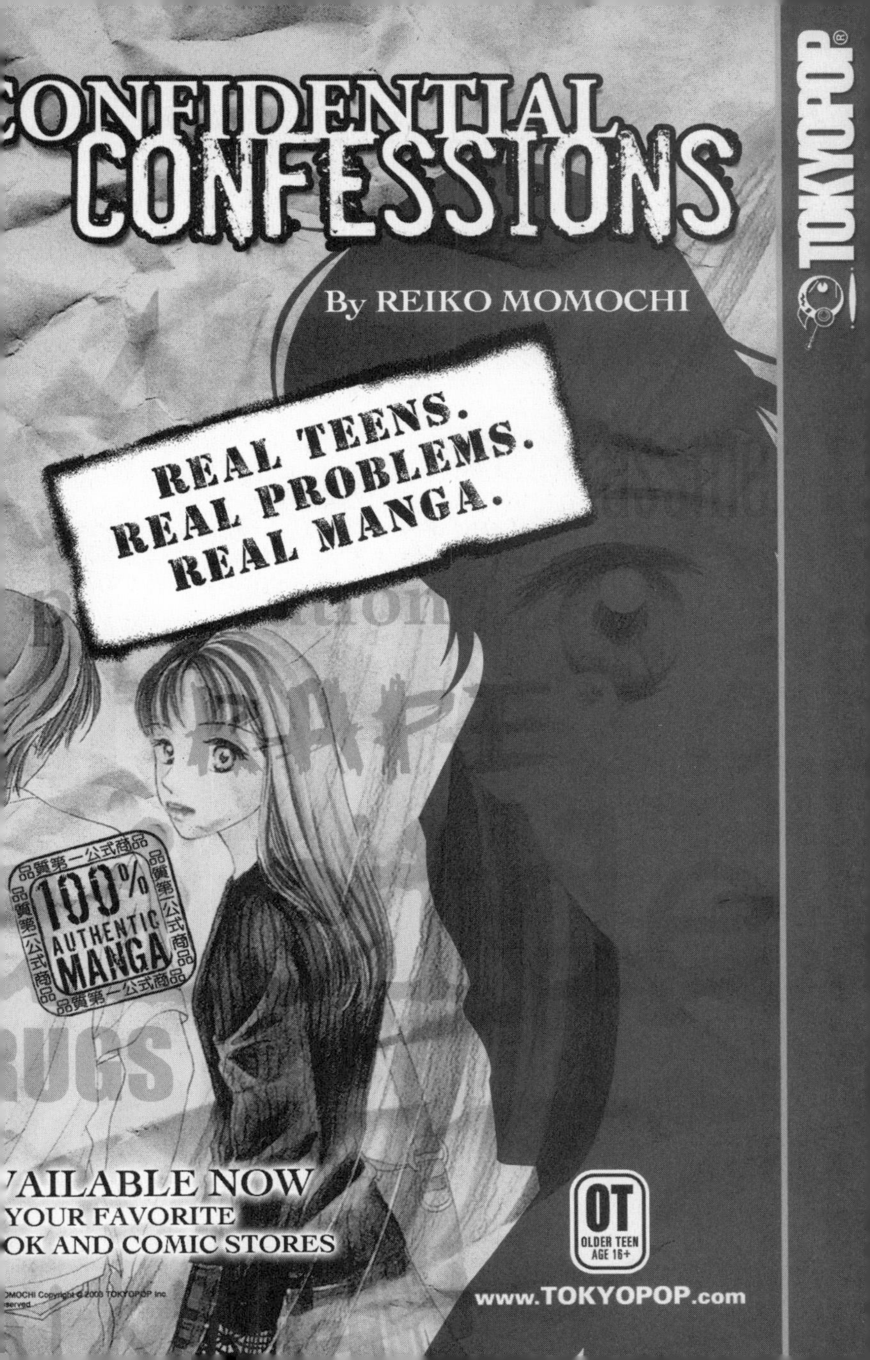

CONFIDENTIAL CONFESSIONS
By REIKO MOMOCHI
REAL TEENS.
REAL PROBLEMS.
REAL MANGA.
100% AUTHENTIC MANGA
品質第一公式商品
VAILABLE NOW
YOUR FAVORITE
OK AND COMIC STORES
OT
OLDER TEEN AGE 16+
TOKYOPOP®
www.TOKYOPOP.com

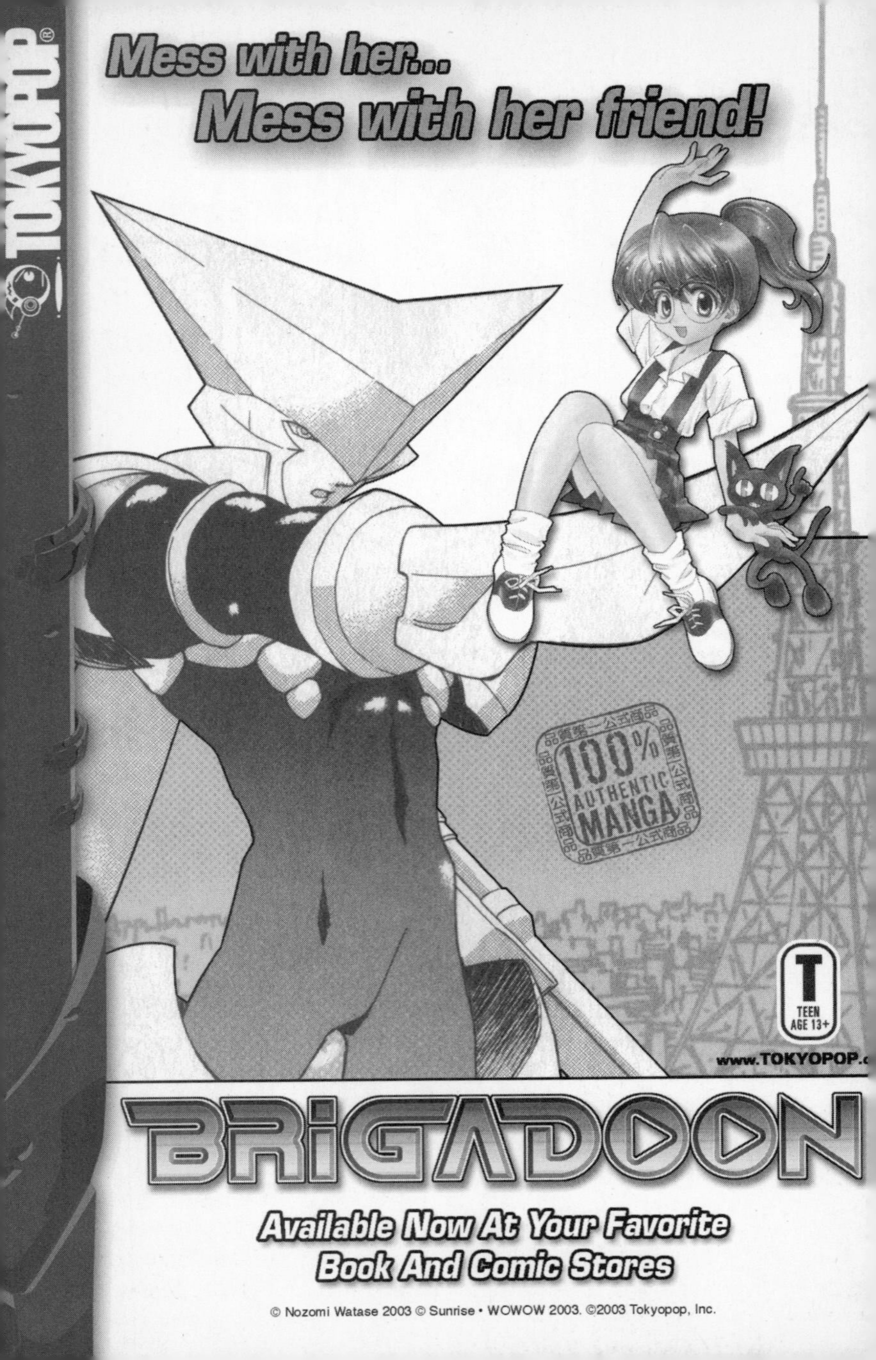
TOKYOPOP®
Mess with her...
Mess with her friend!
100% AUTHENTIC MANGA
T
TEEN AGE 13+
www.TOKYOPOP.c
BRIGADOON
Available Now At Your Favorite Book And Comic Stores
© Nozomi Watase 2003 © Sunrise • WOWOW 2003. ©2003 Tokyopop, Inc.

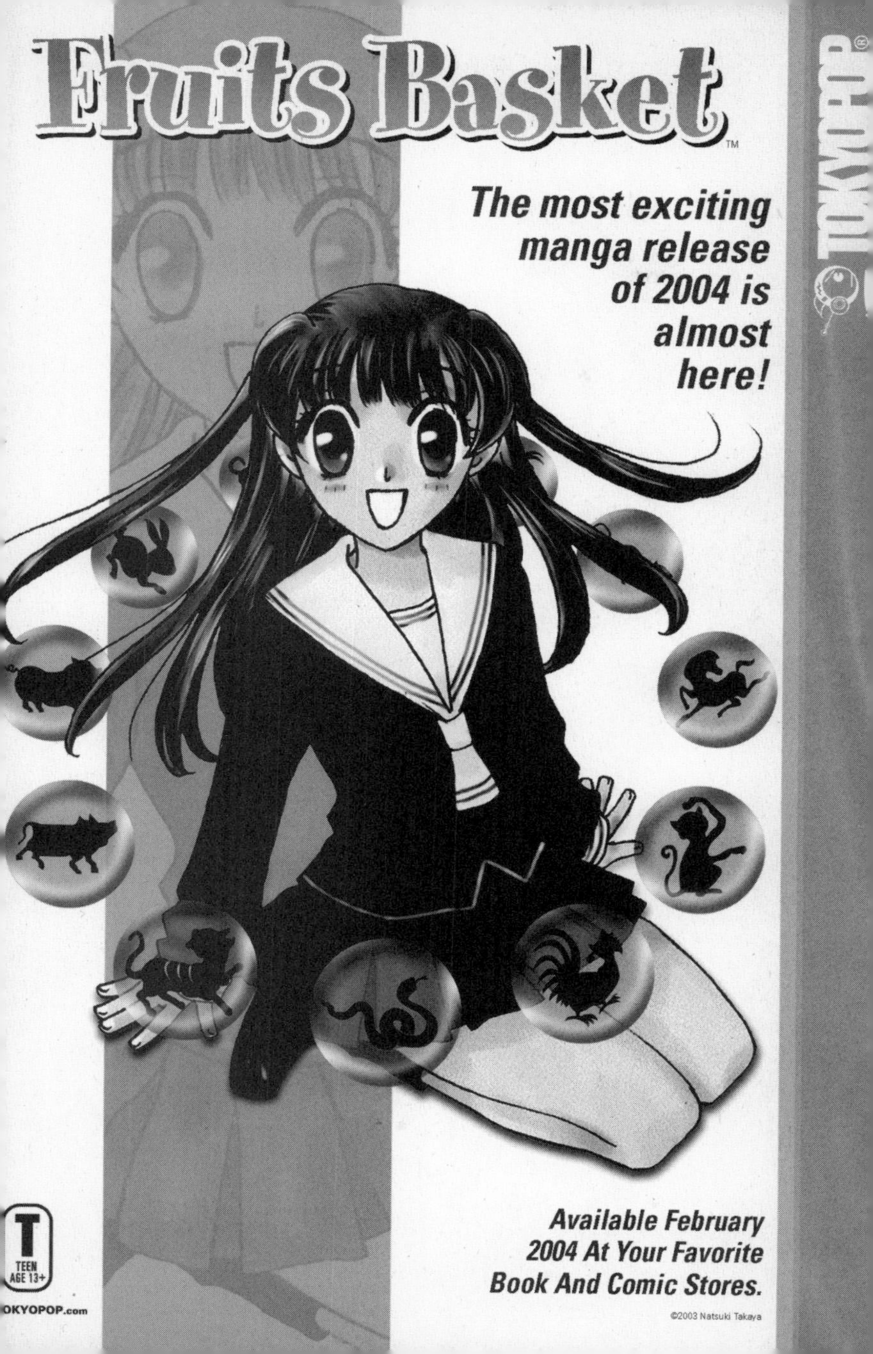

Dancing Was Her Life

Her Dance Partner
Might Be Her Future

Forbidden
Dance

by Hinako Ashihara